PERSONAL & FAMILY FINANCE

ROBERT O. WEAGLEY • **STARLA GREEN IVEY**

Kendall Hunt
publishing company

Kendall Hunt
publishing company

www.kendallhunt.com
Send all inquiries to:
4050 Westmark Drive
Dubuque, IA 52004-1840

Acknowledgments

To our families—the richest resource of all.

About the Authors

Starla Ivey, PhD is an Assistant Teaching Professor in the Personal Financial Planning Department at the University of Missouri. She teaches the introductory Personal and Family Finance course in the undergraduate program for the department. She has taught for Oklahoma State University. She has both her BS and MS from the Department of Personal Financial Planning, and PhD in Education; all from the University of Missouri. Before working as an assistant teaching professor, she worked several years as an academic counselor and also an instructional technology assistant. She has worked for the University of Missouri-Outreach and Extension, State Farm Mutual Insurance, Shelter Insurance, the State of Missouri-accounting department, and Missouri Division of Highway Safety. She is married to Patrick Ivey, who holds a PhD in Sport Psychology and they have two daughters, Paisli and Serena. Hobbies include running, biking, lifting weights, and horse riding.

Robert O. Weagley is Emeritus Chair of the Personal Financial Planning Department at the University of Missouri. He taught courses in Personal Financial Planning: Careers, Investment Management, and Economic Theory of the Household. He holds a BS in Sociology and an MS in Consumer Economics from the University of Missouri, and a PhD from Cornell University. He is a Certified Financial Planner™ registered with Sundvold Financial. He has three children: Daniel, Julianne, and James and two granddaughters Adalie and Madeline. Hobbies include photography, fishing, and walking where he used to run.

If you have suggestions that might improve this workbook, please feel free to contact:

iveysl@missouri.edu

weagleyr@missouri.edu

DISCLAIMER

No endorsement of any product either implied or expressed is intended. Knowledge of the contents is not a substitute for thoroughly seeking current information with regard to financial products and services.

Contents

Preface

Many students find the topics covered in a Personal and Family Finance course to be the most relevant they encounter during college. We agree that the information is valuable and every person can take it and apply it to their financial decisions. We are serious when we say that, if you take the time to learn the material and the analytical skills within this text, the course will pay for itself many times over the course of your life.

This workbook is designed to help the reader understand the usefulness of sound financial planning, with an emphasis on the mathematical concepts encountered in planning one's financial future. To truly benefit from the material, you will need to study the examples and work the problems, as well as try to apply them when engaged with today's financial marketplace. You will only learn this material by actually using it and, as college students, most of you have not had the opportunity to be a purchaser of financial products. Yet, if you look around your class and see some gray hairs in the audience, ask them why they are taking the course and if they find it valuable. It has been our experience that those who have "lived" personal finance find the tools and concepts within these pages to be very valuable. (At least, if you consider their performance on exams to be a valid measure.) We both are "ex-students," and we have seen homework problems as, simply, busy work. Fortunately, in using this text, you may find the homework problems to be "busy" work but you need to trust us when we tell you that the "real world" of personal and family finance requires such work. Financial success requires a fair dose of thinking and problem-solving skills, as well as patience.

Learning the material in a Personal and Family Finance course is similar to conducting an orchestra. You cannot focus on only one section or topic exclusively. For this reason, the topics of Personal and Family Finance are a coherent whole, rather than distinct, separate topics. This workbook is an attempt to simplify and enhance the process of learning the many different topics and formulas necessary to "orchestrate" your financial future. As you work through the course, it is our hope you will avoid the common mistake of focusing too heavily—and at times exclusively—on money and wealth. Money is merely a tool. We invite you to be wise financial stewards, as you pursue the goals and ambitions that you have set for yourself and those around you.

PS: Our department supports a student-led, peer financial counseling center, called the Office for Financial Success. We try to support financial literacy education with links to materials that complement this text. Find out more at http://ofsmizzou.org.

Introduction

GUIDING PRINCIPLES

The study of personal and family finance, while sharing many principles, is quite different from corporate finance or microeconomics. The family is much more than a business enterprise whose value is solely measured by its monetary value. While families do have monetary values, such as their net worth or their income, they are much more than money. Families provide a nurturing environment to develop each generation into leaders of society. Members of families love and trust each other with acts designed to reach mutual goals and to express their uniqueness as a social group. Such characteristics are not present in many of life's relationships outside of the family. Regardless of the truth in these statements, money problems are a major reason why many families end in divorce. There is no reason for this to be the case. Money is not the most important thing in the world, yet it is important. Wherever it is on your list of important things, it is a long way ahead of what comes after it. A key to successful money management is to make the best decisions while you are young. Early mistakes can take years to overcome, thus limiting your potential and constraining the choices you have in life.

Before we begin, we have a little presentation that we sometime present to public audiences and high school classes. It is entitled "How to Get Rich in America." We believe these provide an outline of the important concepts to apply throughout life. We leave it to you to create your future.

Principle 1 Recognize How Lucky You are to be You

First, the odds are very good that you are either an American or are being educated in America. America has an outstanding educational system and you must make the best use of your time in that system. The United States has fallen from a ranking of fifth to seventh in the world, since the last edition of this text, with regard to the percentage of students going to college but seventeen in the world when it comes to the percentage who graduate from college.[1] Over the last 30 years, the proportion of 25–34-year-olds with college degrees is the same as it was 30 years ago. Other industrialized countries did not stand still. Take, for example, South Korea where over 10% of 55–64-year-olds have college degrees, while greater than 60% in the 25–34-age group have a college degree.[2] Why is this? College is expensive and many students cannot manage the costs; either through parental support, savings, part-time work, or loans. Money woes drive more students from college than do academic failures. Speaking of academic failures, you must remember what you learn, in order to apply it in life. What you learn is similar to saving and investing money on which great wealth can accrue. Economists call this "human capital."

---

[1] http://www.google.com/imgres?imgrefurl=http%3A%2F%2Fwww.truthfulpolitics.com%2Fhttp%3A%2Ftruthfulpolitics.com%2Fcomments%2Fu-s-education-statistics-compared-to-other-countries%2F&tbnid=JSqNcNj_dckEbM:&docid=CgIjjyRMQotOSM&h=635&w=387

[2] http://www.middleclasspoliticaleconomist.com/2012/04/america-shows-no-increase-in-college.html

Principle 2 Understand the Power of Compound Interest

Most cannot "get rich" from their earnings. Families and individuals must save money from each paycheck, in order to "get rich." We call this "paying yourself first." Save your money, save religiously, save 10% of your first paycheck, and every paycheck, after graduation until you retire.

Consider this simple example. Say you are 22 years old with a meager $30,000 per year job. To save 10%, you would save $3,000 in the first year. If your income increases at the rate of inflation, say 3% per year, and you are able to earn a rate of return that is 5% greater than the real rate of return, you will have saved $1,811,764 when you retire. If, instead of starting this at 22 years old, you wait until you are 32, you will be able to save only $762,447 by retirement. (See how important it is to start young and take advantage of compound interest?)

Principle 3 Resist the Temptation for Immediate Gratification

Little consumption decisions can cost you a fortune. Fancy coffees, nights on the town, and impulse expenditures can add up and reduce your ability to reach your goals. Do not let your sense of self be tied to what you own. You are more than that. If you think the only way you are going to be able to add to your wealth is to win the Lottery, guess what? You are correct! For, if you waste your money on gambling, you will not be saving your money. You have no control over winning the Lottery. You do have control over your ability to save. We are not saying to never do fun things. What we are saying is that you spend your money on needs to fit in your budget and to support your goals. For example, your reward for saving your target sum for a month, while staying within your budget, could be a nice night out with your favorite dinner partner, a movie, or other entertainment. Once you have established the practice of saving and budgeting, you will be able to have more of the nice things in life and they will likely be things that you truly value—not some consumer skeleton hanging in your closet of impulse purchases.

Principle 4 Take Good Care of Your Health

Exercise and eat well. People who have good nutrition and health habits have lower medical bills, they save more, they make more, and they have greater wealth. It does not take a college degree to figure out that the people who show up at work and who are energized to complete their work are those who are promoted.

Principle 5 Get a Good Education

You are doing that! Remember that only 6.7% of the world's population has a college degree.[3] Think of the opportunity this gives you, as well as the responsibilities it lays before you.

Principle 6 Consider the Financial Benefits of Being Married

It is a fact that married people earn more and have greater wealth than single people. Why? The answer is simple; a married couple has two brains and oftentimes two incomes to work with. Research shows that married people tend to be healthier and happier. Yet, if you marry, marry well. Divorce can undo the best laid financial plan.

---

[3] http://www.huffingtonpost.com/2010/05/19/percent-of-world-with-col_n_581807.html

Principle 7 Establish an Emergency Fund of 3–6 Months Living Expenses

Once you have an emergency fund established, you are able to face many more financial risks that are in front of you. If you have a saving cushion, you are able to have ready cash in the event of a temporary loss of income and you are able to increase your deductibles on your insurance.

Think of the risks you face; getting sick, losing your job, becoming disabled, having an automobile accident, causing harm to another and being sued, or living longer than your money. Each of these has insurance policies that you can, and should, purchase to protect you and your family. (More about this in Sections 6, 7, and 9.)

Principle 8 Do not Try to Beat the Stock Market

Unless you get satisfaction out of buying individual stocks or picking mutual funds, do not try to beat the market. You will find it a very difficult thing to do. Instead, consider using index mutual funds for your retirement and other long-term goals. If you pay others to manage your money, understand what they are doing with your money. Ultimately, your decisions are your responsibility. If you do not understand what you are buying, do not buy it.

Principle 9 Strive for a Balanced Life

Live a principled life that is full of integrity and responsibility. Most universities have a statement of values. Do you know yours? Remember that financial problems are usually behavior problems and, as Yogi Berra,[4] a New York Yankee Hall of Famer, once said, "If you don't know where you are going, you will wind up somewhere else." We encourage you to not "wind up somewhere else."

FISCAL PHILOSOPHY

Gaining a mature philosophy about money, and why we value money, will help you throughout your life. Perhaps surprisingly, money has the potential to produce as many problems as it can solve. Having too much money is often as destructive as not having enough. Ponder the following thoughts:

A heavy purse makes a light heart. (English proverb)

Great riches have sold more men than they have bought. (Bacon, 1561–1626)

It is more difficult to be well with riches, than to be at ease under the want of them. Man governeth himself much easier in poverty than in abundance. (Akhenaton, B.C. 1375)

True security lies not in the things one has, but in the things one can do without. (Og Mandino)

The greatest man in history was the poorest. (Emerson, 1803–1882)

Wealth consists not in having great possessions, but in having few wants. (Epicurus, B.C. 341–270)

Our incomes are like our shoes; if too small they gall and pinch us; but if too large they cause us to stumble and trip. (Colton, 1780–1832)

Money is not required to buy one necessity of the soul. (Thoreau, 1817–1862)

For where your treasure is, there will your heart be also. (Jesus)

In all the world people enjoy salt and money. (Chinese proverb)

More money, more problems (the Notorious BIG)

---

[4] http://baseballhall.org/hof/berra-yogi

WEALTH?

Many people think they are rich if they have a large income. Furthermore, they believe that if their income increases, they are becoming richer. However, despite **nominal** income (the amount of dollars being earned) increasing by 1,258%, **real** income (the purchasing power of those dollars) increased by only 54.2% between 1960 and 2015 in the United States.

Annual Median Family Income

Year	Nominal Income	Consumer Price Index (CPI) (1982–1984 = 100)	Real Income in 1982 Dollars (Nominal income / (CPI/100))
1960	$ 5,620	29.6	$18,986
1965	$ 6,957	31.5	$22,086
1970	$ 9,867	38.8	$25,430
1975	$13,719	53.8	$25,500
1980	$21,023	82.4	$25,513
1985	$27,735	107.6	$25,776
1990	$35,353	130.7	$27,049
1995	$40,611	152.4	$26,648
2000	$50,732	172.2	$29,461
2005	$56,194	195.3	$28,773
2010	$60,236	218.1	$27,619
2015	$70,697	241.4	$29,282
Percentage Change from 1960 to 2015	1,258%	716%	54.2%

Sources: U.S. Census Bureau, Table F-6
http://www.bls.gov/cpi/cpifiles/cpiai.txt
http://www.census.gov/hhes/www/income/data/historical/families/

As shown by the trend in real median family income in recent years, individuals must be careful to not define financial well-being in terms of their income. For this reason, we suggest that well-being should not be defined simply in terms of income. It is our opinion that true wealth includes a wide array of human and material resources, including relationships with family and friends, freedom, health, and opportunity.

True wealth includes much that money cannot (should not) buy.

Time Value of Money

Of all the principles of finance, whether it be personal, family, or corporate finance, none is more central than the **time value of money**. The value of a dollar grows or declines through time, hence the term "time value of money." Over time, a dollar either grows in value due to interest earned or an increase in market value or declines due to the eroding effect of inflation or a decrease in market value.

What is meant by the phrase **time value of money**?

Take a simple example:

Question: Suppose you invested $1,000 on January 1, 2018, and the money earns 7% interest, how much interest will you have earned by December 31, 2018?

Answer: $1,000 * .07 = $70 interest earned

Given an annual interest rate of 7%, it can be said that the *time value* of your $1,000 is 7%.

Now, examine the flip side of the same concept. What if, instead of investing your $1,000, you put it into a jar on your shelf for the whole year? You will earn no interest. During 2013, the average annual rate of inflation was 1.5%. (In other words, the prices of the basket of things we buy [cars, bread, sweaters, pencils, etc.] increased an average of 1.5% between January 1 and December 31.)

What is the *time value* of inflation?

$1,000 at beginning of the year

1.5% inflation during the year

$1,000 * .015 = $15

By the end of 2018, it will take $1,015 to purchase what $1,000 would have purchased on January 1, 2013. In other words, you have lost **purchasing power**.

If you do not invest your $1,000 it ends up being worth $985.22 in purchasing power after 1 year ($1,000/1.015 = $985.22).

- **Mathematics of Money**

$$\text{Formula: } I = P * R * T$$

where: I = Interest earned or interest paid

P = Principal sum of money

R = Annual rate of interest

T = Time period *(where 1 year is the maximum)*

Unless stated otherwise, annual compounding is assumed.

Example Problems

1. You invest $200 into your savings account on January 1, 2018. On December 31, 2018, how much interest will you have earned if the account earns 6.5% compounded annually?

    Year 1   I   = $200   *   .065   *   1   =   **$13.00**

2. You invest $200 into your savings account on January 1, 2018. On June 30, 2018, how much interest will you have earned if the account earns 6.5% compounded semiannually?

    6 months   I   = $200   *   .065   *   .50   =   **$6.50**

3. You invest $200 into your savings account on January 1, 2018. On December 31, 2018, how much interest will you have earned if the account earns 6.5% compounded semiannually? (This example demonstrates the importance of compounding, where returns are earned on previous returns. In this case, the $6.50 that is earned in the first 6 months, in addition to the original principal, earns interest in the next 6 months. The result is an additional $0.21 in return!)

6 months	I	=	$200.00	*	.065	*	.50	=	$ 6.50
6 months	I	=	$206.50	*	.065	*	.50	=	$ 6.71
						Total Interest Earned		=	**$13.21**

4. You invest $200 into your savings account on January 1, 2018. On December 31, 2018, how much interest will you have earned if the account earns 6.5% annual interest *compounded quarterly*?

Qtr 1	I	=	$200.00	*	.065	*	.25	=	$ 3.25
Qtr 2	I	=	$203.25	*	.065	*	.25	=	$ 3.30
Qtr 3	I	=	$206.55	*	.065	*	.25	=	$ 3.36
Qtr 4	I	=	$209.91	*	.065	*	.25	=	$ 3.41
						Total Interest Earned		=	**$13.32**

    Note that in Quarters 2, 3, and 4, you earn interest on interest earned in the previous quarters, or in other words, *compounding of interest* is occurring. Moreover, compared to Example 3, you earn an additional $0.11 as a result of more frequent compounding. The greater the rate of interest and the more frequent it is compounding, the greater will be the value of the money we save in the future.

5. You invest $200 into your savings account on January 1, 2016. On December 31, 2018, what will be your total account balance if the account earns 6.5% compounded annually?

Year 1	I	=	$200.00	*	.065	*	1	=	$ 13.00
Year 2	I	=	$213.00	*	.065	*	1	=	$ 13.85
Year 3	I	=	$226.85	*	.065	*	1	=	$ 14.75
					Interest Earned			=	$ 41.60
					Beginning Balance			+	$200.00
					Total Account Balance			=	**$241.60**

6. You invest $1,000 into your savings account on January 1, 2018. If the account earns 9.5% *compounded semiannually* (1) how much interest will you have earned over the 3-year period and (2) what will your total account balance be on December 31, 2020?

Period 1	I	=	$1,000.00	*	.095	*	.5	=	$ 47.50
Period 2	I	=	$1,047.50	*	.095	*	.5	=	$ 49.76
Period 3	I	=	$1,097.26	*	.095	*	.5	=	$ 52.12
Period 4	I	=	$1,149.38	*	.095	*	.5	=	$ 54.60

Period 5	I	=	$1,203.98	*	.095	*	.5	=	$ 57.19
Period 6	I	=	$1,261.17	*	.095	*	.5	=	$ 59.91

Interest Earned	=	$ 321.08
Beginning Balance	+	$1,000.00
Total Account Balance	=	**$1,321.08**

Assignment 1.1   Mathematics of Banking

Name _____

SHOW YOUR WORK

*** Using the simple I = P * R * T formula, solve the following problems***

1. You invest $3,459 in a savings account which pays 7.2% annual interest. After 1 year how much interest will you have earned?

2. You invest $3,459 in a savings account which pays 7.2% annual interest. After 1 year what will be the total balance in your savings account?

3. You invest $3,459 in a savings account which pays 7.2% annual compound interest. After 3 years how much interest will you have earned?

4. You invest $3,459 in a savings account which pays 7.2% annual compound interest. After 3 years what will be the total balance in your savings account?

5. You invest $500 into a savings account which pays 8.5% annual interest compounded quarterly. How much interest will you earn after 1 year?

6. You invest $500 into a savings account which pays 8.5% annual interest compounded quarterly. What will the total account balance be after 2 years?

7. You invest $1,200 into a 12-month certificate of deposit which will pay 6.6% annual interest. How much interest will you earn if interest is compounded annually?

8. Using the same information from Problem 7, how much interest will you earn with monthly compounding? (When solving for time or "T," be accurate out to four decimal places.)

TIME VALUE OF MONEY FORMULAS

Use of the simple $I = P * R * T$ formula is instructive, but becomes rather tedious as a problem increases in complexity. The solution is algebra (*or ideally a financial calculator!*). Shown below are the algebraic formulas that can be used to solve for future value (FV), present value (PV), length of investment period (n), and needed interest rate (i) for lump-sum investments. Note that these formulas are for lump sums, where a single payment is made or received in the future. Formulas for annuity investments, where multiple, periodic payments are made or received, will be shown later.

Lump-Sum Formulas

FV	=	Future value
PV	=	Present value (as a lump sum)
n	=	Number of investment periods
i	=	Interest rate per investment period

$$FV = PV (1 + i)^n$$

$$PV = FV (1 + i)^{-n} = \frac{FV}{(1 + i)^n}$$

$$i = (FV / PV)^{1/n} - 1$$

$$n = \frac{\ln (FV / PV)}{\ln (1 + i)}, \text{ where } \ln = \text{natural logarithm (however, base 10 will work)}$$

Time Value of Money Instructions—Setting Up Your Calculator

The hardest part of determining time value of money is learning how to set up the formula for given situations. We will give you three tips to help you learn how to set up the problem: Repetition, Repetition, and Repetition. Working through all the practice problems in the workbook and, perhaps, changing the numbers and working them again—while comparing your answers with those of a classmate—are the best ways to learn how to set up time value of money problems. Once you have the problem set up, the computation is really very straight forward.

Many of you have purchased a financial calculator to help you with this class. If so, the following are "important instructions" to help you avoid common mistakes made by students:

1. Always clear your calculator's financial memory after each problem. This insures that the numbers from the previous problem have been removed from your calculator's memory. If you do not do this, your answers will be incorrect. (Refer to your calculator's manual for additional instructions).

To clear the calculator

Hewlett Packard 10BII+	press: orange, then C
Texas Instruments BA II+	press: 2nd, then FV, then 2nd, and then CE/C

2. Money (PV or PMT) *leaving you* (such as a lump-sum investment or a periodic payment) are entered as *negative* numbers when using a financial calculator. Cash flows *coming to you* (e.g., rental income) are entered as *positive* numbers. You have a key labeled $+/-$ on your calculator that you will use to change the sign of a positive number to a negative number, and back again to a positive number if pressed a second time.

   If using the algebraic formula, the sign of numbers is not an issue.

3. When a problem involves compounding more frequently than annually (i.e., monthly compounding, quarterly compounding), it is necessary to adjust **n** and **i** accordingly. For example, if you have 8% interest compounded quarterly for 5 years, you would earn 2% (=8%/4) per quarter, for 20 (=5 ∗ 4) quarters. (NOTE: This assumes your calculator is set for 1 payment per "year." If you change what is entered as your payments per year for each problem, you do not have to divide your interest rate or multiply your years by the number of quarters per year. If you plan to work with these problems as a part of your career, we suggest you begin to change the payments per year for each problem.)

To set your calculator to *one payment per year*

Hewlett Packard 10BII+	press: 1, then orange, then PMT
Texas Instrument BAII+	press: 2nd, then P/Y, then 1, then ENTER

    If you decide to change your payments per year for each problem, follow the information above but instead of 1 change it to the proper number of payment periods for the scenario at hand. For example, if you have 8% interest compounded quarterly for 5 years, you would change your payments per year to 4.

    For many students, especially those taking this course as their only personal finance course, setting your calculator to *one payment per year* is a good practice and you must remember to change your interest rate and number of periods as instructed in #3 above. For those of you that intend to work in the area of finance, we recommend that you now begin to change the number of periods per year with each problem.

4. Enter the interest rate (i) into a financial calculator as a whole number stated as a percent. For example, an interest rate of 8.5% is entered as 8.5, *not* .085. If, however, you are using the algebraic formulas, enter the rate of interest in decimal form as .085, not 8.5%. (If you are choosing to use the algebraic formulas, your mathematical skills are probably good enough that we need not remind you of this.)

5. Set your display to show at least four digits to the right of the decimal.

To set your display to show four digits to the right of the decimal

Hewlett Packard 10BII+	press: orange, then =, then 4
Texas Instrument BAII+	press: 2nd, then ".", then 4, then ENTER, then CE/C

"." is the decimal/period button

6. Yes, the algebraic formulas are as accurate as financial calculators.

7. If you are ever in doubt, assume annual compounding, unless it is stated that you should assume compounding more often than annually.

8. Do not truncate **i** (interest rate) when solving problems. For example, if a problem requires monthly compounding and the annual rate of interest is 11.5%, the monthly rate is

$$11.5 / 12 = .95833333333, \text{ where the 3 keeps repeating.}$$

The only accurate technique for entering such a nontruncating number into the memory of your calculator is to solve the equation (in this case 11.5 / 12) and then immediately enter it as **i**. Do NOT enter an approximation, like .9853. You will not find the correct answer and you will be frustrated.

    When using algebra, you may want to store a nontruncating number in a memory location and recall it when needed.

IF YOU ROUND (i.e., truncate) RATES OF INTEREST, YOUR ANSWERS WILL BE WRONG. The guideline for accuracy is this: *Be as accurate as you want your banker to be with your money.*

9. It is important to know how to set your calculator into *Begin* mode (also referred to as *Annuity Due* mode). Below are the instructions for each calculator commonly used in this course.

To switch from Begin to End Mode

Hewlett Packard 10BII+   press: orange, then MAR (to change Begin/End)

Texas Instrument BAII+   press: 2nd, then PMT, then 2nd, then ENTER, then C

Did you actually complete Steps 1 through 9 on your calculator? Remember the three things you need to know to master time value of money calculations: Repetition, Repetition, and Repetition.

Practice Problems:

If you deposited $2,000 into a savings account that earned 7.5% annual interest (compounded annually means one payment per year or P/Y = 1), how much would you have in the account after 5 years?

The first step in solving such a problem is setting it into the time value of money format.

There are five components of time value of money:

PV	=	Present value
FV	=	Future value
PMT	=	Payment
N	=	Length of time (or number of periods)
I/YR	=	Interest rate
P/YR	=	Payments per year

In this problem the desired answer is the amount of money in the future, hence we are solving for FV. Importantly, the $2,000 is a lump-sum deposit, so we will not use the PMT key.

Solution Using a Financial Calculator

The $2,000 deposit is an investment where money leaves your hands *now* as a lump sum; therefore, it is a PV and is given a negative sign (as shown by <> brackets).

$$PV = -2,000 \text{ or, as accountants write, } <2,000>$$

Next, determine the length of the investment and enter that figure as the *n* input. In this case,

$$N = 5 \text{ years.}$$

Now, enter the annual rate of interest as the *i* input.

$$I/YR = 7.5$$

Is there a PMT involved in this problem? No, there are no repeating cash flows; so PMT is not relevant to this problem.

The complete setup is:

PV	=	<2,000>
N	=	5
I/YR	=	7.5
FV	=	?

If Using the TI BA II+ Financial Calculator

*** Remember to clear the financial register first: **2nd FV 2nd CE/C.**

Keystrokes on TI BA II+ Financial Calculator	2,000	+/−	PV	5	n	7.5	I/YR	CPT	FV

   CPT stands for **compute**. (Not all financial calculators have a CPT button. If yours does not, simply skip that keystroke.)
   Note that the equal sign on your calculator is not needed to enter data or obtain a solution.
   The correct answer for the FV is $2,871.26.

If Using the HP 10B II+ Financial Calculator

*** Remember to clear the financial register first: **orange C (i.e., C ALL).**

Keystrokes on HP 10B II+ Financial Calculator	2,000	+/−	PV	5	N	7.5	I/YR	FV

   The correct answer for the FV $2,871.26.
   If you did not get this answer, check your P/Y setting and try again.

Solution Using ALGEBRA

The setup when using algebraic formulas presents *two important differences* from the setup when using a financial calculator.

- First, the sign (positive or negative) of the data is not important. In this particular case, the PV of $2,000 is entered in the formula as a positive number.
- Second, the rate of interest is ALWAYS expressed in decimal form, never as a whole number percentage.

The setup is as follows:

PV	=	2,000
N	=	5
I/YR	=	.075
FV	=	?

The formula to solve this problem is:

FV	=	PV $(1 + i)^n$

The y^x button on your calculator is used to calculate $(1 + i)^n$. If your calculator does not have a y^x button, you will need to purchase a calculator that does.

$$FV = 2{,}000 \,(1 + .075)^5$$
$$FV = 2{,}000 \,(1.075)^5$$
$$FV = 2{,}000 \,(1.435629326)$$
$$\mathbf{FV} = \mathbf{2{,}871.26}$$

IMPORTANT: As discussed earlier, never truncate numbers that are used in calculations. When solving this problem, do not round 1.435629326 to 1.44. Solve 1.075 raised to the fifth power and immediately multiply that answer by 2,000.

Lump-Sum Example Problems (Annual Compounding)

1. You invest $1,500 as a lump sum into a savings account with *annual compounding*. If the average annual return of the account is 7%, how much will you have in the account after 10 years?

   Using a financial calculator:

PV	=	<1,500>
N	=	10
I/YR	=	7
FV	=	**2,950.73** (notice that interest is entered as a whole number, not a decimal)

   OR

   Using algebra:

   $$FV = 1{,}500 \,(1 + .07)^{10} = \mathbf{2{,}950.73}$$

2. Let's turn the question around. If you want to have $2,950.73 in 10 years, how much will you need to invest in your savings account as a lump sum today if you can earn 7% interest each year? That is, what is the PV? (Clear your TVM memory.)

   Using a financial calculator:

FV	=	2,950.73
N	=	10
I/YR	=	7
PV	=	**<1,500>** (notice that the answer is negative indicating that money is leaving you)

   Using algebra:

   $$PV = 2{,}950.73 \,(1 + .07)^{-10} = \mathbf{1{,}500}$$

3. Now, let us solve for the interest rate. You invest $1,500 today as a lump sum into your savings account. You want to have $2,950.73 in 10 years. What annual rate of return will you need to achieve your goal?

   Using a financial calculator:

PV	=	<1,500>
FV	=	2,950.73
N	=	10
I/YR	=	**7.00**

   Using algebra:

   $$i = (2{,}950.73 \,/\, 1{,}500)^{1/10} - 1 = \mathbf{.07 \text{ or } 7\% \text{ annual rate}}$$

4. Finally, solve for the number of years. You invest $1,500 today as a lump sum into your savings account. If the account has an average annual return of 7%, how many years will it take to have $2,950.73 in the fund?

Using a financial calculator:

PV	=	<1,500>
FV	=	2,950.73
I/YR	=	7
N	=	**10**

Using algebra:

$$n = \frac{\ln(\$2,950.73 / \$1,500)}{\ln(1 + .07)} = \frac{.676587}{.067659} = 10 \text{ years}$$

Lump-Sum Example Problems (Nonannual Compounding)

1. You invest $1,500 as a lump sum into a savings account with *monthly compounding*. If the average annual return of the account is 6.5%, how much will you have in the account after 10 years?

Using a financial calculator:

PV	=	<1,500>
N	=	120 (10 years * 12 months = 120 periods)
I/YR	=	0.54166666666 (=6.50 / 12; if you have P/Y set to 1)
I/YR	=	6.5 (if you change P/Y to 12)
FV	=	**2,868.28**

Using algebra:

FV	=	$1,500(1 + (.065 / 12))^{120}$	=	**2,868.28**

2. If you want to have $5,000 in 10 years, how much will you need to invest in your savings account as a lump sum today if you can earn 12% interest each year *compounded quarterly*?

Using a financial calculator:

FV	=	5,000
N	=	40 (10 years * 4 quarters per year)
I/YR	=	3 (=12 / 4; if you have P/Y set to 1)
I/YR	=	12 (if you change P/Y to 4)
PV	=	**−1,532.78 or <1,532.78>**

Using algebra:

PV	=	$5,000(1 + (.12 / 4))^{-40}$	=	**1,532.78**

3. You invest $1,500 today as a lump sum into your savings account. You want to have $5,000 in 10 years. What *monthly* rate of return will you need to achieve your goal?

Using a financial calculator:

PV	=	<1,500>
FV	=	5,000
N	=	10 years * 12 months per year = 120 months
I/YR	=	**1.0084%** (if you have P/Y = 1, this equals 1.0084 * 12 **12.10% per year**)
I/YR	=	12.100328482% per **year** (if you have P/Y = 12) When you divide this by 12, you will find **1.0084% per month**, as asked for.

Using algebra:

i $\qquad = \qquad (5{,}000 / 1{,}500)^{1/120} - 1 = .010084$ or **1.0084% monthly rate**

OR

$1.0084\% * 12 =$ **12.10% annual rate**

4. You invest $1,500 today as a lump sum into your savings account. If the account has a monthly rate of return of 1.00%, how many *months* will it take to have $5,000 in the fund?

Using a financial calculator:

PV	=	<1,500>
FV	=	5,000
I/YR	=	1 (if you have P/Y set equal to 1)
I/YR	=	12 (if you have P/Y set equal to 12)
N	=	**120.998268509 or 121 months**

Using algebra:

$$n \qquad = \qquad \frac{\ln(\$5{,}000 / \$1{,}500)}{\ln(1 + .01)} = \frac{1.20397}{.00995} = \qquad \textbf{121 months}$$

ANNUITIES

An annuity is a cash flow that takes place more than once. The cash flow (or payment) can be money *received by you* (monthly allowance, bimonthly paycheck, quarterly stock dividend, etc.) or *leaving you* (quarterly deposit into your savings account, monthly payment on a loan, etc.).

Recall that lump-sum problems utilize a PV and a FV. These are lump-sum events, meaning they occur only once. Annuity formulas utilize a **PMT** as well. This PMT occurs on a regular basis (i.e., daily, weekly, monthly, quarterly, biannually, annually).

When equal cash flows occur more than once,
it is an annuity problem.

Cash flows (or payments) that take place at the end of each period (say, at the end of each month) are referred to as *ordinary annuities*. These problems require you to have your calculator set at **END**. (See instruction #9 in the Time Value of Money Instructions above.)

Cash flows that take place at the beginning of the period are referred to as annuity due. Annuity due problems require that you set your financial calculator to **BGN** mode. (Again, see instruction #9 in the Time Value of Money instructions.) Once set, the screen will display the word BEGIN (on the HP 10BII+) or BGN (on the TA BAII+). To reset the financial calculator to ordinary annuity (or END) mode, repeat the same keystrokes and the BEGIN or BEG will be removed from the LCD display.

Remember . . .

1. You have to be very careful to make sure you have the correct P/Y set in your calculator and to adjust your I/YR accordingly. You may need to refer back to the Time Value of Money Directions or consult your calculator's manual.

2. When entering PMT on a financial calculator, you need to assign the *correct sign*. If money is leaving your hands, such as a monthly car payment or a monthly investment, you will enter the PMT as a *negative* number. If money is coming to you, such as withdraw of money each month from a savings account, you will enter the PMT as a *positive* number.

The following pages provide the algebraic formulas used for annuity problems.

They also make the purchase of a financial calculator an easier pill to swallow!

Annuity Formulas (Ordinary Annuities) in End Mode

FV = Future value of an annuity
PV = Present value of an annuity
PMT = Annuity payment
N = Number of investment periods
i = Interest rate per investment period

$$FV = PMT\left(\frac{(1+i)^n - 1}{i}\right)$$

$$PV = PMT\left(\frac{1 - (1+i)^{-n}}{i}\right)$$

$$PMT = \frac{PV}{\left(\dfrac{1 - (1+i)^{-n}}{i}\right)}$$

$$PMT = FV\left(\frac{i}{(1+i)^n - 1}\right)$$

$$n = \frac{\ln(1 + ((FV * i)/PMT))}{\ln(1+i)}$$

$$n = -\frac{\ln(1 - ((PV * i)/PMT))}{\ln(1+i)}$$

Annuity Formulas (Annuity Due) in Begin Mode

FV**ad** = Future value of an **a**nnuity **d**ue
PV**ad** = Present value of an **a**nnuity **d**ue
PMT**ad** = **A**nnuity **d**ue payment
n = Number of investment periods
i = Interest rate per investment period

Annuity due (noted by the small *ad*) means that the periodic investment, or withdrawal, takes place at the *beginning* of the period (week, month, year, etc.) rather than at the *end*.

$$FV = PMTad\left(\frac{(1+i)^n - 1}{i}\right) * (1+i)$$

$$PV = PMTad\left(\frac{1 - (1+i)^{-n}}{i}\right) * (1+i)$$

$$PMTad = \frac{PV}{\dfrac{1 - (1+i)^{-n}}{i}} * \frac{1}{(1+i)}$$

$$PMTad = FV\left(\frac{i}{(1+i)^n - 1}\right) * \frac{1}{(1+i)}$$

$$n = \frac{\ln(1 + ((FV * i)/(PMTad * (1+i))))}{\ln(1+i)}$$

$$n = -\frac{\ln(1 - ((PV * i)/(PMTad * (1+i))))}{\ln(1+i)}$$

Annuity Practice Problem

If you deposited $2,000 AT THE END OF EACH YEAR into a savings account that earned 7.5% annual interest (compounded annually), how much would you have in the account after 5 years?

Solution Using a Financial Calculator

Now instead of a lump-sum deposit (i.e., PV is essentially set equal to 0) you are presented with an annuity problem where an investment is being made each year (i.e., PMT). The investment is made at the end of each year, hence the problem is an ordinary annuity. (Had the investment been made at the beginning of each year it would have been an annuity due problem.)

The complete setup would be as follows:

PMT	=	<2,000>
N	=	5
I/YR	=	7.5, as P/Y = 1
FV	=	?

Solution: **The correct answer for FV is 11,616.78.**

Below are the keystrokes for using a Texas Instruments BAII+ financial calculator. Remember to clear the financial register before entering data.

Keystroke #	1	2	3	4	5	6	7	8	9
Keystrokes on a TI BA II+	2,000	+/−	PMT	5	N	7.5	I/YR	CPT	FV

Pressing CPT followed by FV will display the correct answer, which is $11,616.78.

Below are the keystrokes using a Hewlett Packard 10B II+ financial calculator.

Keystroke #	1	2	3	4	5	6	7	8
Keystrokes on a HP 10B II +	2,000	+/−	PMT	5	N	7.5	I/YR	FV

After pressing FV, the answer of $11,616.78 will be displayed.

NOTE: If you are using a HP 10B II+ or TI BA II+ and are not obtaining the correct answer, please refer to the instructions and repeat, repeat, and repeat.

Now solve the same problem on the financial calculator assuming it was an annuity due problem. The problem would now be worded as follows:

If you deposited $2,000 at the beginning of each year into a savings account that earned 7.5% annual interest (compounded annually), how much would you have in the account after 5 years?

Your calculator needs to be in BEGIN or BEG mode when solving an annuity due problem. The following keystrokes would be used if you have a HP 10B II+ calculator.

Remember to clear the financial register first.

Keystroke #	1	2	3	4	5	6	7	8	9	10
Keystrokes on a HP 10B II+	orange	MAR	2,000	+/−	PMT	5	N	7.5	I/YR	FV

The calculator may be set to BEGIN mode at any point prior to solving the answer by pressing **Orange (the 2nd function button) and then BEG/END (the 2nd function on the MAR key).**
   The answer for FV_{ad} (where the small ad signifies *annuity due*) is $12,488.04. (This is 1 + i greater than the ordinary annuity answer.)

Solution Using ALGEBRA

Solve the ordinary annuity problem first (i.e., in END mode).

If you deposited $2,000 at the end of each year into a savings account that earned 7.5% annual interest (compounded annually), how much would you have in the account after 5 years?

The setup is as follows:

PMT	=	2,000
n	=	5
i	=	.075
FV	=	?

The formula to solve this problem is:

$$FV = PMT\left(\frac{(1 + i)^n - 1}{i}\right)$$

Now, plug in the specific information.

$$FV = 2,000\left(\frac{(1 + .075)^5 - 1}{.075}\right)$$

$$FV = 2,000\left(\frac{.435629326}{.75}\right)$$

$$FV = 2,000 * (5.808391013)$$

$$FV = \mathbf{11,616.78}$$

Ordinary Annuity Example Problems

1. You invest $1,500 at the *end of each year* into a savings account with annual compounding. If the average annual return of the account is 7%, how much will you have in the account after 10 years?
   Using a financial calculator:

PMT	=	<1,500>
N	=	10
I/YR	=	7
FV	=	**20,724.67**

Using algebra:

$$FV = 1,500\left(\frac{(1 + .07)^{10} - 1}{.07}\right) = \textbf{20,724.67}$$

2. If you want to withdraw $1,500 from your savings account at the *end of each year* for the next 10 years, how much money must you deposit today into the savings account if you can earn 7% annual interest? (You will have no money left in the savings account at the end of the 10th year, hence FV = 0.)

Using a financial calculator:

PMT	=	1,500
N	=	10
I/YR	=	7
PV	=	**<10,535.37>**

Using algebra:

$$PV = 1,500\left(\frac{1 - (1 + .07)^{-10}}{.07}\right) = \textbf{10,535.37}$$

3. You deposit $10,535.37 into your savings account today. You would like to withdraw the same amount of money from your account at the *end of each year* for the next 10 years. What is the maximum possible annual withdrawal if you earn 7% annual interest?

Using a financial calculator:

PV	=	<10,535.37>
N	=	10
I/YR	=	7
PMT	=	**1,500**

Using algebra:

$$PMT = \frac{10,535.37}{\left(\dfrac{1 - (1 + .07)^{-10}}{.07}\right)} = \textbf{1,500}$$

4. If you want to have $20,724.67 in 10 years, how much will you need to invest in your savings account at the *end of each year* if you can earn 7% interest each year?

Using a financial calculator:

FV	=	20,724.67
N	=	10
I/YR	=	7
PMT	=	**<1,500>**

Using algebra:

$$PMT = 20,724.67\left(\frac{0.7}{(1 + .07)^{10} - 1}\right) = \textbf{1,500}$$

5. How long will it take to accumulate $20,724.67 if you invest $1,500 at the end of each year into a savings account that earns 7% annual interest?

   Using a financial calculator:

FV	=	20,724.67
PMT	=	<1,500>
I/YR	=	7
N	=	**10**

   Using algebra:

   $$n = \frac{\ln (1 + ((20{,}724.67 * .07) / 1{,}500))}{\ln (1 + .07)} = \textbf{10 years}$$

6. You decide to invest $25,000 into a money market mutual fund. At the end of each year you would like to withdraw $3,000 from the fund. If the fund averages an annual return of 7%, how many years will it take before you withdraw all the money out of the fund?

   Using a financial calculator:

PV	=	<25,000>
I/YR	=	7
PMT	=	3,000
N	=	**12.94 years (or 13 years)**

   (Some financial calculators, such as the HP 12C, do not display a fractional answer for n. For that particular calculator, the correct answer would be 13 years.)

   Using algebra:

   $$n = -\frac{\ln (1 - (($25{,}000 * .07) / $3{,}000))}{\ln (1 + .07)} = \textbf{12.94 years}$$

Annuity Due Example Problems (Annual Compounding)

As previously explained, "annuity due" simply means that the investment, or withdrawal, takes place at the beginning of the period rather than at the end. For example:

1. You invest $1,500 at the *beginning of each year* into a savings account with annual compounding. If the average annual return of the account is 7%, how much will you have in the account after 10 years?

   Using a financial calculator:

   (Remember to set the calculator to *Begin* mode.)

PMTad	=	<1,500>
N	=	10
I/YR	=	7
FV	=	**22,175.40**

   Using algebra:

   $$FV = 1{,}500 \left(\frac{(1 + .07)^{10} - 1}{.07} \right) * (1 + .07) = \textbf{22,175.40}$$

2. You would like to create an "annuity" for your 18-year-old grandson which would pay him $2,000 at the *beginning of each year* for the next 6 years. How much money must you deposit into your money market account to produce the needed annual cash flow if the account earns 5.5% interest (compounded annually)?

Using a financial calculator:

PMTad	=	2,000
N	=	6
I/YR	=	5.5
PV	=	**<10,540.57>**

Using algebra:

$$PV = 2,000\left(\frac{1 - (1 + .055)^{-6}}{.055}\right) * (1 + .055) = \mathbf{10,540.57}$$

Annuity due examples (nonannual compounding)

The concept of nonannual compounding is the same for annuity problems as it is for lump-sum problems. A very common problem scenario is monthly investing, as opposed to making an investment once per year.

1. You invest $250 at the *beginning of each month* into a savings account. If the average annual return of the account is 7% compounded monthly, how much will you have in the account after 10 years?

Using a financial calculator:

PMTad	=	<250>
N	=	120 months (10 years * 12 months per year)
I/YR	=	7 / 12 (if P/Y = 1)
I/YR	=	7 (if P/Y = 12)
FV	=	**43,523.62**

Using algebra:

$$FV = 250\left(\frac{(1 + (.07 / 12))^{120} - 1}{(.07 / 12)}\right) * (1 + (.07 / 12)) = \mathbf{43,523.62}$$

2. If you want to withdraw $1,500 from your savings account at the *beginning of each month* for the next 10 years, how much money must you deposit today into the savings account if you can earn 7% annual interest? Assume monthly compounding. (You will have no money left in the savings account at the end of the 10 years.)

Using a financial calculator: (remember to set the calculator to BEGIN mode)

PMTad	=	1,500
N	=	10 * 12 = **120**
I/YR	=	7 / 12 (if P/Y = 1)
I/YR	=	7 (if P/Y = 12)
PV	=	**<129,943.14>**

Using algebra:

$$PV = 1,500\left(\frac{1 - (1 + (.07 / 12))^{-120}}{.07 / 12}\right) * (1 + (.07 / 12)) = \mathbf{129,943.14}$$

3. You invest $25,000 into an account which will return 9% annually. If you withdraw $200 at the *beginning* of each month, how long will it take before your account runs out of money?

Using a financial calculator: (remember to set the calculator to BEGIN mode)

PV	=	<25,000>
I/YR	=	9 / 12 (if P/Y = 1)
I/YR	=	9 (if P/Y = 12)
PMTad	=	200
N	=	**357 months**

Using algebra:

$$n = -\frac{\ln(1 - ((PV * i) / (PMTad * (1 + i))))}{\ln(1 + i)}$$

$$n = -\frac{\ln(1 - (($25,000 * .0075) / ($200 * (1 + .0075))))}{\ln(1 + .0075)}$$

$$n = -\frac{\ln(1 - (($187.50) / ($201.50)))}{\ln(1 + .0075)}$$

$$n = -\frac{\ln(1 - .930521)}{\ln(1.0075)}$$

$$n = -\frac{-2.666732}{.007472}$$

$$n = -(-356.89) \text{ or } \mathbf{357 \text{ months}} \text{ (the double negative signs cancel each other)}$$

4. You deposit $2,000 into a savings account as a lump sum. *In addition*, you decide to invest $100 at the *beginning of each month* into the same account. After 15 years, how much money will have accumulated in the account if it earns 7% interest per year? (This is a really good problem. Consider if you know how much you have saved and how much you can save per month. If so, you could calculate how much money you would have at a later date, say retirement.)

Using a financial calculator:

PV	=	<2,000>
N	=	15 years * 12 months per year = **180 months**
I/YR	=	7 / 12 (P/Y = 1)
I/YR	=	7 (P/Y = 12)
PMTad	=	<100> per month
FV	=	**37,579.02**

Using algebra (This problem is solved in two steps and, again, makes the purchase of a calculator much less painful.):

First, solve for FV using only PV.

$$FV = 2,000 (1 + (.07 / 12))^{180} = \mathbf{5,697.8935}$$

Second, solve for FV using the only PMTad.

$$FV = 100 \left(\frac{(1 + (.07 / 12))^{180} - 1}{(.07 / 12)} \right) * (1 + (.07 / 12)) = \mathbf{31,881.1243}$$

The final answer is obtained by adding the two future value figures together:

FV = 5,697.8935 + 31,881.1243 = **37,579.02**

Annuity Example

A synonym for annuity is disbursement. An annuity is the disbursement of money on a periodic basis. For example, you may invest $50,000 into an annuity product which will then disburse $400 per month to you for the next 30 years. Annuity products are often marketed by life insurance companies.

What would an annuity product which promised to pay you $1,200 at the end of each year for 10 years cost if the interest rate earned by the annuity was 7% compounded annually?

Same example, different wording . . .

How much money would you need to deposit into your savings account (which earns 7% annually) to enable you to withdraw $1,200 at the end of each year for 10 years? (After 10 years there would no money left in the savings account.)

Write down what you know: PMT = $1,200
                              N   = 10
                              I/YR = 7% (P/Y = 1)

You want to know what?   PV (or the purchase price of the annuity)
Using the correct formula the answer for PV = **<$8,428.30>**
Prove to yourself that the PV is correct by examining the following table.

Year	Starting Balance	Interest Rate	Amount of Interest	Balance	Annuity Payment Withdrawn	Ending Balance
1	$8,429	.07	$590	$9,019	$1,200	$7,819
2	$7,819	.07	$547	$8,366	$1,200	$7,166
3	$7,166	.07	$502	$7,667	$1,200	$6,467
4	$6,467	.07	$453	$6,920	$1,200	$5,720
5	$5,720	.07	$400	$6,121	$1,200	$4,921
6	$4,921	.07	$344	$5,265	$1,200	$4,065
7	$4,065	.07	$285	$4,350	$1,200	$3,150
8	$3,150	.07	$220	$3,379	$1,200	$2,170
9	$2,170	.07	$152	$2,322	$1,200	$1,122
10	$1,122	.07	$79	$1,200	$1,200	0

Assignment 1.2   Time Value of Money Problems

Name _____

SHOW YOUR WORK

1. You have the choice of receiving $15,000 today or $25,000 in 6 years as a down payment from someone who wants to purchase your rental property. If you could expect to earn 11% on invested money (i.e., your time value of money = 11%), which would you choose?

2. What is the present value (or purchase price) of an annuity product which will pay you $2,000 at the end of each year for the next 15 years? Use an interest rate of 9%.

3. You currently have $7,500 to invest. You can invest the full amount now for a period of 9 years, at which time you want to have $15,000. Approximately what rate of return is needed to accomplish this investment goal?

4. You receive an inheritance of $25,000 and promptly invest it in an account which yields an 8% annual return. If you withdraw $2,000 at the *beginning of each year*, how long will the $25,000 last?

5. You are trying to decide between investing $3,000 or $4,000 at the *beginning of each year* for the next 20 years into a retirement account yielding 11%. After 20 years, how much extra money would you have in your account if you invested $4,000 annually versus $3,000 annually?

6. If 4 years of college tuition cost $15,000 in 2015 what did a college education cost in 1990 if tuition increased at 7% per year between 1990 and 2015?

7. If you invest $1,500 at the *beginning of each year* into an account which averages a return of 12%, approximately how long will it take to accumulate $50,000 in the account?

8. [Three-part question] Five years from now you would like to have $25,000 for a down payment on a home. Assuming you could earn 9% interest, how much money would you need to invest today as a *lump sum* to meet your goal? How much money would you have to invest at the end of each year to meet your goal? How much would you need if you invested the payments at the *beginning of each year* with the first payment deposited today?

9. Your eccentric aunt just passed away and she left you $18,000. You decide to invest the full amount (as a lump sum) into a mutual fund which will have a return of 10% per year (compounded monthly) for the next 22 years. You will also invest $125 at the *end of each month* into the same mutual fund account for the full 22 years. How much will you have in the mutual fund account after 22 years? (Hint: this problem must be solved in two stages if you are using algebra.)

10. What would you be willing to pay (on January 1, 2011) for an investment which you could sell on January 1, 2041 for $45,000? Assume that the interest rate between 2011 and 2041 will be 9% annually.

Time Value of Money Practice Problems

1. Today Fred Flintstone purchased an investment-grade diamond for $50,000. He expects it to increase in value at a rate of 15% annually for the next 5 years. How much will his diamond be worth at the end of the fifth year if his expectations are correct?

2. In January of 2018 Prairie Dawn loaned $10,000 to her son at 9.25% interest compounded annually and payable at the termination of the loan. When the son repays the loan in January 2024, how will Prairie receive?

3. Bert and Ernie purchased $75,000 worth of gold coins 9 years ago. The coins have appreciated 4% annually over the time period. How much are the coins worth today?

4. Rocky and Bullwinkle have a balloon payment of $40,000 that is due in 7 years. If they can make the lump-sum payment today (pay off the loan early), how much should they offer the lender if the loan rate is 10.875%?

5. Rocky and Bullwinkle have the same $40,000 balloon note due in 7 years. They cannot afford the lump-sum payment today.

   a. How much would they have to invest at the *end of each year* to have the needed balloon amount in 7 years if they can earn 7% annually?

   b. How much would they have to invest at the *beginning of each year* to have the needed balloon amount in 7 years if they can earn 7% annually?

   c. How much would they have to invest at the *end of each quarter* to have the needed balloon amount in 7 years if they can earn 7% annually with quarterly compounding?

   d. How much would they have to invest at the *beginning of each quarter* to have the needed balloon amount in 7 years if they can earn 7% annually with quarterly compounding?

   e. How much would they have to invest at the *end of each month* to have the needed balloon amount in 7 years if they can earn 7% annually with monthly compounding?

   f. How much would they have to invest at the *beginning of each month* to have the needed balloon amount in 7 years if they can earn 7% annually with monthly compounding?

6. At the end of each year for the past 6 years you have received an annuity payment from your rich uncle of $5,000 which you invested into an account paying 9% annual compound interest.

   a. What is the current account balance?

   b. Your younger sister wants to borrow the money in your account (from 6a) to go to college and she wants to pay you back in four equal payments. If you charge her 12% interest (she is your sister after all), and the first payment is due 1 year from today, what is the size of that payment?

   c. If your sister makes payments to you at the *beginning of each month* (rather than at the end of each year) what will be the size of each payment?

7. A seller offers to finance the sale of a building to you as an investment. The mortgage loan of $280,000 will be for 20 years and requires an annual mortgage payment of $30,672 at the beginning of each year. A local bank offers you a 20-year loan, with annual payments, at an interest rate of 11%. Which source of financing do you prefer?

8. You have the opportunity to purchase, for $550,000, an apartment building with a useful life of 23 years. The current before-tax net rental income is $49,000 per year. The rental income is expected to remain at this level. Since you want a before-tax return of at least 10%, how much should you offer to pay for the apartment building?

9. a. Joe Kappa's grandfather opened a savings account for him with a lump-sum deposit of $500 when Joe was born. The account has a current value of $1,621.50. Approximately how old is Joseph if the deposit has been accumulating at an annual rate of 4% compounded annually?

   b. How much would be in Joe's account if his grandfather made additional deposits of $500 into his savings account at the end of each year? (In addition to the initial deposit of $500.) Use your answer from "9a" as the number of years (n). Assume a rate of interest of 4%.

10. Seven years ago Clarence purchased an Oriental rug for $4,896. Today he sold the rug for $12,250. What annual rate of return did Clarence earn on the rug over the 7-year period?

11. a. If you deposit $10,000 into a savings account and then withdraw $75 at the end of each month, how long will the account last if you earn 7% compounded monthly?

    b. How long will the account last if $75 is withdrawn at the beginning of each month? Assume the same rate of interest.

12. Billy Swine recently won $1,000,000 in Las Vegas. He has the option of receiving $25,000 at the end of each year for the next 40 years or $250,000 as a one-time lump sum today.

    a. If Billy has a time value of money of 9% annually, which payment option should he select?

    b. If Billy invests each annual payment of $25,000 into a mutual fund (at the end of each year) which averages an annual return of 9%, how much will he have in the fund after 40 years?

    c. If Billy chooses the lump-sum payment and invests the entire amount as a lump sum into the same mutual fund, how much would he have after 40 years? (Assume a 9% rate of return.)

Answers to Time Value of Money Practice Problems

1. PV   =   <$50,000>
   N   =   5
   I/YR   =   15% (or .15 using algebra)
   FV   **=**   **$100,568**

2. I/YR   =   9.25%
   PV   =   <$10,000>
   N   =   6
   FV   **=**   **$17,003**

3. PV   =   <$75,000>
   I/YR   =   4%
   N   =   9
   FV   **=**   **$106,748**

4. FV   = $40,000
   N   =   7
   I/YR   =   10.875%
   PV   **=**   **<$19,419>**

5. a. FV   = $40,000
      N   =   7 years
      I/YR   =   7%
      PMT   **=**   **<$4,622.13>**

   b. FV   = $40,000
      N   =   7 years
      I/YR   =   7%
      PMTad   **=**   **<$4,319.75>**

   c. FV   = $40,000
      N   =   28 quarters (7 years * 4 quarters per year)
      I/YR   =   7% / 4 (if P/YR = 1)
      I/YR   =   7% (if P/YR = 4)
      PMT   **=**   **<$1,119.26>**

   d. FV   = $40,000
      N   =   28 (7 years * 4 quarters per year)
      I/YR   =   1.75% (if P/YR = 1)
      I/YR   =   7% (if P/YR = 4)
      PMTad   **=**   **<$1,100.01>**

   e. FV   = $40,000
      N   =   84 months (7 years * 12 months per year)
      I/YR   =   7% / 12 (if P/Y = 1; Do not truncate this answer)
      I/YR   =   7% (if P/Y = 12)
      PMT   **=**   **<$370.37>**

f. FV   = $40,000
   N   = 84
   I/YR   = 7% / 12 (If P/Y = 1)
   I/YR   = 7% (if P/YR = 12)
   PMTad = **<$368.23>**

6. a. N   = 6 years
      I/YR   = 9%
      PMT   = <$5,000>
      FV   = **$37,616.67**

   b. PV   = <$37,616.67>
      N   = 4 years
      I/YR   = 12%
      PMT   = **$12,384.70**

   c. PV   = <$37,616.67>
      N   = 48 months (4 * 12)
      I/YR   = 1% (=12% / 12; if P/Y = 12)
      PMTad = **$980.78**

7. This problem can be solved in several different ways. First, solve the rate of interest for the seller's financing. As it is lower than the bank rate of 11%, the seller's financing is preferable. A second approach is to solve for the loan amount which could be obtained from the bank using i = 11%, PMT = $30,672, and n = 20. Inasmuch as PV for the bank loan is less than PV with the seller's financing, the seller's financing is preferable. Or, assume the same loan amount as the seller financing option, and solve for PMT. As the bank loan leads to a higher PMT, the seller financing is preferable.

Seller's financing		Bank financing	
PV	= $280,000	I/YR	= 11%
N	= 20 years	assume:	
PMT$_{ad}$	= <$30,672>	N	= 20
I/YR	= ???	PMT$_{ad}$	= <$30,672>
i	**= 10.436%**	**PV**	**= $271,119**

Bank financing	
PV	= $280,000
N	= 20
I/YR	= 11%
PMT$_{ad}$	**= <$31,676.74>**

8. PMT   = $49,000
    I/YR   = 10%
    N   = 23 years
    PV   = **<$435,277.70>**

The most you would be willing to pay for this apartment building is $435,277, assuming it produced an annual cash flow of $49,000 and that you require a 10% return on your investment. The seller is asking $550,000—too high a price for you.

9. a. PV   =   <$500>
     I/YR   =   4%
     FV   = $1,621.50
     N   **=   30 years**

   b. PV   =   <$500>
     I/YR   =   4%
     N   =   30 years
     PMT   =   <$500>
     FV   **= $29,664.17**

If using algebra, part b is solved by breaking the problem into two parts. First solve the FV for the initial lump-sum deposit (which was actually given to you in part a).

PV   =   <$500>
I/YR   =   4%
N   =   30 years
FV   **= $1,621.70**

Second, solve for the FV of the $500 annual deposit.

PMT   =   <$500>
I/YR   =   4%
N   =   30 years
FV   **= $28,042.47**

FV is solved by combining answers: **$1,621.70 + $28,042.47 = $29,664.17**

10. PV   =   <$4,896>
    FV   = $12,250
    N   =   7
    I/YR   **=   14%**

11. a. PV   =   <$10,000>
     PMT   = $75
     I/YR   =   7% / 12 (if P/Y = 1)
     N   **=   259 months (or 21.58 years)**

   b. PV   =   <$10,000>
     PMTad   = $75
     I/YR   =   7% / 12 (if P/Y = 1)
     N   **=   255 months**

12. a. PMT   = $25,000
     N   =   40 years
     I/YR   =   9%
     PV   **=   <$268,934>**

Because $268,934 > $250,000, Billy should choose annual payments rather than the lump sum of $250,000.

b. PMT   =   <$25,000>
   N   =   40 years
   I/YR   =   9%
   FV   = $8,447,061

c. PV   =   <$250,000>
   N   =   40
   I/YR   =   9%
   FV   = $7,852,355

Notes:

Personal Financial Statements

There is a burden of care in getting riches;
fear of keeping them; temptation in using them;
guilt of abusing them; sorrow in losing them;
and a burden of account at last to be given concerning them.

Matthew Henry (1662–1714)

NET WORTH STATEMENT

An individual or family can measure financial progress in a number of ways. One common way is by evaluating net worth over time. A **net worth statement** is also commonly referred to as a **balance sheet**.

Net worth is the current market value of your assets (cars, home, electronic equipment, mutual funds, CDs, jewelry, etc.) MINUS the amount of debt you owe (car loans, home mortgage, credit card debt, student loans, IOUs, etc.).

The **current market value** of your assets equals what you could sell them for in today's open market. For an automobile you can use the "Blue Book" value. For your home, ask a realtor for a market price estimate. For securities (stocks, bonds, mutual funds) use the most current market price as listed in the *Wall Street Journal*, *Barron's*, or other financial periodical.

The **total amount of debt** you owe is the total of the outstanding balances for all your debts. Do not use your monthly payment, but rather the total amount of principal you still owe (as of the date on your net worth statement).

Assets − Liabilities = Net worth

For example, a net worth of $1,350 indicates that you have $1,350 more in assets than in liabilities. In other words, if you had to sell everything at its current market value, you would be able to pay off all your debts and have $1,350 left over.

Many liabilities (i.e., debts) will have an offsetting asset. For example, a liability of $75,000 (home mortgage loan) will be more or less "balanced" by an asset of, say, $79,500 (the current market value of the home).

Many students have more liabilities than assets. This is common, particularly when student loans have been acquired. A student loan is a somewhat unique form of debt inasmuch as the offsetting asset is of great value (the knowledge and preparation you gain in college) but is not easily quantified. Therefore, a student loan of $7,500 shows up as a liability on the balance sheet with no offsetting asset. In fact, the "asset" is your increased earning power in the future—but that cannot be shown on the balance sheet.

Example
Net Worth Statement
December, 2018

Assets	Current Market Value	Liabilities (or Debts)	Total Dollar Amount
Car	$1,750	VISA credit card balance	$847.45
Computer	$625	Student loan	$4,500
Clothing	$400	Loan from Dad	$1,350
Checking account balance	$174		
Total Current Value of Assets	$2,949	Total Amount of Liabilities	$6,697.45
Net Worth = Total Assets minus Total Liabilities = $<3,748.45>			

Assignment 2.1   Net Worth Statement

Name _____

Net Worth as of _____, _____

(Day   ,   Month)   (Year)

Assets	Current Market Value	Liabilities (or Debts)	Total Dollar Amount
Total Current Value of Assets		Total Amount of Liabilities	
Net Worth = Total Assets minus Total Liabilities = $_____			

RECORD KEEPING

Never ask of money spent
Where the spender thinks it went.
Nobody was ever meant
To remember or invent
What he did with every cent.

Robert Frost (1874–1963)

Record keeping is simply creating and maintaining a system of preserving or documenting anything of financial, personal, or familial importance. In other words, if it is important, keep it . . . and keep it organized. Below are examples of records worth keeping (and where it is recommended that they be kept).

Financial records worth keeping:

Tax returns for the past 7 years (home)

Warranties for automobiles, appliances, tools, etc. (home)

Wage or salary pay records for 7 years (home)

Insurance policies (safe deposit box)

Household inventories (safe deposit box)

Bank records for 7 years (home)

Medical or drug receipts for 7 years (home)

Credit card statements for 7 years (home)

Deeds, titles (safe deposit box)

Stock and bond certificates (safe deposit box)

Debts you owe and are owed to you (home, safe deposit box)

Personal records worth keeping:

Will, power of attorney, living will (safe deposit box)

Placing your will in a safe deposit box is appropriate in some states, but not all. The power of attorney and living will should ideally be in the safe deposit box of the person who has been granted power of attorney.

Personal journals (home)

Treasured letters or correspondence (home)

Certificates of achievement (home)

Birth certificate, marriage certificate (safe deposit box)

Diplomas, passports, vaccinations (home)

Social security cards, union cards (home)

Military records (home or safe deposit box)

Family records worth keeping:

Photo albums (home with copies elsewhere)

Selected examples of children's drawings and schoolwork (home)

Family and personal journals (home)

Video or audio records (home with copies elsewhere)

Any other treasured record (home with copies elsewhere)

Where should important records be kept? As noted above, the common options are a safe deposit box (at a depository institution) or a fireproof storage safe in your home. As a general rule, if it is not replaceable have a copy somewhere else.

For many types of family records (such as photos) you may want to consider making double prints and sending one set to grandparents, or other family members, with instructions to save them for you. They will enjoy the pictures and you will have a second set in the event that yours are destroyed.

BUDGETING

He is rich whose income exceeds his expenses;
and he is poor whose expenses exceed his income.

Jean de La Bruyere (1645–1696)

Money comes like sand scooped with a needle . . .
Money goes like sand washed by water.

Chinese proverb

The poor stay poor by pretending to be rich,
and the rich stay rich by pretending to be poor.

Anonymous

Budgeting is the process of planning in advance how to spend or use a resource. People often plan how to use their time in advance . . . in other words, they "budget" their time. Unfortunately, many people do a poor job of budgeting financial resources in advance. Successful budgeting requires thoughtful preparation and commitment. The payoff, however, can be substantial. Conscientious budgeting can greatly reduce frivolous or unnecessary expenditures.

Good budgeting skills can have the monetary value of working a second job. After all, there are two ways to increase the money available to save: (1) earn more money or (2) spend less money. Spending less money requires self-control and, therefore, is the road less traveled. Yet, spending less is a road that is always available.

Before any financial progress can be made, budgeting skills must be developed. Purchasing a home and a variety of insurance products, investing in stocks or mutual funds, starting a business, and other "exciting" components of financial planning are *absolutely* dependent upon a sound budgetary plan.

A useful tool in budgeting is an **income and expense statement**. It represents monthly budgets for an extended period of time, usually 1 year. By forecasting monthly income and expenses for a 1-year period it is possible to prepare in advance (i.e., save money) for future months which you estimate will have more expenses than income (i.e., holidays, birthdays, spring break, summer vacations, etc.). **The income and expense statement is a planning tool, not a backward-looking journal of how you spent your money.**

Example
Income and Expense Statement for the Year 2019 on a Monthly Basis

	Jan	Feb	Mar	Apr	May	Jun	Jul	Aug	Sep	Oct	Nov	Dec	TOTAL
Net Income	$700	$850	$850	$850	$850	$2,000	$2,000	$1,400	$850	$850	$850	$700	$12,750
Withdrawal Savings	$3,600		$200					$3,600	$200				$7,600
Scholarship	$5,600		$0					$5,600	$0				$11,200
Saving/Investing	$25	$25	$25	$25	$25	$300	$700	$800	$25	$25	$25	$25	$2,025
Rent or House PMT	$350	$350	$350	$350	$350	$0	$0	$0	$350	$350	$350	$350	$3,150
Food	$125	$175	$175	$175	$175	$0	$0	$80	$175	$175	$175	$125	$1,555
Utilities	$43	$49	$50	$47	$35	$45	$52	$66	$55	$47	$52	$67	$608
Cell Phone	$74	$74	$74	$74	$74	$74	$74	$74	$74	$74	$74	$74	$888
Clothing	$55	$55	$55	$75	$55	$55	$55	$120	$55	$55	$120	$55	$810
Entertainment	$45	$45	$45	$45	$45	$45	$45	$45	$45	$45	$45	$45	$540
Tuition and Books	$9,200							$9,200					$18,400
Credit Card Payment	$45	$45	$45	$45	$45	$45	$45	$45	$45	$45	$45	$45	$540
Insurance			$125						$125				$250
Gasoline	$95	$95	$95	$95	$110	$95	$95	$95	$95	$95	$95	$110	$1,170
Gifts				$55	$25	$25						$200	$305
Total Expenses	$10,057	$913	$1,039	$986	$939	$684	$1,066	$10,525	$1,044	$911	$981	$1,096	$30,241
Monthly Surplus or Deficit	–$157	–$63	$11	–$136	–$89	$1,316	$934	$75	$6	–$61	–$131	–$396	$1,309

Assignment 2.2   Annual Income and Expense Statement

Name _____

Income and Expense Statement for the Year of _____

	Jan	Feb	Mar	Apr	May	Jun	Jul	Aug	Sep	Oct	Nov	Dec	TOTAL
Net Income													
Withdrawals from Savings Account (used as income)													
House PMT or Rent													
Utilities													
Cell Phone													
Donations													
Saving/Investing													
Insurance(s)													
Educ. Expenses													
Medical													
Clothing													
Food													
Debt Payments													
Car/Gas													
Gifts													
Misc.													
Total Expenses													
Monthly Surplus or Deficit													

After your income and expense statement is completed you should do your best to follow it—month by month. This is monthly budgeting. Each month you will need to prepare a monthly budget in which you estimate your income and expenses.

Ideally you simply pull the numbers off your annual income and expense statement and plug them into a monthly budget sheet.

After the month is over you may have to make some adjustments to your income and expense statement if you overspent (or underspent . . . what a crazy thought).

The process of budgeting will never be "done." Regardless of how much money you earn, you should always budget. Whether you record every penny or make rough approximations is up to you. The main idea is to develop a budgeting system that *works for you*, rather than one that *you work for*. Excessively complex budgeting systems will seem like work and may eventually be abandoned. **Remain diligent in your pursuit of the goals that your budget is helping you reach**. However, remain flexible so as to respond to the unpredictable events of life . . . and do not forget to compromise with those whose budget ideas may be different from your own. Among married couples, efforts at budgeting often fail when one partner attempts to force their vision of family spending on the rest of the family.

Start budgeting by simply recording your expenditures for a few weeks or months. Once you understand how much you spend, you can start to plan your spending IN ADVANCE—*which is what budgeting is all about.*

The example monthly budget sheet on the following page shows what one might look like after being filled out during the month. The underlined numbers add up to $1,058 and represent the total amount of money budgeted for all spending categories combined. As money is spent during the month it is subtracted from the allotted, or budgeted, amount in each category. By the end of the month this person had $91.90 left over (the sum of the remaining balances in each category), therefore a total of $966.10 had been spent.

At the start of each month a new budget sheet should be prepared with the total income for that month allotted across the relevant budget categories. As money is spent, simply record the expenditure and keep a running balance per category.

Example Monthly Budget for April

House PMT/Rent 275	Utilities 75	Phone/Cell Phone 48	Donations 50
$275 on April 4 --- Balance = $0 ---	Paid $72 on April 9 --- Balance = $3 ---	Paid $51 on April 11 --- Balance = $-3 ---	Paid $50 on April 6 --- Balance = $0 ---

Miscellaneous 80	Saving/Investing 50	Insurance (Car, Renter's, Health) 90	Education Expenses 25
Wal-Mart $17.50 April 4	T-Rowe Price $50	Paid State Farm $34	None
Wal-Mart $8.89 April 8		Paid All State $22 Paid Aetna $35	
--- Balance = $53.61 ---	--- Balance = $0 ---	--- Balance = -$1 ---	--- Balance = $25 ---

Miscellaneous (cont.)	Medical 30	Clothing 20	Food 190
Bookstore $24.59 April 14	none	Shirt $12	Food 4 Less $128 April 3
Pets-R-Us $13.12 April 23			Albertson's $32 April 11
--- Balance = $15.90 ---	--- Balance = $30 ---	--- Balance = $8 ---	MU Creamery $38
	Debt Payments 45	Car/Gas 50	--- Balance = -$8 ---
	Visa card $45 April 11 --- Balance = $0 ---	Chevron $21 April 8 Gas-R-Us $23 April 25 --- Balance = $6 ---	
	Gifts for Current/ Former Teachers ☺	Other 30 Birthday gift for Pat $14 --- Balance = $16 ---	

Assignment 2.3   Budgeting and Recording Monthly Expenses

Name _____   Month _____

House PMT/Rent	Utilities	Phone/Cell Phone	Donations
_____	_____	_____	_____

Miscellaneous	Saving/Investing	Insurance (Car, Renter's, Health) _____	Education Expenses _____
_____	_____	Medical _____	Clothing _____	Food _____
	Debt Payments _____	Car/Gas _____	
	Gifts for Current/ Former Teachers ☺ _____	Other _____	

FINANCIAL RATIOS

Another way the family or individual can evaluate their financial strength and progress is through the use of financial ratios. These numerical calculations can also be utilized by financial institutions to analyze the household's finances when making loan or credit decisions.

- Provide benchmarks of your current financial position
- Used to spot trouble areas and utilize resources more effectively
- Are helpful to compare over time

Liquidity Ratio

Liquidity is the ease at which an asset can be converted to cash. The liquidity ratio provides an idea of how many months a household could continue to meet expenses should your income stop. Experts suggest a minimum liquidity ratio between 3 and 6 months.

$$Liquidity\ ratio = \frac{Liquid\ assets}{Monthly\ living\ expenses}$$

Examples of liquid assets are cash on hand, checking, and savings accounts. For example, compare the liquid assetson the Net Worth Statement (shown on the next few pages) ($15,000) with the monthly expenses on the Income and Expense Statement (69,200/12).

$$Liquidity\ ratio = \frac{\$15,000}{\$5767} = 2.60$$

Looking at the liquidity ratio, there is living expenses for 2.60 months. A larger amount of income should be deposited into liquid accounts so that at least 3 months worth of income would be saved to pay for expenses should you lose your job.

Debt-to-Total Assets Ratio

This ratio provides a measure of a person or household's ability to pay its debts and determines solvency. Solvency is basically having assets greater than liabilities. However, if a person owes more than they own, they are insolvent. Although the person may be able to pay their current bills with their current income, it would not be enough to cover all of their debts.

$$Debt\ to\ total\ assets\ ratio = \frac{Total\ liabilities}{Total\ assets}$$

Experts suggest having a ratio that is below 1, as 1 means you are insolvent. The lower the calculated number, the more solvent you are.

Calculations based upon the information given show that there is enough assets compared with debts because they owe less than 45% of what they owns.

$$Debt\ to\ total\ assets\ ratio = \frac{\$166,000}{\$369,500} = 0.45$$

Investment Assets-to-Net Worth Ratio

The Investment Assets-to-Net Worth Ratio compares the household's value of investments along with its net worth. Over time, it indicates how well the family is doing toward their goal of wealth accumulation. Experts recommend a ratio that is 50% or higher; however, younger households often have a ratio of less than 20% as they usually have fewer investment assets at this stage in their life.

$$\text{Investment assets to net worth ratio} = \frac{\text{Investment assets}}{\text{Net worth}}$$

Examples of investment assets are such items as stocks, bonds, mutual funds, IRAs, retirement funds. The investment assets total $78,000 from the Net Worth Statement (shown on the next few pages) and a net worth of $203,500 as shown on the Net Worth Statement.

$$\text{Investment assets to net worth ratio} = \frac{\$78,000}{\$203,500} = 38.33\%$$

Example:
Truman Tiger
Net Worth Statement
April 14, 2018

Assets	Current Market Value	Liabilities (or Debts)	Total Dollar Amount
Checking Account	$4,600	Current Bills	$500
Savings Account	$10,400	Credit Card Balance	$500
LIQUID ASSETS	$15,000	CURRENT LIABILITIES	$1,000
Investment Accounts	$7,000		
Retirement Accounts	$71,000		
INVESTMENT ASSETS	$78,000		
Home	$200,000	Home Mortgage	$155,000
Cars	$21,500	Car Loan	$4,500
Other real estate	$55,000	Student Loans	$5,500
REAL ASSETS	$276,500	LONG-TERM LIABILITIES	$165,000
Total Current Value of Assets	**$369,500**	**Total Amount of Liabilities**	**$166,000**
Net Worth = Total Assets minus Total Liabilities = $203,500			

Truman Tiger (FY 2017–2018)
Income and Expense Statement

INCOME

- Paisli income - $130,000
- Tax refunds - $1,500
- Interest and dividends - $2,500
- TOTAL INCOME = 134,000
- Income & FICA Taxes = 30,000
- **NET INCOME = 104,000**

EXPENSES

- House payment - $13,000
- Housing (main, ins, taxes, etc) - $12,000
- Car payments - $5,500
- Car (main, ins, taxes, etc) - $3,200
- Food - $6,500
- Clothing/personal - $10,000
- Childcare - $6000
- Entertainment - $4,000
- Life insurance - $750
- Medical expenses - $1,750
- Charity - $2,000
- Student loan payment - $4,500
- **TOTAL EXENSES = 69,200**

EXPENSES

- House payment - $13,000
- Housing (main, ins, taxes, etc) - $12,000
- Car payments - $5,500
- Car (main, ins, taxes, etc) - $3,200
- Food - $6,500
- Clothing/personal - $10,000
- Childcare - $6000
- Entertainment - $4,000
- Life insurance - $750
- Medical expenses - $1,750
- Charity - $2,000
- Student loan payment - $4,500
- **TOTAL EXENSES = 69,200**

Assignment 2.4   Financial Ratios

Name _____

SHOW YOUR WORK

Bill Bugsby wants to assess his financial strength; below is his financial information. The total expenses for the year from his Income and Expense Statement were $64,786.

Checking account balance	$2,660
Student loan balance	$1,400
Savings account	$1,760
House	$176,000
Mortgage loan balance	$92,000
Retirement account	$750
Car	$20,500
Stocks	$2,800
Mutual funds	$106,200
Car loan	$7,700
Credit card debt	$1,665

1. Use the information above to provide the following financial ratios: liquidity ratio, debt-to-assets ratio, investment assets-to-net worth ratio.

Section Two Practice Problems

1. In what ways is a net worth statement different from an income and expense statement?

2. What are some compelling reasons to keep good records?

3. The current market value of your car is $3,200. Your checking account balance is $422 and your savings account balance is $2,403. You have a student loan balance of $8,500 and your VISA credit card balance is $291. What is your current net worth?

4. If Fred's net worth is <$23,529> and his assets total $48,500, what are his current liabilities?

5. Marcia is applying for a loan, and the bank has asked her for some financial information. The total expenses for the year from her Income and Expense Statement were $48,000. Use the following data to calculate her *net worth*.

Annual salary	$ 34,000
Checking account balance	$ 800
Student loan balance	$ 1,400
Savings account	$ 700
House	$120,000
Mortgage loan balance	$ 90,000
Retirement Account	$ 750
Car	$ 5,500

6. Use the information above to provide the following financial ratios and briefly describe each based on the answers received: liquidity ratio, debt-to-assets ratio, investment assets-to-net worth ratio.

Section Two Practice Problem Answers

1. An income and expense statement covers a period of time, typically 1 year. It is based on best estimates of future income and future expenses. Preparing an income and expense statement helps in the process of preparing monthly budgets.

   A net worth statement looks back in time by accounting for the value of all assets minus the amount of all accumulated debts up to that point in time. As such, it has a very short shelf life because the value of certain assets (e.g., investment accounts) can change on a daily basis.

2. There are many reasons to keep good records. Consider the following:
   - Quality of life issues: Documenting the life cycle of a family is very important. It gives family members a greater sense of identity and a feeling of belonging. Family photographs, awards, and other precious records strengthen family ties and can enrich future generations by creating a sense of continuity and heritage.
   - Financial Records: As one example, good financial records are needed to qualify for a home loan. Also, keeping accurate records is critical to correctly complete annual income tax forms.
   - Medical Records: A history of medical problems, medications, and other health-related issues—for each family member—is important. Doctors are greatly assisted by patients who know their medical history.

3.

Assets	Current Market Value ($)	Liabilities (or Debts)	Total Dollar Amount ($)
Car (current value)	3,200	Student loan	8,500
Checking account balance	422	VISA credit card balance	291
Savings account balance	2,403		
TOTAL	6,025		8,791

Net Worth = Assets − Liabilities = $6,025 − $8,791 5 **<$2,766>**

4. **Liabilities 5 $72,029**

   $48,500 − × = **<$23,529>**   (Brackets "< >" indicate a negative number)

   × = 72,029

5. **Net Worth Statement (Balance Sheet)**

   ASSETS   LIABILITIES
   Checking = 800   Student loan = 1,400
   Savings = 700   Mortgage = 90,000
      Liquid assets = 1,500

   Retirement account = 750
      Investment assets = 750

House = 120,000
Car = 5,500
     Total Real Assets = 125,500

TOTAL ASSETS = 127,750   **TOTAL LIABILITIES = 91,400**
Net worth = Assets − Liabilities = 127,750 − 91,400 = 36,350

6. Liquidity ratio = (Liquid assets / Monthly living expenses)
        (1,500) / (48,000 / 12) = 1,500 / 4,000 = 0.38
              Experts suggest at least 3 months worth saved up

Debt-to-assets ratio = (Total liabilities / Total assets)
        91,400 / 127,750 = 0.72
              Experts suggest under 1 in order to be solvent

Investment assets-to-net worth = (Investment assets / Net worth)
        750 / 36,350 = 2.06%
              Experts suggest a ratio around 50%

   Notes:

Cash Management

In investing money, the amount of interest you want
should depend on whether you want to eat well or sleep well.

J. Kenfield Morley (1838–1923)

'Tis against some men's principles to pay interest,
and it seems against others' interest to pay the principal.

B. Franklin (1706–1790)

WHAT TYPE OF BANK SHOULD I CHOOSE?

Large National and Multinational Banks: Big name banks, such as Bank of America and Citigroup, offer several physical branch locations almost anywhere in the United States. If you travel a lot it may be beneficial to be able to find a bank location in any state; however, large banks have many customers and often do not offer the best rates on their accounts.

Online-Only Banks: Online-only banks do not offer brick-and-mortar bank locations. Due to this, they may offer higher interest rates than large national banks. So if you would like to visit your local branch or speak to someone face to face about your accounts, then you may not like an online-only bank. ING Direct and Ally Bank are examples of a few online-only banks.

Community Banks: Community banks are usually smaller than national banks but pride themselves on customer relations. If you travel a lot or move frequently, you should understand that community banks may have fewer locations and not have offices outside of the community. Thus, you may not be able to find the exact same bank while travelling or if you move.

Credit Unions: Credit unions are very similar to community banks as you generally do not have locations in multiple states; however, they usually offer better interest rates on loans and checking and savings accounts than other banks. Not everyone can be a member of a credit union as you must meet specific requirements to join. Similar to community banks, you probably would not find branches when you travel or if you move out of state or out of your local community.

SELECTING A BANK—WHAT SHOULD I LOOK FOR?

Compare the following across institutions:

- Online banking to check your account balances online for various accounts (checking, savings, mortgage, automobile, commercial, investments etc.), arrange transfers for various accounts both within and outside the bank, viewing checks paid, and online bill pay, purchasing/selling stocks, ordering checks, and more.

- Fees (for checking, overdrafts, copies of checks, etc.).
- Effective annual yield (the "actual" amount of interest paid on the account).
- Interest rates charged on loans.
- Federal Insurance (FDIC for banks and S and L's, NCUA for credit unions). To check to see if the bank is FDIC insured: http://research.fdic.gov/bankfind/
- Direct deposit options (having your paycheck deposited directly into your checking or savings account).
- Overdraft protection options.
- Convenience options such as automated transactions. This refers to electronic funds transfer (EFT) for payroll deposits or payments (such as your monthly house payment or monthly investments into a mutual fund).

REGULATION

The Banking Act of 1933 increased stability in the banking industry by forbidding interest rates on checking accounts, establishing maximum interest rates on savings accounts, restricting certain types of loans, and forbidding sales of securities to the public by banks. In short, this act separated investment and commercial banking activities and set forth strict regulations on banks. A primary criterion when selecting a bank was the type of banking business being conducted.

The Depository Institutions Deregulation and Monetary Control Act of 1980 altered traditional roles by allowing some leniency to "banking institutions." The main results were that banks now could provide interest on checking accounts and had flexibility on how much they could set for interest rates on savings accounts and loans. It also increased the federal deposit insurance amount from $40,000 to $100,000.

A portion of the Banking Act of 1933 was changed through the passing of the Financial Services Modernization Act of 1999 which extended the freedoms of banks. The new act allowed these institutions to blend a variety of products and services together that were once restricted. Therefore, the unique identities of commercial banks, savings and loans, and mutual savings banks have become less distinct. For example, a commercial bank can now sell investments like stocks and bonds, and also insurance products along with personal and commercial products.

The primary outcome of the Depository Institutions Deregulation and Monetary Control Act of 1980 and the Financial Services Modernization Act of 1999 was to make choosing a bank no longer a matter of the nature of their business. Consumers have since began to select banks that best meet their needs.

PUBLIC GUARANTY INSURANCE

The Federal Deposit Insurance Corporation (FDIC) established in 1934 covers deposits in insured banks for up to $250,000 per account. Simply put, if the bank fails, you get your money back.

If you have more than $250,000 to deposit, you must either open accounts at different banks or creatively deposit at your own bank to maintain $250,000 insurance on each account. For example, if you had $1,000,000 (just pretend!) you could deposit it in the following accounts.

$250,000 in your own name	$250,000 in spouse's name
$250,000 in an Individual Retirement Account	$250,000 in a joint account

For deposit insurance purposes, money in joint accounts is evenly allocated to each person. Therefore, in this scenario, only $750,000 would be insured because each individual (you and your spouse) already have $250,000 insured. To "insure" the money currently in the joint account, it would need to be transferred to another bank, or deposited into a child's account.

Multiple retirement accounts (IRA, Keogh, Self-Directed Defined Contribution Plan, etc.) at the same depository institution ("bank") are insured separately for their combined total up to $250,000.

Types of Bank Accounts	
FDIC Insured	**Not FDIC Insured**
Checking Accounts	Mutual Funds
NOW Accounts	Stocks
Money Market Demand Account (MMDA)	Bonds
	Life Insurance Policies
Savings Accounts	Annuities
Certificates of Deposit	US Treasury Bills, Bonds, or Notes

TYPES OF "BANK" CHECKING ACCOUNTS

Checking Accounts: A demand deposit account (the official name of a "checking account") that uses a legal document (a check) demanding that the bank transfer funds from the payer to the payee.

Share Draft Accounts: Checking accounts at a credit union.

Money Market Deposit Accounts (MMDAs): Federally insured money market accounts offered by banks and savings and loans. Typically, a MMDA pays the highest rate of any bank account on which checks can be written. However, there is typically a limit on the number of transactions per month.

TYPES OF "BANK" SAVINGS ACCOUNTS

Savings Accounts: An account designed for saving money where the money is readily available. Savings accounts have no maturity and no limit to the number of transactions (withdrawals or deposits) the account owner can make per month. Because of this, they pay a low rate of interest and may have a minimum deposit requirement.

Certificates of Deposits (CDs): A very safe time deposit where you deposit your money for a specified period of time (3 months to 5 years) for a guaranteed rate of return. Normally, the greater the time until maturity, the greater the rate of interest. If you withdraw the money before the end of the time period, there is an interest penalty.

Several Alternative CDs:

> **7-Day Certificate,** minimum deposit requirement, matures every 7 days and interest rolls into your checking account or compounds to the CD.

> **Brokered CDs** are sold by stockbrokers with the commission paid by the issuing institution. These offer yields that are from one-quarter to one-half percent higher than those offered by a bank. Brokered CDs may be sold prior to maturity without an interest penalty. However, given their marketability, there is a risk of loss of principal if interest rates increase in the market.

Bump-Up CDs have rates of interest that may increase over time. If market rates of interest go up, you are allowed to ask the bank to change the rate of interest on the CD. Typically, this is allowed only once or twice during the contract.

Variable-Rate CDs are longer term CDs with variable rates tied to a market rate of interest index.

Risk-Free CDs give the flexibility to access funds prior to maturity date without penalty. Similar to a savings account but usually provides a higher interest rate and a short term.

CD Management Ideas:

Laddering: Using this technique you would place portions of your money in several different CDs that mature at different times. Then, when the shortest term CD matures, you would "roll it" into a new, longer term CD. As greater rates of interest are typically paid the longer the term of the investment, this management approach allows one to always have money invested at the greater, longer term rates of interest. Moreover, the owner always has a CD maturing in the near term which provides liquidity to the investment.

Divide and Conquer: If you have the money, instead of placing it all in, say, one $100,000 CD, split it into three CDs of $33,333. In this way, if you need the money from a CD, you have to break the contract on only a part of your funds.

Borrow: If you need the money from your CD, inquire about borrowing the money from the bank with the CD as collateral. Such collateral will reduce the cost of borrowing and you will not have to break the contract.

NOMINAL VERSUS EFFECTIVE RATES OF INTEREST

Nominal refers to a rate of interest using annual compounding. **Effective** refers to the interest rate that actually occurs given that compounding occurs more than once per year. Take, for example, the following advertisement in a financial section of a newspaper:

12-Month Certificate of Deposit
Rate   8.80%
Yield   9.095%
Quarterly Compounding
Offered by Slippery Bucks Savings & Loan

If you invest $1,000 into this CD, how much interest will you earn—$88 (using the 8.80% rate) or $90.95 (using the 9.095% yield)?

The answer is $90.95. The CD in this example compounds interest each quarter (every 3 months). Therefore, even though the annual rate is 8.80% (which assumes annual compounding) the effective rate (or yield) equals 9.094683%. The effective rate is called the **effective annual yield** and must be reported to the consumer (as of January, 1993).

Prove it to yourself by using time value of money.

PV   = <1,000>
I/YR = 8.8 / 4
N   = 1 × 4 = **4**
(I/YR = 8.8, if P/Y = 4)
FV   = 1,090.95

$$\text{Effective Annual Yield} = \frac{\text{Amount of interest earned}}{\text{Amount invested}}$$

$$= \frac{\$90.95}{\$1,000} = .09095 \text{ or } 9.095\%$$

Or

$$\text{Effective Annual Yield} = \frac{FV - PV}{PV}$$

$$\frac{1,090.95 - 1,000}{1,000} = .09095 \text{ or } 9.095\%$$

Another approach to solving for the effective annual yield is to use the formula.

$$\text{Effective Annual Yield} = ((1 + i/n)^n) - 1$$

To solve the problem using this formula, remember to use quarterly compounding.

$$((1 + .088/4)^4) - 1 = .09095 \text{ or } 9.095\%$$

Let's try the problem again assuming *monthly compounding*.

```
PV    =  <1,000>
I/YR  =  8.8 / 12
N     =  1 * 12 = 12
(I/YR =  8.8, if P/Y = 12)
FV    =  1,091.64
```

$$\text{Yield} = \frac{1,091.64 - 1,000}{1,000} = .09164 \text{ or } 9.164\%$$

Or

$$((1 + .088/12)^{12}) - 1 = .09164 \text{ or } 9.164\%$$

As expected, the effective percentage yield increases when there are more compounding periods.

Nominal versus Effective Rate Example 1

What is the effective annual yield after 1 year for an investment of $2,500 in to a CD if the interest rate is 7.75% compounded quarterly?

Solution 1:

$$((1 + .0775/4)^4) - 1 = 0.07978 = 7.978\%$$

Solution 2:

Solve for your FV and then use for formula (FV−PV)/PV

```
PV    =  <2,500>
I/YR  =  7.75/4
N     =  1 × 4 = 4
(I/YR =  7.75, if P/Y = 4)
FV    =  2,699.45
```

$$\text{Yield} = \frac{2,699.45 - 2,500.00}{2,500.00} = 0.07978 \text{ or } 7.7978\%$$

Nominal versus Effective Rate Example 2

What is the effective percentage yield of 9.4% compounded semiannually?

$$((1 + .094/2)^2) - 1 = .09621 = 9.621\%$$

CALCULATING INTEREST EARNED ON CHECKING AND SAVINGS ACCOUNTS

Interest paid on a checking account (or share draft account at a credit union) each month is determined by first calculating the average balance in the account during the month. Since 1993, all depository institutions must use the average daily balance method.

Average Daily Balance Example

The simple illustration below demonstrates how the average daily balance would be calculated for a checking account during the month of April.

The account pays 5% annual interest compounded monthly.

Balance in checking account			Multiplied by number of days		Total
April 1–10	$562	×	10	=	$ 5,620
April 11–22	$430	×	12	=	$ 5,160
April 23–30	$ 38	×	8	=	$ 304
					$ 11,084
					÷ 30 days
					$ 369.47

So, the average daily balance equals **$369.47**.

Now, use the versatile I = P × R × T formula to calculate the interest earned *during the month of April* (in this case, T = 30 days) (365 days = .08219).

In this example:

P = Average daily balance
R = The annual rate of return in the checking account
T = Time period

Interest earned during April = 369.47 × .05 × .08219 = **$1.52**

Another example...

Tightwad County Bank pays 4.75% annual interest, *compounded monthly*. How much interest will you earn if you have the following transactions for the month of March? (March has 31 days.)

		Balance
March 1	Beginning balance	$4,000
March 16	Withdraw $1,500	$2,500
March 28	Deposit $700	$3,200

Step 1. Determine the average daily balance.

March 1–15	$4,000	×	15 days	=	$ 60,000
March 16–27	$2,500	×	12 days	=	$ 30,000
March 28–31	$3,200	×	4 days	=	$ 12,800
					$ 102,800
					÷ 31 days
		Average Daily Balance			$3,316.13

Step 2. Use the $I = P \times R \times T$ formula to calculate the interest earned during the month of March (where P = average daily balance).

Interest earned = $3,316.13 × .0475 × (31/365) = **$13.38**

Daily Compounding Example

Spendthrift County Bank pays 4.75% annual interest, *compounded daily*. How much interest will you earn if you have the following transactions for the month of March? (March has 31 days.)

		Balance
March 1	Beginning balance	$4,000
March 16	Withdraw $1,500	_____
March 28	Deposit $700	_____

Daily compounding adds a bit of complexity to this problem. The average daily balance method does not apply when interest is calculated on a daily basis. The technique to solve this problem is to use the following time value of money equation (or a financial calculator).

Algebra formula: $\mathbf{FV = PV(1 + i)^n}$

OR

Financial calculator setup: Enter PV, N, and I/YR and solve for FV

Dates	Beginning Balance	Algebra Equation	Ending Balance	Interest Earned
March 1–15	$4,000	$4,000 (1 + (.0475 / 365))^{15}$	$4,007.82	$ 7.82
$1,500 is withdrawn on March 16				
New balance on March 16: $4,007.82 − $1,500 = $2,507.82				
March 16–27	$2,507.82	$2,507.82 (1 + (.0475 / 365))^{12}$	$2,511.74	$ 3.92
$ 700 is deposited in the account on March 28				
New balance on March 28: $2,511.74 + $700 = $3,211.74				
March 28–31	$3,211.74	$3,211.74 (1 + (.0475 / 365))^{4}$	$3,213.41	$ 1.67
Total Interest Earned during March				$13.41

Though the difference in interest earned is relatively small, daily compounding does produce more interest than monthly compounding.

"NONBANK" SAVINGS ALTERNATIVES

Money Market Mutual Funds (MMMFs) are mutual funds where you buy shares. Typically, one dollar buys one share of the fund that invests the proceeds in a pool of short-term debt obligations. These include treasury securities, high-quality bank CDs, and top grade commercial paper. MMMFs, as compared to money market deposit accounts, do not carry federal insurance but are extremely safe. Their assets are short-term securities with little interest rate risk but the risk allows them to pay more than a bank MMDA. These accounts are included in the investment category of *cash investments*.

Series EE U.S. Savings Bonds are sold on a discount basis and redeemed at face value. The difference in selling price and redemption value is interest earned and no interest is received until the bonds are redeemed. They are offered in face values of $50 through $10,000 with a purchase price of one-half of the face amount. Series EE bonds pay a variable rate of interest (compounded semiannually) as long as you hold them at least 5 years. Typically, the interest earned is tax deferred (federal tax) until the bond is redeemed unless the owner chooses to pay taxes as they accrue. There is no state income tax on interest earned from Series EE bonds.

As of January 1990, interest earned on Series EE savings bonds is exempt from federal taxation if the bonds are purchased and owned by parents and used for the college tuition and fees of their children or purchased by an adult 24 years old or older and used for their own tuition. The bond must be in the name of a parent and the parent(s) must have an adjusted gross income that is sufficiently low, otherwise the interest earned is federally taxed.

U.S. Treasury Bills (T-Bills) are short-term debt obligations of the U.S. government with a maturity of 1 year or less. T-Bills have a minimum face value of $10,000 and are sold on a discount basis where the interest is deducted from the face value at sale and the face value paid at maturity. Interest earned is exempt from state income tax, but is taxed by the federal government.

Assignment 3.1 Savings Account Mathematics

Name _____

SHOW YOUR WORK

1. Republic Bank pays 3.25% interest, *compounded monthly*. How much interest will you earn if you have following transactions for the months of March and April? (March has 31 days, April has 30 days.)

Date	Account Activity	Balance
March 1	Beginning balance	$ 6,500
March 16	Withdraw $1,500	$ 5,000
March 28	Deposit $700	$ 5,700
April 3	Deposit $1,100	$_____
April 25	Withdraw $1,400	$_____

2. Dominion Bank also pays 3.25% annual interest, *compounded daily*. If you had the same pattern of withdrawals and deposits as in problem #1, calculate the amount of interest you would have earned at Dominion Bank. (Hint: the answer will be larger than in question #1.)

3. What is the effective annual yield after 1 year for an investment of $3,065 in to a CD if the interest rate is 1.75% compounded monthly?

4. You are comparing savings accounts, which has the higher effective annual yield and why?

   7.2% compounded quarterly,

   7.2% compounded monthly, or

   7.2% compounded semiannual

Section Three Extra Practice Problems

1. What is the effective annual yield after 1 year for an investment of $2,500 into a CD if the ending account value is $2,630?

2. Use the following information to find the effective annual yield.

12 Month Certificate of Deposit
Annual Interest Rate = 7.75% Initial Investment = $2,000 Quarterly Compounding

3. Find the average daily balance and the total interest earned during the month of January using the following information:

	Balance in Account
January 1–11	$445
January 12–20	$332
January 21–25	$285
January 26–31	$ 57

The account pays 8% annual interest compounded monthly.

4. You have a checking account at Cheapskate County Bank that pays you 6% annual interest compounded *monthly*. How much interest will you earn with the following 2 months' transactions?

July 1	Beginning Balance	$1,340
July 4	Withdraw	$ 600
July 16	Deposit	$1,200
July 21	Deposit	$1,400
July 29	Withdraw	$ 850
August 4	Deposit	$1,200
August 19	Withdraw	$ 300
August 26	Deposit	$1,850
August 30	Withdraw	$4,500

5. What is your total account balance at Cheapskate County Bank on September 1?

6. You find another bank just down the street, Big Bucks City Bank, that will pay you 6% annual interest compounded *daily*. How much interest will you earn using the same transactions as in problem #4?

7. What is your total account balance at Big Bucks on the morning of September 1?

Section Three Practice Problem Answers

1. Effective Annual Yield = **5.2%**

   Effective Annual Yield = Amount Interest Earned / Amount Invested

   Effective Annual Yield = 130 / 2,500 = .052 or **5.2%**

2. Effective Annual Yield = **7.98%**

P	$\times$	R	$\times$	T	=	I
2,000.00	$\times$	.0775	$\times$	.25	=	38.7500
2,038.75	$\times$	.0775	$\times$	.25	=	39.5008
2,078.25	$\times$	.0775	$\times$	.25	=	40.2661
2,118.52	$\times$	.0775	$\times$	.25	=	41.0463
				TOTAL	=	159.5632

Effective Annual Yield = Amount Interest Earned / Amount Invested

Effective Annual Yield = 159.56 / 2,000 = .07978 or **7.98 %**

Using a **FINANCIAL CALCULATOR**:

PV   =   <2,000>
n   =   4 quarters
I/YR =   7.75 / 4 = 1.9375 quarterly rate
FV   =   2,159.56

Interest earned = FV − PV
                = 2,159.56 − 2,000
                = **159.56**

Effective Annual Yield = Amount Interest Earned / Amount Invested

Effective Annual Yield = 159.56 / 2,000 = .07978 or **7.98%**

Using **ALGEBRA**:

FV   =   PV $(1 + i)^n$
FV   =   2,000 $(1 + .0775/4)^4$
FV   =   **2,159.56**

Interest earned = FV − PV
                = 2,159.56 − 2,000
                = **159.56**

Effective Annual Yield = Amount Interest Earned / Amount Invested

Effective Annual Yield = 159.56 / 2,000 = .07978 or **7.98%**

3. Average Daily Balance = **$311.29**

Interest earned during January = **$2.12**

	# of days		Balance in account		Total
January 1–11	11	×	445	=	4,895
January 12–20	9	×	332	=	2,988
January 21–25	5	×	285	=	1,425
January 26–31	6	×	57	=	342
					9,650
					÷ 31 days
					$ 311.29

P	×	R	×	T	=	I
311.29	×	.08	×	(31/365)	=	**$2.12**

4. *Remember that July and August both have 31 days.

July 1–3	1,340	×	3 days	=	4,020
July 4–15	740	×	12 days	=	8,880
July 16–20	1,940	×	5 days	=	9,700
July 21–28	3,340	×	8 days	=	26,720
July 29–31	2,490	×	3 days	=	7,470
					56,790
					÷ 31 days
					1,831.94

Use	P	×	R	×	T	=	I
	1,831.94	×	.06	×	(31/365)	=	**$9.34**

The starting balance in August is the last balance in July ($2,490) plus the interest earned in July ($9.34).

August 1–3	2,499.34	×	3 days	=	7,498.02
August 4–18	3,699.34	×	15 days	=	55,490.10
August 19–25	3,399.34	×	7 days	=	23,795.38
August 26–29	5,249.34	×	4 days	=	20,997.36
August 30–31	749.34	×	2 days	=	1,498.68
					109,279.54
					÷ 31 days
					3,525.15

$3,525.15 × .06 × (31/365) = **$17.96**

Total Interest for July and August: $9.34 + $17.96 = $27.30

5. Closing balance in August + Interest earned in August

   749.34 + 17.96 = **$767.30**

6. *Remember that the month end does not matter when using daily compounding.

				Interest Earned
July 1–3	$1,340 (1 + (.06 / 365))^3$	=	1,340.66	.66
July 4–15	$740.66 (1 + (.06 / 365))^{12}$	=	742.12	1.46
July 16–20	$1,942.12 (1 + (.06 / 365))^5$	=	1,943.72	1.60
July 21–28	$3,343.72 (1 + (.06 / 365))^8$	=	3,348.12	4.40
July 29–Aug 3	$2,498.12 (1 + (.06 / 365))^6$	=	2,500.58	2.46
Aug 4–18	$3,700.58 (1 + (.06 / 365))^{15}$	=	3,709.72	9.14
Aug 19–25	$3,409.72 (1 + (.06 / 365))^7$	=	3,413.65	3.93
Aug 26–29	$5,263.65 (1 + (.06 / 365))^4$	=	5,267.11	3.46
Aug 30–31	$767.11 (1 + (.06 / 365))^2$	=	767.36	0.25
				$27.36

7. **$767.36**

   Notes:

Credit and Loans

Money often costs too much.

R. W. Emerson (1803–1882)

People come to poverty in two ways:
accumulating debts and paying them off.

Jewish proverb

If you would know the value of money,
go and try to borrow some.

Benjamin Franklin (1706–1790)

You may think that credit is a good thing to have, but many people find themselves in financial difficulty because of his or her use of credit. Millions of Americans face monthly consumer debt payments that add up to 20% or more of their take-home pay. These people are the financially overextended. These are individuals who have either used too much credit or who have encountered circumstances beyond their control that strip them of their financial stability, such as unemployment or catastrophic illness. Unfortunately, these numbers are rising and those receiving financial counseling or entering bankruptcies are increasing every year.

Consumer credit debt (credit card debt, auto loans, etc.) is not bad. Neither is it good. It does have a place in the life of America. Like a medicinal drug with some addictive properties, however, consumer credit can create a false sense of prosperity as consumers speed toward a reality of financial disaster.

Consumers in all age, income, and occupational groups use consumer credit. However, we see the greatest use by families, particularly newly married couples, who use consumer credit to acquire home furnishings and other necessary consumer durables. Increasingly, young single adults (*college students*) are using consumer credit to fund their lifestyles.

WHAT IS CREDIT?

Consumer credit debt includes automobile loans, single payment loans, mobile home loans, credit card debt, and other consumer loans. The only major category of debt not included in consumer credit debt is home mortgage loans. Consumer credit debt is divided into three categories:

Installment Debt—(equal, periodic payments)
- auto loans
- furniture or appliance loans

Noninstallment Debt—(single payment or full payment each period)
- single payment loans
- full payment due on a travel or entertainment card (such as American Express or Diners Club)

71

Open-End Credit—(single repayment or series of equal/unequal payments)
- credit card debt

THE FIVE C's OF CREDIT

You may want to use credit. Besides being careful of overindebtedness, you must meet the lending criteria of the lender. Lenders use the five C's of credit to judge loan applicants: character, capital, capacity, collateral, and conditions.

Character is determined by the amount of integrity you demonstrate with respect to money matters. It is your honesty, reliability, willingness to pay, and your record of financial accountability. When you set up a budget and maintain your household in a business-like manner, you demonstrate your commitment to the integrity of your financial matters.

Capital is measured by your assets—housing equity, automobiles, personal property, savings, emergency fund, investments, and life insurance. Capital can be demonstrated by your net worth statement.

Capacity is your ability to repay the debt from your income. This is a measure of your earned income—both present and expected—combined with a measure of your current level of debt payments.

Collateral is whether you have an asset that can be pledged against the loan. Lenders will be more likely to make a loan that is secured by, say, an automobile than to loan you money to take a Caribbean cruise. However, if you were to pledge a certificate of deposit (in this case collateral) against the loan for the cruise, the lender would probably make the loan. In the event you do not repay the loan, the lender takes the collateral.

The economic **conditions** of the nation or community at the time of the loan request may affect the lender's loan decisions as well. If the local economy is in a nosedive and massive layoffs are expected, the lender may not be willing to make a loan even to a borrower who meets the other four C's.

THE CREDIT APPLICATION

Your application for future credit will require you to report on your work history (earnings and length of tenure), place of residency, your banking relationship(s), and your current credit accounts or debts outstanding. In this process, the lender is trying to establish his or her willingness to trust you with his or her (the lender's) money. You are a person worthy of that trust if you are current with the payment of your debts, have a strong employment history, have maintained your residency, and can demonstrate your commitment to the management of your financial life.

In the process of a loan application the lender is restricted from denying credit based upon your race, sex, marital status, religion, age (assuming you are an adult), national origin, or because you receive public assistance income. In addition, the lender cannot require you to renegotiate a loan that has been granted should you reach a certain age, or if credit life insurance is unavailable to someone who is retired. These rules are described in the **Equal Credit Opportunity Act**. It does not guarantee you credit. It simply assures that the lender's decision is based upon your credit worthiness—not the lender's biases.

If you are married, the Equal Credit Opportunity Act requires the credit history to be reported in the name of both the husband and wife. While both good and bad reports will be maintained in both files, the creditor must disregard information that you prove is present as a result of the behavior of your spouse. This is especially important in the case of a divorce. Finally, whether married or single, you have the right to apply for credit in your own name. As such, the decision to grant you credit will be based solely on your credit worthiness, not that of your spouse.

The Act also requires that you be notified of your acceptance or rejection within 30 days of applying. If you are rejected, you must be told (or have access to) the specific reason(s) for the rejection.

If you do not understand the rejection, contact the lender for further explanation. In addition, if you are rejected or the charge for credit is increased due to information contained in the files of the credit bureau, the **Fair Credit Reporting Act** requires the lender to tell you the name and address of the reporting agency that furnished the report. Within 30 days of being denied credit due to the information at the credit bureau, you are able to visit the credit bureau to review your credit history free of charge. If you have not been denied credit, the credit bureau may charge a small fee before you are granted permission to review your credit.

The credit bureau will reinvestigate any information that you question. If it is found to be incorrect, it will be deleted. If the reinvestigation does not result in a satisfactory change in your credit history, you may file a brief statement of your side of the story to be included with future reports. Most negative information—bad debts, arrest records, suits, judgments, etc.—can remain on your record for 7 years. Information about a straight bankruptcy is maintained in your file for 10 years.

You can obtain a copy of your credit report once every 12 months at no charge. The centralized website for this service is located at:

https://www.annualcreditreport.com

YOUR CREDIT HISTORY

You may have experience with credit. If so, you have started to establish your credit history. If you do not have experience with credit, you need to establish a history that suggests that you are a responsible borrower. How do you establish yourself as a borrower that a lender would be willing to trust? Below are several recommended steps.

Manage your finances. Prepare your net worth statement, do your budget, maintain a household inventory, and place all of your financial records in their proper place. Maintain a record of where they are stored. Be able to demonstrate to the lender that you are conducting your financial affairs in a business-like manner.

Open a checking and savings account. Every applicant is asked about their banking history. You must have one to report. The ability to manage your cash is what the lender is looking for. Do not overdraw your checking account. Rather, make regular deposits to your savings plan to demonstrate your discipline in making payments to yourself and living within your means.

Open a retail charge account. Retail charge accounts are easy to obtain. Use your credit card to purchase small, needed items that you would have purchased with cash. Then pay the bill *in full* when it is received to avoid the finance charge.

Apply for a bank card. These all-purpose credit cards are honored most everywhere and are a convenient form of credit. Use it sparingly and pay the bill *in full* when it is received to avoid the finance charge. If you do not pay the bill off in full each month (i.e., carry a balance), *always* pay more than the minimum required monthly payment to minimize the interest you will pay.

CREDIT CHECKLIST

- Establish an emergency fund of 6 to 12 months' living expenses.
- In addition to rent or mortgage payments, pay no more than 15% of your *take-home pay* on monthly credit payments. If you are anticipating a change in your family, reduce this amount to allow for the additional expense.
- Always repay one major debt before taking out another.
- Reexamine your desire to purchase the good or service. Could you make the *credit* payments to yourself and buy the good later with cash?
- Keep a running total of the amounts you have charged and set a limit.

- Do not shop when you are feeling discouraged.

- Do not go shopping unless you need something. If you see something on impulse that you want, *do not touch it*! Wait a day or two. By then, the "want" may have disappeared. Use the HALT principle. Do not make major purchases (or decisions) if you are Hungry, Angry, Lonely, or Tired.

- Shop for credit. A difference of even 1% point in the annual percentage rate (APR) can create savings. If you must borrow, typically the least expensive sources of borrowing (from least to most expensive) are family and friends, cash advance from employer, life insurance company, credit union, bank or savings and loan, consumer finance company, pawn shop, and title loan lenders.

WHEN YOU BORROW

The federal **Consumer Credit Protection Act**, or the **Truth in Lending Act**, requires that all lenders and merchants provide the consumer with certain information before they sign the credit contract. This information must be conspicuously displayed and contain two important pieces of information relative to the cost of the credit: the total *finance charge* expressed in dollars and the APR of interest.

The finance charge will inform the consumer of the total dollar cost of using borrowed money to make the purchase. By law, the finance charge must include all charges: interest, loan fees, service charges, loan investigation fees, and premiums for credit life insurance. Comparing the dollar amount of finance charges between different lenders is meaningful but only if the loans are for the same amount of money for the same length of time.

The APR is the cost of credit in percentage terms. If you compare two contracts for the same amount of money with the same repayment schedule for the same time period, the lender with the lowest APR would be preferred.

The **Truth in Lending Act** states that lenders cannot require you to purchase credit life insurance from them. They can, however, require that you have life insurance to insure the performance of your loan in the event of your death. If you have a choice, consider your need for additional life insurance to cover this loss. You may have sufficient life insurance if you have an adequate life insurance program. Conversely, if you need additional life insurance to cover this debt, consider its costs both from the lender and from other sources. The lender's policy typically will not require proof of insurability. This may be advantageous if you are unable to buy life insurance elsewhere. However, if you are young and in good health, you might be able to purchase a declining term-life insurance policy to cover this loss at reduced cost.

The **Credit Card Act of 2009** was passed in order to help consumers understand their credit cards better. Credit card companies are required to disclose how long it will take to pay off the entire balance by only making the monthly minimum payments and they must also specify how much the consumer needs to pay each month in order to pay off their debt in 1–3 years, including the amount of interest they would be paying. Also, for those under the age of 21 it may be harder to obtain a credit card as they must cosign with someone over 21 or prove independent means of income. Below are some other important pieces of this legislation that are beneficial to consumers.

- Promotional rates must last at least 6 months and regular rates cannot be raised for at least 1 year

- Rate hikes require 45 days notice (instead of 15)

- Rates cannot be raised on existing balances (unless payment is more than 60 days late)

- Companies must send statements 21 days before the payment is due (instead of the prior 14 day requirement)

- Double-cycle billing banned

- Credit card companies cannot charge an over-limit fee unless the consumer approves it (those who do not agree will have their transactions rejected)

- Companies can only charge one over-limit fee per billing cycle

- Payments received by the due date (Or next business day) cannot be subject to late fees

CAN YOU AFFORD TO USE CREDIT?

In contemplating the use of credit in your future, first you must decide whether you can afford to use credit. The best way to determine this is to review your budget. Ask yourself the following questions: *What income do I have to spend each month? What are my fixed and flexible expenses, including money for my emergency fund, savings, and a monthly amount set aside for irregular payments?* and *How much do I have left after these are all paid?*

    Your answers will categorize you within one of the three cases below.

Case 1: Your expenses are greater than your income. If this is true, you have no credit capacity and your answer to credit use is an emphatic *NO!*

Case 2: Your income meets your expenses, but there is nothing extra. You should postpone the use of credit until you have some obligations repaid or your income increases. However, if you have an emergency that requires you to use credit you will have to reduce some expenses or increase income in order to avoid the potential of credit difficulty.

Case 3: You have money left after paying for your living expenses and savings. In this fortunate scenario you have to decide what to do with the excess income. Proper financial planning may result in deciding that the extra cash be used to prepay other obligations, or to increase your savings/investment program. On the other hand, Case 3 represents the only case where you have the potential to meet the credit payments should you decide to borrow.

DANGER AHEAD!

Financial difficulties have a way of coming to those who cannot turn their back on credit, like the recovering alcoholic or smoker who thinks that one drink or one cigarette will not hurt. But soon it is two, then three, then a fifth or a pack or a carton. Do not become a *credit-holic*. Should any of the following danger signals occur, stop using credit and get your financial life together.

    Are total consumer credit payments over 20% of your monthly budget?

    Is an increasing portion of your income going to debt repayment?

    Are your credit cards at or near their limit?

    Are you always late on one or more bills?

    Are you borrowing to pay for things you used to pay for with cash?

    Have you taken out a new loan to repay an old loan?

    Is your net worth decreasing?

    If you lost your job, would you make it for 6 to 12 months?

    Are creditors threatening to repossess?

If you answered *yes* to any of the above questions, you may be headed toward a crisis. Your money problem could come from inexperience, an emergency, marital problems, or a number of other problems that could inhibit your family's ability to meet credit obligations. Whatever the cause, you must act promptly to avoid any serious problem that is around the corner.

    You may find a way to increase income. Perhaps, a second earner could enter the workforce or an earner could find a better paying job, or a job with better benefits which could reduce costs. An older child may be willing to find a job and help see the family through this difficult time.

    Under pressure we can reduce our living expenses. Say *goodbye* to your cable television and *hello* to a book from the library. Stop buying something, anything, everything that is not necessary for your family's maintenance and well-being. Examples would be clothes, expensive cuts of meat, and brand name toiletries. Try riding your bike or walking and driving your car less. Do this for 2 to 3 months. It may put you back on track and get you out of trouble. However, if these changes do not help, seek additional support before the problem gets out of hand.

First, contact your creditor. Many problems can be resolved by negotiations between the creditor and the borrower. Creditors can often understand a legitimate reason why you are having problems with your debt repayment. They may defer payments, reduce the finance charge, or lower the monthly payment to help you make it through a difficult time. The worst thing you can do is to avoid your creditors when you begin to have trouble.

If negotiations with individual creditors do not solve the problem, then, perhaps, a debt consolidation loan would be useful. Such a loan consolidates all your loans into one loan that is renegotiated and payments are set at a level that can be met. If, however, you choose this alternative, be sure that you stop using your credit cards. The fact that you have lower monthly payments does not mean that you have just received additional debt capacity.

RUNNING AGROUND

If all else fails and your family's financial ship crashes against the shore—either through mismanagement or an unforeseen emergency—then you may have to seek other solutions. One of the best services to help you with this problem is the Consumer Credit Counseling Service. They can help the overextended borrower work out a plan to repay his debts without going into bankruptcy.

While a Consumer Credit Counseling Service may exist in your town, do not confuse a private, profit-making enterprise with the nonprofit credit counseling service. If you have doubts, ask your local Better Business Bureau or Chamber of Commerce for information about the nearest member of the National Foundation for Consumer Credit.

SUNK

The **Bankruptcy Abuse Prevention and Consumer Protection Act of 2005** represents the largest reform ever made to the U.S. Bankruptcy Act of 1978. The goal of the change is to increase the integrity of bankruptcy law and practice by restoring personal responsibility. As such, the law has the greatest impact on personal bankruptcies, with minor changes for corporations, farmers, and small businesses.

Bankruptcy reform was deemed necessary due to several factors: escalating bankruptcy filings, significant creditor losses, and perceived loopholes that created a moral hazard leading to abusive personal bankruptcy filings. The tone, if you will, was that there exists a lack of personal accountability for some segments of consumers. To address these issues, the Act changed the responsibilities of those who administer bankruptcies, as well as those who counsel debtors to seek bankruptcy.

The prime change is to make it more difficult for a consumer to file a **Chapter 7 bankruptcy**. A Chapter 7 bankruptcy, often called a *straight bankruptcy*, is one where all of the bankrupt entity's property, with few exceptions, is taken by the court and sold. Then, the proceeds from the sale are used to repay the creditors. If there are insufficient assets to repay the creditors in full, the balance of the loan is discharged. Exceptions to debts able to be discharged are alimony, child support, back taxes, debts that creditors successfully have reaffirmed, and some student loans. In a sense, a Chapter 7 allows the consumer to begin anew.

The Bankruptcy Abuse Prevention and Consumer Protection Act of 2005 ceases the presumption that a debtor is entitled to a Chapter 7 bankruptcy, and applies a test of simple, as opposed to substantial, abuse. To determine abuse, a means test is applied to project household income and expenses over the next 5 years. Expenses must be reasonable expenses, varying by family size, as determined by Internal Revenue Service standard allowances for food, clothing, personal care, and entertainment with regional adjustments where possible. Simply put, if a debtor has $166.67 in current monthly income in excess of current monthly expenses, abuse is presumed regardless of the debtor's unsecured debt level. At the other end, if a debtor has at least $100 in current income in excess of expenses, abuse is presumed if their income is deemed sufficient to pay at least 25% of the unsecured debt over 5 years.

If simple abuse is found, the Chapter 7 bankruptcy claim is dismissed or, with the consent of the debtor, converted to a **Chapter 13 bankruptcy** (formerly referred to as the *wage earner plan*). A Chapter 13 bankruptcy allows a debtor to discharge his or her credit obligations by a court-supervised repayment plan. The plan may extend from 3 to 6 years.

Bankrupt consumers are responsible to perform additional tasks and report them to bankruptcy court. They must provide the court a certificate of completion for a completed credit counseling session and a financial literacy course. Bankrupt consumers must submit their pay stubs, any anticipated income or expenditure increases, an itemization of monthly net income, their most recent federal tax return to any affected creditor and to continue to provide future tax returns to the court, an annual documentation of their budget statement, and a disclosure of any educational savings plans to the court. Needless to say, not following the precepts of goal setting, budgeting, and the necessity of living within one's means creates a world where the bankrupt consumer is increasingly obligated to the larger society. The consumer's privacy and freedoms are clearly reduced while he or she works to restore their financial life.

It is often asked, "Can a person who has filed for bankruptcy ever receive credit?" The answer varies from lender to lender, but the answer is probably *yes*. By removing all debts from a consumer's net worth statement (their financial ledger), he or she is able to begin anew. The record of the bankruptcy, however, remains on the borrower's credit history for 10 years. This will lower the likelihood of low-risk lenders (read this as *lower-cost lenders*) being willing to lend to said consumer. Bankruptcy is an extreme step and, while some consumers cannot avoid it following a catastrophic loss, an uninsured health episode, or divorce, others could have avoided bankruptcy by being more prudent in their expenditures and practicing the principles of personal financial management as laid out in this text and others. It is crucial for young consumers who are just embarking on their financial journey to get started the right way if they aspire to have a strong and successful financial foundation.

BANKRUPTCY – DEBTS THAT MAY BE DISCHARGED

A bankruptcy discharge frees you from the obligation of paying back the remaining debt. Each household's situation is unique in regards to the type of bankruptcy that is filed, the household's income level and the type of debt. This information is used to determine which items may be discharged and which items must be repaid (and how much). Not all debts are treated equally in bankruptcy and therefore, some debts are forgiven as other may never go away (even if you file for Chapter 7 bankruptcy). The table below gives some general guidelines of which debts may be discharged and ones that may not.

Debts that can be Discharged	Debts that cannot be Discharged
Credit Card Debt	Federal Student Loans
Medical Debt	Federal Income Taxes
	Alimony
	Child Support
	Debts from DUI charge

THE GROWTH OF CONSUMER CREDIT DEBT

The table on the next page demonstrates the tremendous growth in the amount of consumer credit debt since 1970. Total consumer debt is comprised of credit card debt, automobile debt, mobile home loans, student loans, and other miscellaneous loans. Mortgage debt (ie home loans) is *not* included in consumer debt. In 2000, total credit card debt in the United States accounted for about 40% of the total consumer debt at $682 billion, however, by the middle of 2018, total credit card debt had increased to $840 billion but its percentage of total consumer debt had decreased to 21%. The rise in auto, student, etc debt can be

Growth of Consumer Credit Debt in the United States: 1970–2018

Year	Total Consumer Debt (billions)	Credit Card Debt (billions)	Percentage of Total Consumer Debt	Auto, Student, etc. Debt (billions)	Percentage of Total Consumer Debt	U.S. Population (millions)	Consumer Debt per Capita	U.S. Median Family Income	Consumer Debt as Percentage of Income for Family of four	Consumer Price Index (CPI) (1982–1984 = 100)	U.S. Median Family Income in 1982–1984	Total Consumer Debt in 1982–1984 (billions)	Consumer Debt Per Capita in 1982–1984
								Nominal Data (Not Adjusted for Inflation)			**Real Data (Adjusted for Inflation)**		
1960	$60	—	—	$60	100	180.7	$332	$5,620	23.6	29.6	$18,986	$203	$1,122
1965	$96	—	—	$96	100	194.3	$494	$6,957	28.4	31.5	$22,086	$305	$1,567
1970	$132	$5	4	$127	96	205.1	$644	$9,867	26.1	38.8	$25,430	$340	$1,659
1980	$352	$55	16	$297	84	227.7	$1,546	$21,023	29.4	82.4	$25,513	$427	$1,876
1990	$808	$238	29	$570	71	250.1	$3,231	$35,353	36.6	130.7	$27,049	$618	$2,472
2000	$1,722	$682	40	$1,039	60	282.4	$6,098	$50,732	48.1	172.2	$29,461	$1,000	$3,541
2005	$2,295	$826	36	$1,468	64	296.9	$7,730	$56,194	55.0	195.3	$28,773	$1,175	$3,958
2009	$2,500	$900	36	$1,600	64	307.0	$8,143	$52,175	62.4	214.5	$24,324	$1,166	$3,796
2013	$2,940	$680	23	$2,260	77	317.0	$9,274	$52,100	71.2	233.0	$22,361	$1,262	$3,981
2018	$3,950	$840	21	$3,100	79	329.0	$12,006	$62,175	59.6	252.9	$24,585	$1,562	$4,748
Percentage Change from 2000 to 2018	129%	23%	−48	198%	32%	17%	84%	23%	24%	47%	−17%	56%	34%

Total consumer debt includes: Auto Loans, Mobile Home Loans, Credit Card Debt, Student Loans, Other Loans

Source: U.S. Census Bureau (http://www.census.gov)

attributed to the sharp increase in student loan debt which has increased by over 450% since 2000. Also the median family income in America has decreased, therefore limiting the ability of households to repay debt. It is predicted that by the end of 2018 total consumer debt will amount to $4 trillion (this number was just at $1.722 trillion in 2000).

So, how does this break down? (as of June 2018):

- The average household owes $7,328 on their credit cards (US average in 1980 was $670) ($15,482 on their credit cards for average indebted household—this basically means that a small number of households have a lot of credit card debt causing the indebted average to be much higher)
- Americans have paid over $100 billion in credit card interest and fees which is an increase of 35% since 2013

TOTAL DEBT COMPOSITION (INCLUDING MORTGAGES)

If you include mortgage loans, the American consumer owes (June 2018) $13.29 trillion totally. We are truly a nation of debtors.

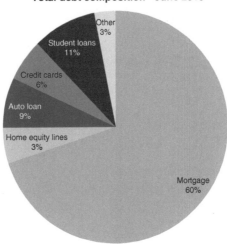

Total debt composition - June 2018

Source: U.S. Census Bureau (http://www.census.gov)

It is important to note that student loan debt was the only non-mortgage debt among those listed that increased during the Great Recession (December 2007–June 2009). Student loan debt is now the second largest balance after mortgage debt amassing a devastating total of over $1.5 trillion as of June 2018. This equates to over $39,000 owed per student in the 2017 graduating class.

EVALUATING CREDIT CARDS

The following should be considered when evaluating credit cards:

Annual fee (ranging from none to $100s).

Grace period (no interest is charged on new purchases if you pay your bill in full on time each month).

Interest rate charged on outstanding balances expressed as an annual percentage rate (APR).

0% introductory fee, how long is it.

Foreign transactions fees if you are traveling abroad

Understand the rewards program and what is its interest rate - compare that to the interest rate on a non-rewards program account

Requirements of payment (entire balance must be paid each month versus minimum payment).

If you . . .

. . . **carry a balance** on your credit card (meaning that you *do not* pay off the balance due each month) you should **select a credit card with the lowest possible APR**. Whether or not the card has a grace period is irrelevant because a grace period only applies if you pay the full balance each month.

. . . **pay your credit card bill in full** each month you should **choose a card which has a grace period and a low annual fee**. The APR is irrelevant because you never carry a balance.

Obtaining a credit card for status is vain. Obtaining a credit card to pay off another credit card is stupid unless its APR is lower. Obtaining a credit card for convenience makes some sense. Carrying a balance is expensive. While the average number of credit cards held by a consumer in 2017 has fallen to 2.7 (consumers held seven in the year 2000), indebtedness is still an issue among American households. Use of credit is essentially spending future income before you actually earn it. This may be sensible *if* you can guarantee your future income . . . but can you?

LIABILITY FOR LOST CREDIT CARDS

limited to $50

LIABILITY FOR LOST DEBIT CARDS

$50 if the card is reported lost of stolen within 2 days

$500 if the lost or stolen debit card is reported within 60 days.

Failure to tell your bank within 60 days after your bank statement is received puts your entire checking and overdraft account at risk.

ONLINE PAYMENT SERVICES – CONTACTLESS CARDS

Do you carry your phone with you everywhere? Who doesn't these days. Have you every forgotten your wallet when going to the grocery store or while dining with friends? Why not create a system where you can pay for purchases like groceries or food at a restaurant using your smartwatch? How about an easy way to repay friends without going the atm or stopping by the bank by using your smartphone? Instead of carrying around checks or credit/debit cards or cash, digital wallets are quickly replacing these archaic ways to pay for things. Peer to peer systems and digital wallets like Pay Pay, Apple Pay, Google Pay, Venmo, and Zelle utilize your existing checking or credit card accounts to offer a seamless way to pay through devices you already own and take everywhere with you. Some of these online payment services offer more secure systems than credit cards as your personal information is never shared thus making it harder for thieves to use your card fraudulently. Simply hold your smartphone or smartwatch near the reader where you usually swipe/dip your credit card. Instantly your payment is transmitted electronically.

Peer to peer systems allow you to send and receive money to and from friends. Some of these are social systems and the transactions can be found online (if you like to snoop on your friends). Digital wallets replace the need to carry around credit or debit cards to pay for a latte or dinner out with friends

Digital Wallets

- *PayPal – one of the first digital wallets, popular with E-Bay
- *Apple Pay – can only be used with Mac products
- *Google Pay – can only be used with Android systems
- Samsung Pay – Samsung phones can use Google Pay or Samsung Pay
- Chase Pay
- Masterpass
- Visa Checkout

(* acts as both a digital wallet and a peer to peer system)

Peer to Peer Payment Systems

- Venmo – used by more millennials
- Zelle – used by most adults

It is important to note that for the convenience these products add, there are also some negatives. Some systems do not allow you to cancel transactions, so if you accidentally send $100 instead of $10, you may be out of luck. Also, there may be costs associated with each transaction if you are associating your digital wallet with a credit card instead of a checking account. Another item to note is that if you leave your iPhone unlocked and you haven't logged out of your peer to peer account, someone could send themselves money from your account to there's very easily. Make sure and log out of all of your apps when you are finished with them and lock your iPhone so others cannot access your information and make unauthorized charges.

IF YOU LOSE YOUR PURSE OR WALLET

We have probably all heard horror stories about fraud that is committed using your name, address, social security number, credit, and so on. Here is some critical information to limit the damage in case this happens to you or someone you know. As everyone always advises, cancel your credit cards immediately, but the key is having the toll-free numbers and your card numbers handy so you know whom to call that information in an easily accessible location. File a police report immediately in the jurisdiction where it was stolen. By doing this, it proves to credit providers that you were diligent, and it serves as a first step toward an investigation (if there ever is one).

But here is what is perhaps most important: Call the three national credit reporting organizations immediately to place a fraud alert on your name and social security number. The alert means any company that checks your credit knows your information was stolen and they have to contact you by phone to authorize new credit.

If you suspect that you are a victim of credit fraud or identity theft, contact the appropriate agency listed below.

Credit Bureau Fraud Departments
TransUnion   Fraud Victim Assistance Department   P.O. Box 6790   Fullerton, CA 92834   http://www.transunion.com   Phone: 800-680-7289
Equifax Credit Information Services   Consumer Fraud Division   P.O. Box 740256   Atlanta, GA 30374   http://www.equifax.com   Phone: 800-525-6285
Experian   Experian's National Consumer Assistance   P.O. Box 2002   Allen, TX 75013   http://www.experian.com   Phone: 888-397-3742
Government Agencies
Social Security Administration (fraud line): 1-800-269-0271   http://sss.ssa.gov
U.S. Postal Inspection Service: http://www.usps.com/ postalinspectors
To Report Fraudulent Use of Your Checks
Check Rite/Global Payments: Phone: 800-638-4600
SCAN: Phone: 800-262-7771
Tele-Check: Phone: 800-710-9898
Chex Systems: Phone: 800-428-9623
Scam Alerts
http://www.consumer.ftc.gov/scam-alerts
Identity Theft
Federal Trade Commission: Phone: 877-ID-THEFT   http://www.consumer.gov/idtheft

COST OF CREDIT

You receive a check from Count-a-Buck Bankcard which you may cash for $1,200. "Wow, I can spend that!", you say. We are sure you can . . . and probably more.

By cashing the check, you have agreed to the terms of the Bankcard and all too soon it is time to start repaying the debt. The APR on this line of credit is 21%. If you pay the minimum monthly payment of $40 it will take you 43 months (or 3.6 years) to repay the $1,200.

But, the total amount of your repayment is not $1,200, it is around $1,720 ($40 × 43 months = $1,720). *You will pay $520 in interest alone.* Your $100 sweater actually ended up costing $143 ($100 is 1/12th of $1,200 and $43 is 1/12th of $520). What a steal . . . for Count-a-Buck Bankcard, Inc.

Here is the mathematics of this loan using a financial calculator:

PV   =   1,200
PMT   =   <40> monthly (entered as a negative on your financial calculator)
I/YR =   21/12 months = 1.75% per month
(I/YR =   21, if P/Y = 12)
N   =   **42.91 or approximately 43 months**

Or, solve for n using the following algebraic formula:

$$n = - \frac{\ln\left(1 - \left(\left(PV \times i\right) / PMT\right)\right)}{\ln\left(1 + i\right)} \quad \text{where } \ln = \text{the natural logarithm}$$

$$n = - \frac{\ln\left(1 - \left(\left(1,200 \times 0.175\right) / 40\right)\right)}{\ln\left(1 + .0175\right)}$$

$$n = - \frac{-.74444}{.017349} = -(-42.91) = \textbf{42.91 or approx. 43 months}$$

CREDIT LIFE INSURANCE

Credit life insurance is insurance that pays off your debt if you (the borrower) or the co-borrower die. In some cases it will also pay off your debt if you are disabled. Is it a good deal? Usually not. Credit life insurance turns out to be *very expensive insurance*. The cost per $1,000 of credit life insurance coverage is much higher than a good term-life insurance policy.

For example, a 25-year-old person could purchase a $100,000 term-life insurance policy for roughly $100 per year. Contrast that to a 3 year consumer loan of $8,000 which would charge a lump sum premium of $170 for joint-life credit insurance (insurance for the borrower and co-borrower).

Inasmuch as the two insurance policies described above are not equal in size ($100,000 versus $8,000) directly comparing the premium for each policy would be inappropriate (or as the saying goes, it would be comparing apples to oranges!).

The solution is to compare insurance policies on the basis of their *annual cost per $1,000*. Comparing the annual cost per $1,000 for insurance is identical in principle to comparing the *cost per ounce* of grocery items. For example, when comparing a large jar of peanut butter to a small jar of peanut butter, the small jar will obviously cost less total money—but it will usually be *more expensive per ounce*. The same is true with life insurance products. Large policies will cost more money in total—but will be *less expensive per $1,000 of coverage*.

Shown below is the formula to determine the approximate *annual cost per $1,000* of insurance (any kind of insurance).

$$\frac{\text{Annual Insurance Premium}}{\textbf{Number of \$1,000s of Insurance}} = \textbf{Annual Cost per \$1,000}$$

The "Number of $1,000s of Insurance" equals the amount of insurance divided by 1,000 (the amount of insurance is more accurately referred to as the death benefit). For example, the number of $1,000s of insurance for a $100,000 term-life insurance policy would be:

$$\$100,000 / 1,000 = \textbf{100}$$

TERM-LIFE INSURANCE

The annual premium for the $100,000 life insurance policy is **$100**.
  Annual cost per $1,000 for $100,000 of term-life insurance:

$$\frac{\$100 \text{ annual premium}}{100} = \$1.00 \text{ per \$1,000 for term-life insurance}$$

CREDIT LIFE INSURANCE

The one-time premium for 3 years of joint credit life insurance is $170. The approximated annual premium is **$56.67 (or $170 / 3)**. (This approximation ignores the time value of money. However, to do so is a bias in favor of the credit life policy!).
  Annual cost per $1,000 for $8,000 of joint-life credit insurance:

$$\frac{\$56.67 \text{ "annual" premium}}{8} = \$7.08 \text{ per \$1,000 of joint credit life}$$

As can be seen, the joint-life credit insurance is seven times more expensive than the term-life insurance for a 25-years old person. Moreover, the joint-life credit insurance declines in value as the loan is gradually paid off. If either the borrower or co-borrower dies, say, after 2 years, only the loan balance of $3,123.86 would be paid off—not $8,000. (The declining balance schedule of this particular loan is shown on page 85).
  You might consider purchasing credit life insurance if you do not qualify for a life insurance policy due to advanced age or poor health. Otherwise, avoid credit life insurance.
  General guideline: Insurance is usually a better deal in greater face-value amounts. In other words, buy in bulk and save!

SIMPLE INTEREST INSTALLMENT LOANS

An installment loan is a loan that is repaid in equal installments, such as a loan to purchase a car, furniture, or home. Most installment loans are calculated using **simple interest**. This means that *interest is charged only on the outstanding (or unpaid) balance* of the loan. As you gradually pay the loan off your interest payment becomes smaller and smaller (as shown in the table on the following page). Simple interest is favorable for the consumer (unless you can get an interest-free loan).

Below is an example of an $8,000 installment loan. The lender convinced the borrower to purchase credit life insurance for $170 (which was added to the loan amount), so the total loan balance equals $8,170. Recall that the borrower will only receive $8,000. The APR of this loan is 14.50% (the monthly rate equals .145 / 12). The loan is to be repaid in 3 years, or 36 months (with payments at the end of each month).

Solution if using a financial calculator

PV   = $8,170
N   = $3 \times 12 = 36$ months
I/YR =   14.5 / 12 = 1.208333333
(I/YR =   14.5, if P/Y = 12)
PMT =   **<281.22>**

Solution if using algebra

$$PMT = \frac{PV}{\left(\dfrac{1 - (1 + i)^{-n}}{i} \right)}$$

$$PMT = \frac{\$8,170}{\left(\dfrac{1 - (1 + (.145 / 12))^{-36}}{.145 / 12} \right)} = \mathbf{\$281.22}$$

The portion of the monthly payment that goes to interest is determined by multiplying the loan balance by the monthly rate of interest. For the first month the interest payment would be $8,170 \times (.145 / 12) =$ $98.72.

The portion of the monthly payment that goes to pay off principal is simply the monthly payment minus the interest payment, or (in month 1) $281.22 − 98.72 = $182.50 in principal repaid. The new loan balance is the loan balance at the start of the month minus the payment to principal, or in this case $8,170 − 182.50 = $7,987.50.

Month	Loan Balance	Monthly Payment	Payment to Interest	Payment to Principal	New Loan Balance
1	8,170.00	281.22	98.72	182.50	7,987.50
2	7,987.50	281.22	96.52	184.70	7,802.80
3	7,802.80	281.22	94.28	186.94	7,615.86
4	7,615.86	281.22	92.02	189.20	7,426.67
5	7,426.67	281.22	89.74	191.48	7,235.18
6	7,235.18	281.22	87.43	193.79	7,041.39
7	7,041.39	281.22	85.08	196.14	6,845.25
8	6,845.25	281.22	82.71	198.51	6,646.75
9	6,646.75	281.22	80.31	200.91	6,445.84
10	6,445.84	281.22	77.89	203.33	6,242.51
11	6,242.51	281.22	75.43	205.79	6,036.72
12	6,036.72	281.22	72.94	208.28	5,828.44
13	5,828.44	281.22	70.43	210.79	5,617.65
14	5,617.65	281.22	67.88	213.34	5,404.31
15	5,404.31	281.22	65.30	215.92	5,188.39
16	5,188.39	281.22	62.69	218.53	4,969.86
17	4,969.86	281.22	60.05	221.17	4,748.70
18	4,748.70	281.22	57.38	223.84	4,524.86
19	4,524.86	281.22	54.68	226.54	4,298.31
20	4,298.31	281.22	51.94	229.28	4,069.03
21	4,069.03	281.22	49.17	232.05	3,836.98
22	3,836.98	281.22	46.36	234.86	3,602.12
23	3,602.12	281.22	43.53	237.69	3,364.43
24	3,364.43	281.22	40.65	240.57	3,123.86
25	3,123.86	281.22	37.75	243.47	2,880.39
26	2,880.39	281.22	34.80	246.42	2,633.97
27	2,633.97	281.22	31.83	249.39	2,384.58
28	2,384.58	281.22	28.81	252.41	2,132.17
29	2,132.17	281.22	25.76	255.46	1,876.72
30	1,876.72	281.22	22.68	258.54	1,618.17
31	1,618.17	281.22	19.55	261.67	1,356.51
32	1,356.51	281.22	16.39	264.83	1,091.68
33	1,091.68	281.22	13.19	268.03	823.65
34	823.65	281.22	9.95	271.27	552.38
35	552.38	281.22	6.67	274.55	277.83
36	277.84	281.22	3.36	277.86	−.03
Total	N/A	10,123.92	1,953.89	8,170.00	
Average	4,491.71				

The APR on a simple interest loan can be calculated by the following formula:

$$\text{APR} = \frac{\text{Average Annual Finance Charge *}}{\text{Average Loan Balance}}$$

$$* \text{ where: Average Annual Finance Charge} = \frac{\text{Total Interest Paid}}{\text{Length of Loan (in years)}}$$

$$\text{APR} = \frac{\$1,953.89\,/\,3}{\$4,491.71} = \frac{\$651}{\$4,491.71} = \mathbf{14.50\%}$$

As can be seen, with a simple interest loan the actual APR is the same as the stated rate of interest. Therefore, solving the APR using the above calculation was redundant because the *actual APR* for a simple interest installment loan is always the same as the *stated interest rate*.

Assignment 4.1   Credit Calculations

Name _____

SHOW YOUR WORK

1. You decide to use your department store charge card . . . a lot! After 7 weeks you have racked up $1,400 of debt. Your minimum monthly payment is $45, and is paid at the end of each month. If the APR is 16.80%, how long will it take you to pay the loan off? (Assume that you make the minimum payment until the debt is entirely paid off).

2. You have the opportunity to purchase a $150,000 term-life insurance policy for $145 per year for the next 4 years. Your bank has offered you credit life insurance in conjunction with a $12,000 four-year (48 months) loan you are applying for. The credit life insurance premium would be a one-time up-front fee of $325. What is the annual cost per $1,000 of insurance for (a) the term-life insurance and (b) the credit life insurance?

3. Assume you obtain the $12,000 loan (without the credit life insurance). It is a 4-year simple interest installment loan with an annual interest rate of 12.50%. First, what would be the monthly payment? Second, how much total interest will you pay over the 4 years? Third, what is the APR of this loan?

4. You are interested in buying a car. One dealer will sell you a car for $17,000 and is offering 3.9% APR financing. The other dealer's price for the same car is $15,000, but with financing at 7.9% APR. Both loans will be for 5 years. Which is the better deal (as determined by monthly payment)?

5. You borrow $10,000 for education expenses (i.e., a student loan). Six months after graduation you need to start making monthly payments on your loan.

   a. If the loan repayment period is 10 years and the APR is 4.9%, how much is your monthly payment?

   b. If you make the normal monthly payments over the 10-year period, how much total interest will you pay over the 10 years?

   c. If, instead, you make a payment of $150 each and every month, how much interest will you save?

Section Four Extra Practice Problems

1. How long will it take you to pay off your $1,846 credit card bill if you pay the minimum $40 per month and the card charges 14.0% APR? Secondly, how much total interest will you pay if you pay only $40/month until the loan is repaid in full? Always assume ordinary annuity for credit payment problems.

2. You have a simple interest installment loan of $26,000 for your new car. You need to pay back the loan in 6 years at 8% APR. What is your monthly payment?

3. Compare the annual cost per thousand of a $150,000 term-life insurance policy that costs $125/year, to a 4-year $9,000 credit life policy that charges a lump sum premium of $195.

4. What is the APR of a 4-year simple interest installment loan of $15,000 with an annual interest rate of 9.5%?

5. You borrow $7,500 for education expenses (i.e., a student loan). Six months after graduation you need to start making monthly payments (at the end of each month) on your loan. The loan repayment period is 10 years and the APR is 5.9%.

   a. If you make the normal monthly payment over the 10-year period, how much total interest will you pay over the 10 years?

   b. If you add an extra $50 to the payment each and every month, how much interest will you save over the life of the loan?

Section Four Practice Problem Answers

1. a. PV   = 1,846
    I/YR   = 14 / 12 (or .14 / 12 if using algebra)
    (I/YR   = 14, if P/Y = 12)
    PMT   = <40>
    N   = **66.65 months or 5.5 years**

    b. (PMT × N) − PV = Total Interest Paid
      (40 × 66.65) − 1,846 = **$820**

2. PV   =   26,000
   N   =   6 × 12
   I/YR   =   8 / 12 (or .08 / 12 if using algebra)
   (I/YR   =   8, if P/Y = 12)
   PMT   =   **<$455.86> per month**

3. Annual Insurance Premium / Number of $1,000s of Insurance
   Term Life: 125/150 = **$0.83 per $1,000**
   Credit Life: 195/4   = 48.75

            48.75/ 9 = **5.42 per $1,000**

4. 9.5%. The APR of a simple interest installment loan is *always* the same as the stated interest rate.

5. a. PV   =   7,500
    N   =   10 × 12
    I/YR   =   5.9 / 12   (or .059 / 12 if using algebra)
    (I/YR   =   5.9, if P/Y = 12)
    PMT   =   **<82.89> per month**

    $82.89 × 120 months = $9,946.80 total repayment to lender
    $9,946.80 − 7,500 loan = $2,446.80 total interest paid to lender

    b. PMT   =   <132.89>
       PV   =   7,500
       I/YR   =   5.9 / 12   (of .059 / 12 if using algebra)
       (I/YR   =   5.9, if P/Y = 12)
       N   =   **66.27 months**

    66.27 × $132.89 = $8,806.62 − $7,500 = $1,306.62 total interest
    $2,446.71 − $1,306.62 = **$1,140.09 interest saved** by adding an extra $50 to each monthly payment.

Notes:

Taxes

One thing is clear: The Founding Fathers never intended a nation where citizens would pay nearly half of everything they earn to the government.

Ron Paul

To compel a man to furnish funds for the propagation of ideas he disbelieves and abhors is sinful and tyrannical.

Thomas Jefferson

We contend that for a nation to try to tax itself into prosperity is like a man standing in a bucket and trying to lift himself up by the handle.

Winston Churchill

A democracy cannot exist as a permanent form of government. It can only exist until the people discover they can vote themselves largess out of the public treasury. From that moment on, the majority always votes for the candidate promising the most benefits from the public treasury, with the result that democracy always collapses over a loose fiscal policy to be followed by a dictatorship.

Alexander Fraser Tytler

As we peer into society's future, we—you and I, and our government—must avoid the impulse to live only for today, plundering for our own ease and convenience the precious resources of tomorrow. We cannot mortgage the material assets of our grandchildren without risking the loss also of their political and spiritual heritage. We want democracy to survive for all generations to come, not to become the insolvent phantom of tomorrow.

Dwight D. Eisenhower

FEDERAL EXPENDITURES

We hear a lot of talk about the federal deficit and what to do about it. One side of the congressional aisle has great trouble working with the other side of the aisle. Both sides of the aisle say they want the best for our country, though the means they choose to reach those ends are quite different. There is much division between the two largest political parties, but they also have much in common. Both parties want to spend money that benefits their supporters, while levying taxes on those who are less likely to support their agendas. This methodology is quite natural, especially when one is trying to get reelected in efforts to preserve his or her position of influence in our country. I might label both of them as spendthrifts. For, as the following graphs demonstrate, there has been very few times in recent history when revenues exceeded expenditures and, during that brief period, the Democrats were in charge. This leads me to conclude that economic cycles have as much, if not more, to do with federal budgets than do those we elect to lead our country.

As you can see, the US federal government budget had estimated outlays of $3.98 trillion dollars during fiscal year 2017, representing 25.8% of our gross domestic product (GPD). Unfortunately, the federal government had projected receipts of only $3.2 trillion. Thus, there was an anticipated deficit of $665 billion in 2017, or $2,033 for every person living in the United States. This represents 3.4% of the Gross Domestic Product (GDP) of the United States.

When our government engages in deficit spending, the government must choose between borrowing money, raising taxes, or lowering expenditures. Given the reality of politics, the latter two are rarely chosen. As a result we, as Americans, have a federal debt totaling $20.21 trillion, or 104.2% of GDP. Given the US population of 310.5 million, total per person federal government indebtedness is over $64,803, compared to $49,000[1] in 2015.

The Federal Reserve Bank and the US Treasury work as the major players in financing the country's activities. If the federal government is going to borrow money, one of their primary means is to sell Treasury bills and bonds to individual investors and nations to cover its budget deficit. Buyers of US Treasury bills and bonds are lending money to the government to finance the national debt (see charts below). As a result, interest of approximately $310.3 billlion was paid to the owners of the debt in fiscal year 2018.[2]

Although rare, when the government has a surplus of receipts over expenditures, the leaders of our country must decide whether to spend the excess on governmental activities or return the excess funds, typically through reduced taxes. On the other hand, leaders could debate whether the excess in receipts should be used to pay back some of the money they have borrowed or to spend it to supplement areas of social need, such as Social Security, health care, national defense, transportation, or another area of public expenditure that our elected representatives support.

The charts below show the historical trend in deficits and surpluses. It is clear that surpluses have been few in number and deficits have been the rule.[3] It is not a pretty picture, yet our collective decisions have created our present view. Our collective decisions will always build our future.

---

[1] https://www.usgovernmentspending.com/
[2] http://www.treasurydirect.gov/govt/reports/ir/ir_expense.htm
[3] http://www.kowaldesign.com/budget/

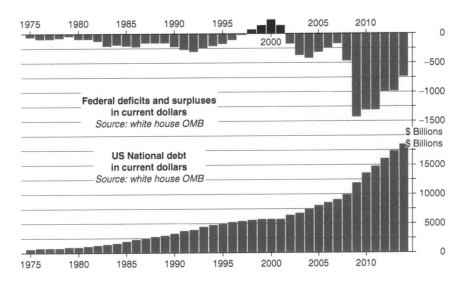

The following graph demonstrates actual changes in the proportion of federal revenues, for the fiscal years 1934–2017. A close examination will reveal that payroll taxes (Social Insurance and Retirement Receipts) have made up an increasing proportion of our total taxes, while corporate taxes and excise taxes make up a decreasing proportion of our total taxes, and individual income taxes have remained relatively constant since the 1940s. Given the importance of taxes to our overall well-being, and the large cost they are to individual taxpayers, one must understand the current tax system to help one pay his or her fair share without having to pay one dime more!

Federal Tax Revenue by Source

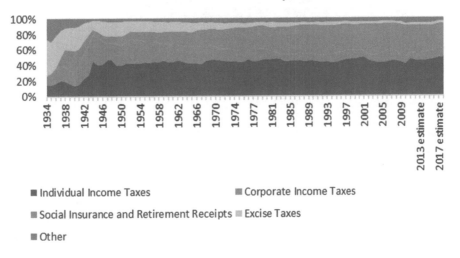

It is interesting to note that, while taxes are a burden, taxes make up a relatively smaller percentage of the US GPD than taxes do in other developed countries. In 2015, when we consider taxes at all levels, taxes in the United States were, on average, 26% of GDP. This is compared to an average of 34% of GDP for the 30 member countries of the Organization for Economic Cooperation and Development (OECD).[4] Take a minute to observe which countries have relatively high tax burdens and which countries have relatively low tax burdens.

---

[4] http://www.taxpolicycenter.org/briefing-book/background/numbers/international.cfm

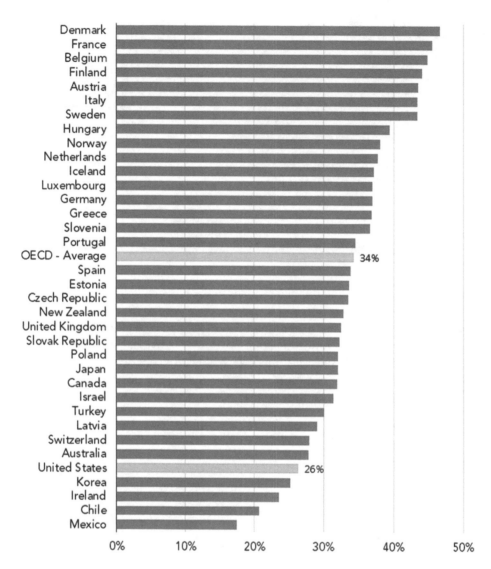

Figure 1 Taxes as a Share of Gross Domestic Product OECD, 2015

Source: OECD Stat Extract. These are provisional estimates. 2014 data are used for Australia, Japan, and Poland. The OECD average is over the most recent available data.

Many people wonder why the federal government spends our money in the manner in which they do. If we mimicked the logic of our forefathers, however, we might question whether our elected officials are acting on our collective values to allocate expenditures in a manner that creates the greatest benefit to the people of the United States. The following pie chart demonstrates expenditures for fiscal year 2010. The largest category of expenditures is Social Security (19.63%), followed by Defense (18.74%), Mandatory Welfare and Unemployment Expenditures (16.13%), and Medicare (12.79%). Are the allocations made on your behalf consistent with where you would like to see your money spent? If they are, relax. If they are not, become active in the electoral process and work for the changes you believe need to occur. If you believe in democracy, this is truly your responsibility.

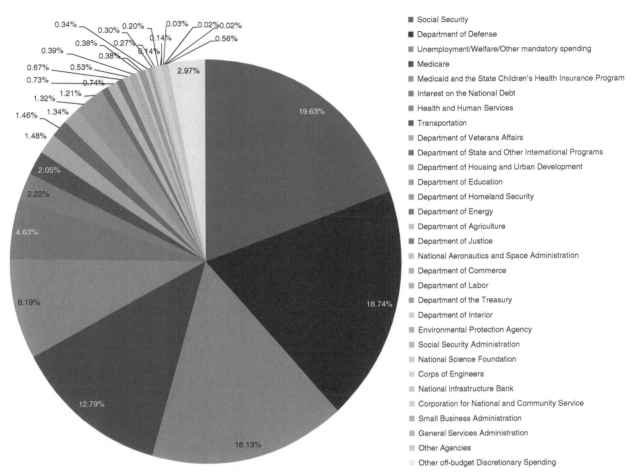

- Social Security
- Department of Defense
- Unemployment/Welfare/Other mandatory spending
- Medicare
- Medicaid and the State Children's Health Insurance Program
- Interest on the National Debt
- Health and Human Services
- Transportation
- Department of Veterans Affairs
- Department of State and Other International Programs
- Department of Housing and Urban Development
- Department of Education
- Department of Homeland Security
- Department of Energy
- Department of Agriculture
- Department of Justice
- National Aeronautics and Space Administration
- Department of Commerce
- Department of Labor
- Department of the Treasury
- Department of Interior
- Environmental Protection Agency
- Social Security Administration
- National Science Foundation
- Corps of Engineers
- National Infrastructure Bank
- Corporation for National and Community Service
- Small Business Administration
- General Services Administration
- Other Agencies
- Other off-budget Discretionary Spending

http://www.publicagenda.org/charts/federal-budget-expenditures

CRITERIA USED TO ASSESS TAX *FAIRNESS*

As long as we are considering your responsibilities in a democracy, it is a good time to consider the two philosophical bases for judging the appropriateness, or fairness, of a tax. These two criteria are: benefits received and ability to pay. They have been employed for years by policy makers to help them decide the appropriateness of a method of taxation. You need to remember that these criteria are neither right nor wrong. It is right, however, for an educated citizen to be able to understand perspectives with regard to taxation. (Hopefully, this occurs prior to voting to elect our representatives. They are, after all, the creators of our tax system.)

Benefits Received

This criterion states that people should pay taxes in proportion to the benefits that they receive from those tax revenues. Those who receive the greatest benefit from the tax should pay the greatest tax. We see this being applied in quantity taxes, such as fuel taxes, where those who use the roads the most, primarily funded by fuel taxes, pay the greatest amount of fuel taxes. Similarly, "sin" taxes on tobacco and alcohol are paid by those who smoke and drink. In other cases, this criterion cannot be adhered to due to other variables. For example, the recipient of food stamps may not directly pay any federal taxes, as their income is low.

Ability to Pay

The second criterion states that citizens with differing amounts of income (or wealth) should pay different amounts of taxes. This criterion is used to categorize taxes as being progressive, proportional, or regressive. As an informed, educated citizen, you need to understand these differences and work to see your preferred method applied in the marketplace.

Progressive tax: A progression tax is a tax where tax *rates* increase as taxable income increases. For example, federal income tax rates increase as taxable income increases. The tax rate charged on your last dollar of taxable income is known as your marginal tax rate.

Proportional tax: A proportional tax is a tax that is applied at a constant rate to all levels of taxable income. For example, recent "flat-tax" proposals are an example of applying the proportional income tax criteria.

Regressive tax: A regressive tax is where the rate of taxation decreases as a percent of taxable income as income increases. For example, sales taxes are regressive. This can be understood by observing how lower income households have a tendency to spend all their income and, thus, pay sales taxes on every dollar spent, while higher income household have greater rates of savings. Social Security taxes, a payroll tax, is also regressive as Social Security taxes are not collected after income exceeds the $132,900, the 2019 limit on Old Age Security and Disability Security taxes. (There is no income threshold for Medicare taxes, however.)

TYPES OF TAXES

Taxes on Purchases

Sales or *ad valorem* taxes: Sales taxes are a percentage tax that is applied to the purchase price of taxable goods. In some states, not all purchases are subject to sales taxes. Food, some services, and prescription drugs are often excluded from sales taxes in an effort to prevent the taxation of essential items.

Excise or quantity taxes: Excise taxes are levied against certain specific products or services on a per unit basis. Examples would be fuel taxes (per gallon), liquor taxes (per gallon or barrel), or cigarette taxes (per pack).

Taxes on Property

Property taxes are another example of an *ad valorem* tax. Property taxes are levied on the assessed value of the land and buildings owned by real property owners, such as homeowners and landlords.

Personal property taxes are assessed on specific personal assets, such as automobiles, trucks, farm equipment, cattle, recreational vehicles, and so on. Prior to registering a car—in most states—a car owner must demonstrate that he or she has paid property taxes on the vehicle for the preceding year(s).

Taxes on Wealth

Federal estate and gift taxes are charged on the value of a person's estate upon their death when the estate is sufficiently large. In 2019, there is effectively no federal estate tax on an estate valued at $11,400,000, or less. The future of this tax, however, is not known and political wrangling over the estate tax is present in every election.

Similarly, an **inheritance tax** may be levied on money and property received by heirs. This type of tax is collected by many, but far from all, states.

---

[5] Tax laws change as a result of decisions by our elected officials. Simply, they wish to encourage some behaviors while discouraging others by use of the tax code to provide subsidies or additional cost to particular behaviors. Each year a copy of Publication 17 from the Internal Revenue Service will provide detailed, current information.

Taxes on Earnings

Social Security and **income taxes** are levied against the earnings of workers, while corporations pay taxes on earnings.

US PERSONAL INCOME TAX PLANNING[5]

The objective of **tax planning** is to *legally maximize* the amount of money you keep by *legally minimizing* the amount of money you pay in taxes. Effective tax planning requires a household to merely have a basic understanding of how personal income taxes are determined. There are frequent changes in tax law and, admittedly, a myriad of complex rules exist which seems to have the effect of discouraging people from even attempting to understand taxes. Since taxes are how we fund the services provided by our government, and the government is by the people and for the people, we have an obligation to understand taxes. If you understand the basics of taxation, you will make improved financial decisions. You might be surprised to discover that the basic foundations of taxation are easy to understand.

The objective is simple. You want to minimize taxable income by being sure that items that should be subtracted from gross income are accounted for and are subtracted from gross income. You do not spend money without purpose. You maximize legitimate *adjustments to income* particularly when the adjustment to income is, in reality, savings. A common adjustment is to make deposits into one's retirement account(s) (IRA, 401k, 403b, etc.).

Why is this important? Any dollar that is "spent" on an *adjustment to income* or a tax *deduction* lowers the amount of income that is subject to income taxes by a dollar. Not being subject to taxes, the one dollar reduction in taxable income, multiplied by the taxpayer's marginal tax rate, is the tax savings to the taxpayer. For example, a person in the 25% marginal tax bracket makes a $100 contribution to her pre-tax 401k plan which reduces her taxes by $25. Had she not made the deposit as an adjustment to income, her monthly income would have been $75 greater, as $25 in taxes would have been paid on the $100. This adjustment not only reduced her taxes by $25, it allowed her to deposit those "unpaid taxes" in an account for her retirement. One should account for all dollars of legitimate deductions and adjustments to income.

Let us continue our overview by considering the basic formula for the United States' personal income tax, to be followed by a brief examination of each piece, one-by-one.

The following are the required steps for effective tax management.
Pay attention.
It is quite simple …

The basic formula for "doing your taxes" is quite simple:

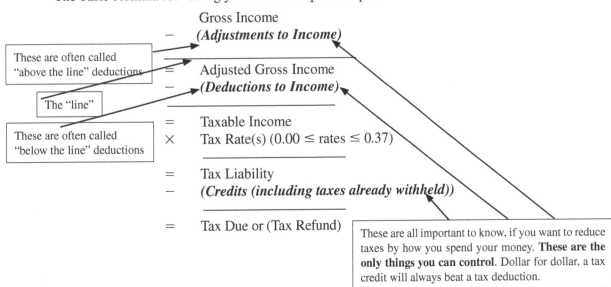

Gross Income
− *(Adjustments to Income)*

These are often called "above the line" deductions

= Adjusted Gross Income
− *(Deductions to Income)*

The "line"

These are often called "below the line" deductions

= Taxable Income
× Tax Rate(s) ($0.00 \leq$ rates ≤ 0.37)

= Tax Liability
− *(Credits (including taxes already withheld))*

= Tax Due or (Tax Refund)

These are all important to know, if you want to reduce taxes by how you spend your money. **These are the only things you can control**. Dollar for dollar, a tax credit will always beat a tax deduction.

One should attempt to take full advantage of all the items that are subtracted (adjustments to income and deductions) in order to lower the amount of income subject to income taxes (i.e., taxable income) and, thus, lower one's tax liability. To reiterate, this does not mean that you should spend a dollar, as a deduction, to save that dollar multiplied by your marginal tax rate. If you are in the 25% federal marginal tax rate bracket and, if you spend a dollar, you are only saving $0.25 in taxes. (If you like that "deal", I will gladly give you a quarter for every dollar you want to give me!)

Principle: Spending should come from necessity, the heart, or seeking financial profit; not from tax considerations. Many adjustments, deductions, and credits derive from industries that are subsidized by the tax code.

Now, let us look at each step in the process:

+ GROSS INCOME

Add each of the following to calculate gross income:

- Wages and Salaries (compensation for services, including fees, commissions, some fringe benefits)
- Taxable interest income
- Ordinary dividends (taxed at a lower rate than income)
- Net capital gains (capital gains after subtracting capital losses), including capital gain distributions from mutual funds. It is possible to deduct $3,000 in net capital losses from ordinary income. It should be noted that long-term net capital gains are taxed at a lower rate than short-term net capital gains which are taxed as ordinary income
- Investment income over $2,100 for children who are either under 19 or full-time students under the age of 23 is taxed to the parents
- Taxable gain on sale of one's personal residence (up to $250,000 for individuals or $500,000 for a married couple as long as you have owned the home and lived in the home for a minimum of 2 years)
- Taxable refunds, credits, or state and local tax refunds
- Royalties
- Unemployment compensation
- Gambling and lottery winnings, net of losses
- Employee productivity awards or prizes (or other prizes or awards)
- Scholarships and fellowships in excess of fees, tuition, books, supplies, and equipment
- Cancelled debt, unless you, taxpayer, are bankrupt
- Business and/or partnership net income (loss)
- Rental income
- Farm income
- Juror duty fees
- Distributed, qualified state tuition program earnings (not the principal)
- Reimbursements for previously deducted expenditures
- Pension and annuity income
- Sick pay
- Barter income
- Illegal income
- Income in respect of a decedent
- Interest income from an estate or trust

The sum is gross income.

− ADJUSTMENTS

Subtract adjustments to income from one's gross income to calculate *adjusted gross income* **(AGI):**
Adjustments to income are particularly valuable, since you do *not* have to itemize your deductions to subtract them from gross income. Sometimes referred to as "above-the-line" deductions, they precede the calculation of AGI.

Adjustments:

Retirement savings (possible from earned income sources only)

- Qualified IRA deposits (up to $6,000 per year for qualifying individuals, up to $7,000 if age 50 or older during 2019)

- Payments to a Keogh or SEP retirement plan (you may deduct the lesser of $52,000 or 25% of income)

- Payments to tax-deferred retirement accounts such as 401k or 403b plans (general limit of $19,000 per year for employee contributions) or SIMPLE retirement plans (limit of $13,000 per employee contribution)

Other adjustments to income

- Student loan interest of up to $2,500, if AGI is less than $70,000 ($145,000 if married filing jointly). Above those AGI limits, the deduction is phased out

- Amounts that are owed to you that you cannot collect

- Penalty charged on early withdrawal of savings from a time deposit, such as a certificate of deposit

- Health savings account contribution deduction (minimum/maximum = $1,350 / $6,750 for individuals, $2,700 / $13,500 for families)

- Moving expenses, if you meet the distance (50 miles) and time (must work 39 of 52 weeks) tests

- One-half of self-employment taxes

- Self-employment health insurance premiums

ADJUSTED GROSS INCOME AGI (VERY IMPORTANT VALUE)

Then, one subtracts deductions from AGI

− Deductions

Taxpayers should deduct the greater of the applicable standard deduction or the sum of their itemized deductions. (Remember this! You want to remove as much income from being subject to tax as possible.) These are the standard deductions for 2019:

Standard Deductions for 2019

Single Filer	$12,200
Head of Household	$18,350
Married Filing Jointly	$24,400
Married Filing Separately	$12,200

If a taxpayer is blind, or 65 years of age, the taxpayer may claim an additional $1,300 if married for each occurrence. This amount is increased to $1,600 if the individual is also unmarried and not a surviving spouse. For example, a blind single person over the age of 65 could deduct an additional standard deduction of $3,200, for a total standard deduction of $15,200 = $12,000 (for being single) + $1,600 (for being over age 65) + $1,600 (for being blind). The $15,200 would be the individual's standard deduction.

Itemized deductions: Sum all itemized deductions to determine the benefit of itemizing versus taking the standard deduction. The taxpayer will deduct either the standard deduction or the sum of itemized deductions, *whichever is greatest*. (Remember?) There are three types of itemized deductions:

1. Expenses which are fully deductible
2. Medical expenses that exceed 10% of AGI
3. Real estate losses

1. Expenses that are deductible in full:

Qualified home mortgage interest for first and second homes
   a. Purchase indebtedness up to $750,000 mortgage, for homes purchased after December 14, 2017

Real estate taxes, property taxes and state and local taxes up to a limit of $10,000 total

Charitable contributions of to 60% of adjusted gross income

Interest on loans for investment and business

Gambling losses, to the extent of winnings

Estate taxes to the extent that income is taxed to the estate

Impairment-related work expenses of the handicapped

Pro rata share of some costs paid by a housing cooperative or condominium association

Unrecovered cost of a pension

Amounts included in income in previous years and since returned

Soil and water conservation expenditures

Nonbusiness casualty and theft losses

Student loan interest up to $2,500, which begins to phase out for single taxpayers at an adjusted gross income of $70,000 and is $0 at $140,000

2. Medical expenses:

The portion of *nonreimbursed* medical expenses in excess of **10%** of AGI is deductible. For example, if you have $7,000 of nonreimbursed medical expenses (including insurance premiums) and your AGI = $66,666.66, then 10% would be $6,666.66 (66,666.66 × .10 = $6,666.66) and you may deduct only $333 = $7,000 (expenses) − $6,667 (10% of AGI) in medical expenses as an itemized deduction. The 10% threshold is reduced to 7.5% for taxpayers who are 65 years of age, or older.

3. Real estate losses

You may deduct only up to $25,000 in rental real estate losses from other income if you actively participated in real estate activities. If the taxpayer's AGI > $100,000, this amount is reduced $1 for each $2 of AGI and, therefore, equals $0 at an AGI of $150,000.

TAXABLE INCOME

After subtracting adjustments to income and deductions, the net result is **taxable income** to be used to determine how much tax is owed to the federal government. Once taxable income is known, a table, similar to the one below, may be used to determine the taxes owed. You will note that the percentage of income due in taxes increases as taxable income increases. Hence, federal income taxes are progressive taxes. Following the table is an example which should clarify the concept.

2019 Federal Income Tax Rates					
Joint Returns			**Single Returns**		
Taxable Income		**Tax Rate (%)**	**Taxable Income**		**Tax Rate (%)**
Over	but Less Than		Over	but Not Over	
$ 0	$ 19,400	10	$ 0	$ 9,700	10
$ 19,400	$ 78,950	12	$ 9,700	$ 39,475	12
$ 78,950	$168,400	22	$ 39,475	$ 84,200	22
$168,400	$321,450	24	$ 84,200	$160,725	24
$321,450	$408,200	32	$160,725	$204,100	32
$408,200	$612,350	35	$204,100	$510,300	35
Over $612,350		37	Over $510,300		37

Standard Deductions for 2019:

Single filers   = $12,200
Married, filing jointly   = $24,400

Tax Example:
Married couple (i.e., joint return) with *taxable income* of $100,000.
Using the joint return tax rates:

1. The tax rate on the first $19,400 is 10%. The taxes due would be calculated by:

$$\$19,400 \times .10 = \$1,940$$

The tax rate on the amount between $19,400 and $78,950 is 12%, or $7,146, as calculated by:

$$\$78,950 - \$19,400 = \$59,550 \times .12 = \$7,146$$

2. The tax rate on the remaining income of $26,200 is 25%, resulting in a tax of $6,550, as calculated by:

$$\$100,000 - \$78,950 = \$21,050 \times .22 = \$4,631$$

3. The total tax owed for 2019, in this example, is $16,712.50 as calculated by:

$$\$1,940 + \$7,146 + \$4,631 = \$13,717$$

(For the same income, in 2014, the tax would have been $16,712.50)

(In 2006, the tax would have been $17,375)

In steps 2 and 3, the concept of **marginal tax rate** is demonstrated. At higher income brackets, the tax *rate* increases—but only on the income in that particular bracket. One's marginal tax rate is the rate of tax paid on the next dollar earned. In this case, the marginal tax rate is 22% on the last $21,050 of taxable income.

The **average federal tax rate** in this example is 16.7125%, as calculated by total federal tax owed divided by total taxable income, or $13,717 / $100,000 = 0.13717 or 13.717%.

— TAX CREDITS

Tax credits reduce the taxes you owe *dollar for dollar*. This means a $1 tax credit reduces your tax bill by $1. (Reminder: Adding $1 more to your itemized deductions only decreases your tax bill by a maximum of 37 cents [the highest marginal tax rate].) After federal income tax has been calculated, you determine if (1) any tax credits can be applied and (2) how much federal income tax you have already paid during the year through payroll deduction.

Examples of tax credits are:

- Earned income credit (EIC) for lower income, working parents[6].

- Child tax credit ($2,000 per child under the age of 17 and/or $500 for dependents other than children, phased out beginning at higher income levels

- Child-care credit (depending on your income, 20%−35% of up to $3,000 in expenses per child, for up to two children).

- Low-income housing credit

- Adoption credit (up to $14,080 for 2019).

- Education tax credits:
  - American Opportunity Tax Credit / Hope ($2,900 credit with phase out beginning at AGI = $180,000 (joint); $90,000 (all others))
  - Lifetime leaning credit ($2,000 credit with phase out at AGI = $130,000 (joint); $65,000 (all others))

In the example of the married couple with taxable income of $100,000, if we assume this couple had one child they would qualify for a $2,000 child tax credit. If we also assume that they had $21,500 in federal taxes withheld during the year, they would receive a 2019 tax year refund of $9,783.00.

$13,717.00	Taxes owed
− $ 2,000.00	Child-care tax credit
− $21,500.00	Federal tax withheld during year
$ 9,783.00	Refund

CAPITAL GAINS AND QUALIFYING DIVIDENDS

Tax rates on net long-term capital gains and qualifying dividends will always be changing. Sometimes tax rates on investment returns are raised to reduce the deficit and often they are reduced as an economic stimulus—encouraging people to sell assets and put the money into the economy. Long term refers to assets that are purchased and held for a minimum of one year. Gains on sales of assets owned for less than one year are short-term gains. These short-term gains are taxed the same as ordinary income. For 2019, the following tax rates apply.

---

[6] For more information about the EIC go to www.irs.gov and look up Publication 596. The maximum EIC is $3,526 for taxpayers filing jointly with one child, $5,828 for two children, $6,557 for three or more children, and $529 for no children. Check: www.irs.gov.

Tax Situation	Tax Rate on Capital Gains and Qualifying Dividends (%)
Taxpayers in 10% or 12% marginal tax bracket	0
Taxpayers in the 22%, or higher, but below the 39.6% marginal tax rate	15
Taxpayers in the 37% tax bracket	20

SPECIAL TAX CONSIDERATIONS FOR COLLEGE STUDENTS

$2,500 American opportunity tax credit (replaced the HOPE tax credit)

Students who are eligible during the first 4 years of post-secondary education may receive a tax credit of 100% of the first $2,000 of tuition, fees and course materials paid during the taxable year, and 25% of the second $2,000. Tax liability is reduced dollar for dollar of the eligible credit. If the credit is more than the tax liability, the extra amount of the credit is refundable up to a maximum of 40% of the amount of the eligible credit. For joint (single) filers, the credit is phased out when AGI is $160,000 ($80,000 for single filers).

Lifetime learning credit for qualified expenses

Students who are engaged in taking classes beyond their first 2 years of education, those taking courses part-time, or those wishing to upgrade their job skills, the job skills of the student or their family, if they are a dependents, can receive a 20% tax credit for the first $10,000 of tuition and fees. Again, this credit is available only for tuition and fees that have been paid for post-secondary enrollment, after those have been reduced by any grants received. The lifetime learning credit is available on a taxpayer/family basis, and begins to phase out at AGIs of $107,000 (joint) and $53,000 (others).

Coverdell education savings accounts (Coverdell ESA)

Families with children under the age of 18 may deposit up to $2,000 per year into a Coverdell ESA. Money that is deposited accumulates tax free with the added benefit that no taxes are due when the money is withdrawn if the expenditures are for the education of the child (Kindergarten through graduate school). This is phased out for joint filers with AGI above $190,000 and single filers with AGI above $95,000. For more information go to: http://www.savingforcollege.com

Student loan interest deduction

An adjustment to gross income (often called an above-the-line deduction) may be taken for interest paid on student loans used for post-secondary educational expenses. This is solely for interest paid during the first 60 months of loan repayment on either private or government-backed loans. The maximum deduction is $2,500 and is phased out for higher income. The expenses eligible for the deduction are any expenses related to post-secondary expenses for tuition, fees, books, equipment, room, and board. One may not claim both the Student Loan Interest Deduction and the American Opportunity Tax Credit.

IRA withdrawals

Taxpayers may withdraw funds from an IRA, without paying the 10% penalty tax, for the higher education expenses of the taxpayer or the taxpayer's dependents (spouse, child, or grandchild). As with the other plans, the amount is limited to post-secondary expenses for tuition, fees, books, equipment, and room and board reduced by grants received. The amount may be subject to taxation, if it is a traditional IRA (pretax contributions).

Community service loan forgiveness

Any loan amounts that are forgiven by nonprofit, tax-exempt charitable or educational institutions may be excluded from gross income that is subject to taxation. Examples of nonprofit, tax-exempt activities that qualify are teaching, nursing, Americorps, and the Peace Corps. The rules vary by program.

Tax forms (Forms you may need can be found on http://www.irs.gov)
Commonly used federal income tax forms:

Form 1040

Form 1040A

Form 1040EZ

Schedule A   Itemized Deductions

Schedule B   Interest and Dividend Income

Schedule D   Capital Gains and Losses

Publication 596   Earned Income Credit

Publication 970   Tax Benefits for Education

2019 tax example for a single filer

Ben A. Weincork is single with wages from his regular job of $45,000 during 2019, earnings of $15,000 from his weekend job, and $5 from tips. He received $500 in interest from his taxable savings account during 2019. Since he has no pension plan at work, he contributed $4,000 to a regular (deductible) IRA. His qualified home mortgage interest for 2019 was $6,400 and his property taxes were $1,700.
What is Freddie's gross income?

	$45,000	Income from first job
+	$15,000	Income from second job
+	$ 5	Tip income
+	$ 500	Interest income
	$60,505	**Gross Income**

What is Freddie's AGI?

	$60,505	Gross Income
	$ 4,000	IRA adjustment
	$56,505	**AGI**

The standard deduction for a single taxpayer in 2019 is $12,200 and the personal exemption is $3,950. What are Freddie's deductions and taxable income?

Standard Deduction	**Itemized Deductions**	
$12,200	$6,400	Mortgage interest
	+ $1,700	Property taxes
	$8,100	**Total itemized deductions**

Since the $12,200 standard deduction is more than $8,100, Freddie will use the $12,200 standard deduction. This results in a taxable income of:

$56,505   AGI
$12,200   Standard deduction
—————
$44,305   Taxable income

Using the following tax table, calculate Freddie's 2019 tax. If he owes any, it will be due by April 15, 2020.

2019 Federal Income Tax Rates					
Joint Returns			**Single Returns**		
Taxable Income		**Tax Rate (%)**	**Taxable Income**		**Tax Rate (%)**
Over	**but Less Than**		**Over**	**but Not Over**	
$ 0	$ 19,400	10	$ 0	$ 9,700	10
$ 19,400	$ 78,950	12	$ 9,700	$ 39,475	12
$ 78,950	$168,400	22	$ 39,475	$ 84,200	22
$168,400	$321,450	24	$ 84,200	$160,725	24
$321,450	$408,200	32	$160,725	$204,100	32
$408,200	$612,350	35	$204,100	$510,300	35
Over $612,350		37	Over $510,300		37

Freddie's $44,305 taxable income utilized three different tax brackets. His 2014 federal income tax is $, as calculated by:

The first $9,700 is taxed at 10%, or $970

The next $29,775 is taxed at 12%, or $29,775 × .12 = $3,573

The final $4,830 is taxed at 22%, or $4,830 × .22 = $1,062.60 (round to $1,063)

Freddie's 2014 Federal income tax is: $970 + $3,573 + $1,063 = $5,606

Freddie will owe money to the Internal Revenue Service (IRS) if he had less than $5,606 of Federal income taxes withheld from his pay during 2019.

Freddie will be entitled to a tax refund if he had more than $5,606 of Federal income taxes withheld during 2019.

2019 Tax example for married filing jointly

Michael and Leah Swansong are married with three children from Leah's first marriage, ages 3, 6, and 7. They file taxes jointly. Michael's wages from his job were $76,495, while Leah earned $35,900 as a part-time secretary at the university. They also received $4,000 in qualified corporate dividends, $550 in interest on a money market deposit account (MMDA), and $500 in interest from their municipal bond mutual fund. Michael has a pension plan at work where he contributed $5,500 to his 401k plan. Their qualified home mortgage interest for 2019 was $6,500, they contributed $1,400 to their church, Michael paid $6,000 alimony to his first wife, their state income taxes totaled $2,725, and they paid $1,900 in other taxes (real estate and personal property). Total federal income tax withheld during 2019 was $8,120 ($6,036 for Michael and $2,084 for Lucy).

What is the Swenson's gross income?

	$76,495	Mike's wage income
+	$35,900	Lucy's wage income
+	$ 4,000	Dividend income
+	$ 550	MMDA interest
	$116,945	**Gross income**

Note that the interest received from the municipal bond mutual fund was not included in determining gross income. Interest received from municipal bonds is exempt from federal tax and, possibly, state tax if the bondholder lives in the state that issued the bond(s). (The latter varies by state.)

The corporate dividends (as well as capital gains, if there were any) of $4,000 will be taxed at a lower rate; they are included in gross income but, later, we will "pull them out" when we calculate the taxes on the remaining income. Then, we will calculate the tax on the dividends and add them to the other tax total.

What is the Swansongs' AGI?

	$116,945	Gross income
−	$ 5,500	401k contribution
	$111,445	**AGI**

The standard deduction for a married couple filing jointly in 2019 is $24,400. What are the Swenson's deductions and subsequent taxable income?

Standard Deduction	**Itemized Deductions**	
$22,400	$ 6,500	Mortgage interest
	$ 1,400	Charitable contributions
	$ 2,725	State income taxes
	$ 1,900	Real estate property taxes
	$12,525	**Itemized deductions**

As $12,525 is less than $22,400, they will use the $22,400 itemized deduction which results in a taxable income of:

	$111,445	AGI
−	$ 22,400	Itemized deductions
	$ 89,045	**Taxable income**

Using the "joint returns" information in the following tax table, calculate the Swansongs' 2014 federal income tax.

2019 Federal Income Tax Rates					
Joint Returns			**Single Returns**		
Taxable Income		**Tax Rate (%)**	**Taxable Income**		**Tax Rate (%)**
Over	**but Less Than**		**Over**	**but Not Over**	
$ 0	$ 19,400	10	$ 0	$ 9,700	10
$ 19,400	$ 78,950	12	$ 9,700	$ 39,475	12
$ 78,950	$168,400	22	$ 39,475	$ 84,200	22
$168,400	$321,450	24	$ 84,200	$160,725	24
$321,450	$408,200	32	$160,725	$204,100	32
$408,200	$612,350	35	$204,100	$510,300	35
Over $612,350		37	Over $510,300		37

First, we will remove the $4,000 in corporate dividends.

$$\$89,045 - \$4,000 = \$85,045; \text{ remaining taxable income after subtracting dividends}$$

Of the $85,045 taxable income, the first $19,400 they will be taxed at a rate of 10%:

$$\$19,400 \times .10 = \$1,940$$

The next $59,550 (as calculated by $78,950 - $19,400 = $59,550) will be taxed at a rate of 12%:

$$\$59,550 \times 0.12 = \$7,146$$

Finally, the remaining taxable of $6,095 ($85,045 - 19,400 - 59,550 = $6,095) will be taxed at the rate of 22%:

$$\$6,095 \times .22 = \$1,341$$

For the $4,000 in corporate dividends they will need to pay taxes of $600 ($600 = $4,000 × .15). Remember:

Tax Situation	Tax Rate on Capital Gains[1] and Qualifying Dividends (%)
Taxpayers in 10% or 15% marginal tax bracket	0
Taxpayers in higher brackets	15

[1]For capital gains longer than 1 year.

The Federal Income tax liability for the Swenson's (before applying tax credits and payments) is:

$$\$1,940 + \$7,146 + \$1,341 + \$600 = \$11,027$$

The next step is to subtract the child tax credit and the amount of federal income taxes paid (i.e., withheld) during 2010. Three children at $1,000 credit per child = $3,000 child tax credit

$11,027 Tax liability
− $ 6,000 Child tax credit ($2,000 multiplied by three children)

$ 5,027
− $ 8,120 Federal income tax withheld during 2009

$ 3,093 Federal income tax refund to Michael and Lucy

TAXABLE-EQUIVALENT YIELDS

Some investments produce interest income that is not taxed. Most common among such investments are municipal bonds (discussed later in Section 8). Investments that are not federally taxed offer a lower rate of return than taxable investments for the same level of risk. However, their **taxable-equivalent yield** can be less than, equal to, or exceed the return of taxable investments of similar risk. The formula for determining taxable-equivalent yield is shown below:

$$\text{Taxable-Equivalent Yield} = \frac{\text{Tax–Free Rate of Return}}{(1-\text{Marginal Tax Rate})}$$

Example: You just inherited $10,000. You want to use it as savings for your vacation home. You are considering two savings options: (1) Fund Blue, a taxable bond mutual fund paying 7.5% interest annually or (2) Fund Green, a tax-exempt bond fund paying 5.8% interest annually. You are in the 24% marginal tax bracket.

Which fund will you choose so as to maximize your after-tax interest earnings?

$$\text{Fund Green's taxable-equivalent yield} = \frac{.058}{1 - .24} = 7.63\%$$

$$\text{Fund Blue's taxable yield} = \textbf{7.5\%}$$

Fund Green is the better choice (other things being equal) because it has a higher after-tax yield (7.63%). Another way to look at it is to ask, "How much would be the after-tax return be for Fund Blue?"

Fund Blue after-tax return = .075 × (1 − .24) = .057.

5.7% is less than the 5.8% return from Fund Green.

After 13 years how much would you have in Fund Green and in Fund Blue?
Tax-exempt Fund Green:

$$\$10,000 \times (1.058)^{13} = \textbf{\$20,811.99}$$

Taxable Fund Blue:

First, the after-tax yield must be calculated as follows:

Before-tax yield × (1 − marginal tax rate) = After-tax yield
7.5% × (1 − .24) = **5.7% or .057**

Second, determine interest earned using the after-tax yield:

$$\$10,000 * (1.057)^{13} = \textbf{\$20,557.71}$$

After 13 years, the tax-exempt Fund Green would produce $254.28 more interest than the taxable Fund Blue. Obviously, as a person's marginal tax bracket increases (say, to 37%) the benefit of tax-free investments increases, as is shown in the table below.

Tax-Exempt Yields and Their Taxable Equivalents

Tax-Exempt Yield (%)	Federal Marginal Tax Bracket						
	10%	**12%**	**22%**	**24%**	**32%**	**35%**	**37%**
3	3.33%	3.41%	3.85%	3.95%	4.41%	4.62%	4.76%
4	4.44%	4.55%	5.13%	5.26%	5.88%	6.15%	6.15%
5	5.55%	5.68%	6.41%	6.58%	7.58%	7.35%	7.69%
6	6.66%	6.82%	7.69%	7.89%	8.82%	9.23%	9.23%
7	7.77%	7.95%	8.97%	9.21%	10.29%	10.77%	0.77%

In the above table, it is clear that the advantage of owning a tax-free municipal bond is greater, as the taxpayer's marginal tax bracket is higher. Thus, lower marginal tax bracket consumers are better off investing in taxable bonds for, after they pay their taxes, they will have more money in their checking account to pay for life's necessities and niceties.

Principle: Whenever there is a segment of a market for investments that has a clear advantage with respect to taxes, that segment will be the segment that controls prices.

Assignment 5.1   Federal Income Tax Calculations

Name _____

ATTACH A SHEET SHOWING YOUR CALCULATIONS

Using the forms at http://www.irs.gov, complete the following assignment for the *2019 tax year*:

   Bruce and Robin Wayne

   Three children living at home under the age of 17

   $78,000 gross annual combined salaries

   $2,000 invested in Bruce's IRA during 2019

   $580 in savings account interest

   $400 in dividends from Bats Incorporated

   300 shares of Guano stock sold for $27 per share on July 2, 2019. The stock was purchased for $10 per share in 2010. There was a $50 brokerage commission associated with both the purchase and sale of the stock.

   $4,300 in medical expenses

   $9,000 in home mortgage interest

   $3,000 given to charity

   $2,500 paid in state income taxes

   $1,750 paid in local property taxes

   $7,460 federal income tax withheld during 2019

1. What is the Waynes' gross income?

2. What is their AGI?

3. Will Bruce and Robin itemize or take the standard deduction? If so, show the correct amount for whichever one they choose.

4. What is (a) their taxable income and (b) their federal income tax liability?

5. After applying credits, will they owe the government money or will they receive a refund? (Remember to take into account the income taxes they have already paid during the year.)

Section Five Extra Practice Problem

Pat Twirlygig, single, age 39

One child living at home, age 7

$39,100 gross salary in 2019

Pat invested $600 into her (deductible) IRA during 2019 (see Section 9 for more information about IRA accounts)

$35 of interest was earned during 2019 in her savings account

$6,000 in uninsured casualty losses to her automobile

$4,500 in home mortgage interest

$500 given to charity

$700 paid in state income taxes

$500 paid in local property taxes

$1,580 federal income tax withheld during the year

1. What is Pat's gross income in 2019?

2. What is her AGI?

3. Will Pat itemize or take the standard deduction? Show the correct amount.

4. What is her 2019 taxable income and her 2019 federal income tax liability?

5. Does she still owe the government money or will she receive a refund? If so, how much does she owe?

Section Five Practice Problem Answers

1. What is Pat's gross income?

$$\$39,100 + \$35 = \mathbf{\$39{,}135}$$

2. What is her AGI?

$$\$39{,}135 - \$600 \text{ IRA contribution} = \mathbf{\$38{,}535}$$

3. Will Pat itemize or take the standard deduction? Show the correct amount.

Itemize:	**Standard Deduction:**
$6,000 casualty loss on auto	$18,350 as head of household
$4,500 mortgage interest	
$ 500 charity	
$ 700 state income taxes	
$ 500 local property taxes	

$12,200 Itemized expenses

Therefore, take the **standard deduction** as $18,350 > $12,200.

Head of Household Returns 2019		
Taxable Income		**Tax Rate**
Over	**but Less Than**	**(%)**
$ 0	$ 13,850	10
$ 13,850	$ 52,850	12
$ 52,850	$ 84,200	22
$ 84,200	$160,700	24
$160,700	$204,100	32
$204,100	$510,300	35
Over $510,300		37

4. What are her 2019 taxable income and her 2019 federal income tax liability?

Gross income:		$39,135
minus Adjustments:		$ 600
equals AGI		$38,535
minus Deductions		$18,350
equals Taxable income		$20,185
Taxes due:	$13,850 × .10 =	$ 1,385
(20,185 – 13,850=	$ 6,335 × .12 =	$ 760
2019 Federal income tax liability		**$ 2,145.00**

5. Does she still owe the government money or will she receive a refund? If so, how much does she owe?

Federal income tax liability	$2,145
minus Child tax credit	−$2,000
minus Taxes already paid via withholding tax	−$1,580
Refund due Pat	($1,435[7])

Notes:

---

[7] One important issue that this simple example did not explicitly consider is the Earned Income Credit. Her AGI was too large for her to qualify for EIC benefits.

Risk Management and Insurance

All losses are restored and sorrows end.

Shakespeare (1564–1616)

RISK

Household risk management is designed to ensure that the family is able to reach economic goals despite potential economic catastrophes. **Risk** is a condition in which there is a possibility of an adverse deviation from a desired outcome that is expected or hoped for.

This definition of risk allows for human expectations and natural possibilities. If you invest money in the stock market, your *desired outcome* (or hope) is that the market increases and you earn a profit. However, there is a *possibility* that you could lose money—obviously an *adverse deviation* from your desired outcome.

In the context of insurance, risk has two main components: perils and hazards.

Perils: A peril is the cause of a loss. In other words, it is the actual loss-causing event. Falling, crashing, choking, fire, wind, hail, lightening, water, volcano, or falling objects are all examples of perils.

Hazards: A hazard is a condition or situation that increases the likelihood of a peril occurring (e.g., texting while driving).

Physical hazards: Ice on the sidewalk, a muddy windshield, smoking, skydiving, and so on.

Moral hazards: Dishonesty (burning the warehouse of your bankrupt company to collect insurance money), insuring someone else's life for $2,000,000, naming yourself as the beneficiary, and then killing them.

Morale hazards: Careless attitude toward the occurrence of a loss (associated with a peril) because "no problem, insurance will pay for it. . . ." Repeated elective surgery or refusing to wear a helmet when driving a motorcycle are examples.

RISK MANAGEMENT TECHNIQUES

Risk control	Risk financing
Avoidance	Retain
Reduction	Transfer (Insurance)

For example, the financial and personal safety risks of driving an automobile are many.

1. You may break the traffic rules and be required to pay a fine.
2. You may injure or kill yourself.
3. You may injure or kill other people.
4. You may cause property damage.
5. You may be found guilty of any of the above and spend some time in jail.

Avoid risk: "Just say no" to driving.

Retain risk: Maintain enough money in a savings account to cover losses resulting from accident or injury incurred while driving. This will be very difficult to do.

Reduce risk: Wear seat belts, do not drive too fast, do not drive drunk, and drive cars that are in safe condition.

Transfer risk: Purchase **insurance** for possible losses in which you could not afford to pay for damage to the injured person or damaged property.

Implementation of the appropriate risk management technique depends on **loss frequency and loss severity.**

	Low-Frequency Peril	**High-Frequency Peril**
Low-Severity Peril	(Losing your shoes) Retain	(Breaking dishes) Retain, Reduce
High-Severity Peril	(Home fire) Transfer	(Lung cancer caused by smoking) Avoid, Reduce

BASIC RULES OF RISK MANAGEMENT

Transfer catastrophic losses of which the potential severity cannot be reduced.

Do not transfer those risks for which the probability of occurrence is very high. Utilize other risk management techniques, such as reduction, avoidance, or retention.

Maintain a reasonable relationship between the cost and benefit of insurance. Going into excessive debt to pay insurance premiums would be foolish.

INSURANCE (TRANSFERRING RISK)

Insurance is not gambling. In gambling, there is a chance for gain. Moreover, in gambling, you choose to participate in the gambling event.

Insurance provides **indemnification** (reimbursement), not financial gain, from losses (perils) for which the probability of occurrence cannot entirely be avoided.

Insurance allows the dollars of many to pay for the losses of the few.

*Pay a **small, certain** premium to avoid the possibility of a **large, uncertain** financial loss.*

For example: In a small neighborhood, there are 100 houses worth $10,000 each ($1,000,000 total value). Based on historical data, 5 homes are expected to burn each year. Without insurance, every homeowner must "self-insure" their home for $10,000 (the cost to rebuild the home). With insurance (a mutual cooperative technique) each homeowner must only pay $500 into the insurance fund:

$$5 \text{ homes burn} \times \$10,000 = \$50,000$$

$$\$50,000 \div 100 \text{ homeowners} = \mathbf{\$500} \text{ premium}$$

Appropriately transferring risk (i.e., purchasing insurance) must be preceded by identifying the specific risks involved. In the following table, specific risks are identified. In the middle column, likely financial "perils" are presented. In the right-hand column, common forms of insurance are listed which allow the insured to "transfer" risk of financial loss to an insurance company (which in turn transfers it back to the group of insured persons).

In a cooperative sense, insurance companies act as the "risk transfer liaison" between the individual insured party (a person, household, or company) and the entire group of insured parties.

Risk	Financial "Peril"	Insurance
Disability/Illness	Loss of income Medical expenses Personal maintenance	Disability income Major medical Hospital insurance Long-term care insurance
Death	Loss of income Medical/funeral expenses Unpaid debts	Life insurance Credit/mortgage insurance
Extended Life Span	Loss of income, lower level of living	Annuities Retirement planning Personal investments
Damage or Loss of Property	Replacement or repairs	Homeowner's or renter's policies (property insurance) Automobile collision and comprehensive coverage
Legal Liability	Damages awarded to an injured party	Comprehensive personal liability Liability coverage in personal automobile policy

ELEMENTS OF AN INSURABLE RISK (FROM THE INSURANCE COMPANY'S VIEWPOINT)

Law of large numbers

A large, homogenous group of insured people allows for more accurate prediction of losses. Moreover, financing the losses is possible.

Flip a coin six times, you may not get 50% tails.

Flip a coin 600,000 times, the percentage of tails will be 50%.

Loss must be accidental

A "planned" accident is not an insurable event. Intentionally burning down a warehouse full of merchandise so as to collect a settlement is contrary to the purpose of insurance.

Loss must be definite and measurable

Mental illness is more difficult to measure than a broken arm. Likewise, medical malpractice is often less definite than a smashed car. An X-ray of a broken arm is more objective and "definite" than subjective opinions about some forms of mental illness.

Peril must not be catastrophic to the insurance company

For example, there is a "war exclusion" in life and property insurance policies.

Cost of insurance must be affordable

The cost of the insurance product must be reasonably priced for the law of large numbers to operate.

PROVIDERS OF INSURANCE

1. Private insurance company types:
   a. Capital stock insurance companies—owned by stockholders (Traveler's, Allstate)
   b. Mutual insurance companies—owned by policyholders (State Farm, Northwestern)
   c. Reciprocals
   d. Lloyd's associations
   e. Health expense associations (e.g., Blue Cross/Blue Shield [BC/BS])

2. Social insurance
   a. Federal Social Security (OASDHI)
      OA = Old Age (retirement income)
      S   = Survivors (survivors' income insurance)
      D   = Disability (dependents' income insurance)
      HI = Health Insurance (Medicare)
   b. Worker's compensation
      This program provides monthly income to a worker who is unable to work because of an injury sustained while on the job. It is operated at the state level. Premiums are paid by the employer.
   c. Flood insurance
      Property owners who live in flood-prone areas can purchase flood insurance from the federal government. Damage to a home due to flooding is generally *not covered* in a standard homeowners insurance policy, hence the government's involvement.

3. Public guarantee insurance
   a. FDIC (Federal Deposit Insurance Corporation)
   b. NCUA (National Credit Union Administration)
   c. SIPC (Securities Investor Protection Corporation)

SELECTING AN INSURANCE COMPANY

1. Compare the costs for coverage (compare equivalent policies).
2. Compare service.
3. Select a financially secure company (as rated by Standard & Poor's, Duff & Phelps, Moody's, A.M. Best, Weiss Research). Financial strength is critical inasmuch as the insurance company is making a promise that they will be around to pay should you experience a loss.
4. If in doubt, or if you have a complaint, contact the Division of Insurance in your state.

FACTORS THAT LIMIT AN INSURER'S LIABILITY

Insurable interest

An insurance contract is valid only if the insured (you, for example) has a financial interest in the person or property being insured. For example, you cannot insure your neighbor's home because you would not suffer a financial loss if it burned down. However, you would experience a financial gain if you were allowed to insure it and it subsequently burned down—a clear violation of the principle of indemnification.

Actual cash value

Indemnification under an insurance contract is governed by the notion of reimbursement of the actual dollar loss. Actual cash value allows the insured to receive the amount of money necessary to replace the damaged or destroyed property.

Other insurance

Prevents overlapping of payments on the same claim by multiple insurance companies. This eliminates the possibility of double payment by one, or more, insurance companies.

Face amount

Specifies the maximum amount of money that the insurer would be required to pay the insured. A term life insurance policy with a face amount of $100,000 indicates that the insurer will pay $100,000 (no more and no less) if the insured dies.

Coinsurance

Specifies how costs will be shared between the insurer and the insured. For example, a health insurance policy with a coinsurance clause of 80/20 indicates that the insurer will pay 80% of the medical bills and the insured will pay 20% (up to a specified maximum).

Subrogation

If a loss is caused by negligence, the insured may be indemnified (reimbursed) by the insurance company, but relinquishes the right to sue the guilty party to the insurance company. The principle of subrogation applies in property and liability insurance, occasionally in health insurance, but never in life insurance. For example, in the following examples the truck driver is negligent.

Bob is hit by a truck and killed—his survivors can collect the *life insurance* AND sue the truck driver (subrogation does not apply).

Bob is hit by a truck and disabled—he can collect disability insurance from his *health and disability insurer* AND can sue the truck driver for damages (subrogation does not apply in some cases when dealing with health insurance).

Bob is hit by a truck, he is fine but his car is totally demolished—he can be reimbursed by the *automobile insurance* company (either the truck driver's or his own company based on a variety of circumstances). Bob cannot sue the truck driver for damage caused to his car but his insurance company can. This is a case in which the principle of subrogation applies.

Deductible

A deductible is the amount of money paid by the insured before the insurer is liable to pay. For example, Jim has a homeowner's insurance policy with a $250 deductible. A hailstorm causes $2,500 damage to his roof. Jim will pay the first $250 to repair the roof (his deductible) and his insurance company will pay the remaining $2,250.

UNDERWRITING

The primary purpose of underwriting is to minimize "adverse selection." Adverse selection refers to the tendency for people who are exposed to particular hazards and perils to purchase insurance against those particular hazards and perils.

People who live in a flood plain want flood insurance.

People who have terminal cancer want to purchase life insurance.

People who have serious health problems would like to purchase health insurance.

LIFE INSURANCE

The concept of **life insurance** is to reimburse the financial loss of one or more persons resulting from the death of the insured. Life insurance is not for you (the insured). Life insurance death benefits are for survivors. *It replaces your earnings if you (as the wage earner) die*. If your death will not cause financial loss to anyone, you do not need life insurance.

However, life insurance can be used to serve other purposes:

- build a savings account (generally a poor choice)
- maintain estate liquidity (generally not necessary)
- provide a gift to a favorite charity at death

The term "life" insurance is an oxymoron. The *event* of death is not what is being insured, but rather the *timing* of death. Life insurance is not a waste of money if you do not die—its purpose is to provide the assurance that your dependents will be provided for in the event that you die. (Is property insurance a waste if your house never burns?)

Life insurance should be compared to life insurance; investments should be compared to investments. Comparing life insurance policies to investment products is tempting, but is not a "fair" comparison.

Purchasing life insurance is an emotional event for some people because it reminds them that they will die. As a result, some people delay purchasing life insurance . . . until it is too late.

Purchasing life insurance for a child makes sense if the child may not be insurable later in life (due to illness, disease, etc.) or if the child(ren) produce(s) an income on which the family is dependent.

FOUR QUESTIONS REGARDING LIFE INSURANCE

The purchase of life insurance involves four questions:

1. Do I need life insurance?
2. How much insurance should I purchase?
3. What kind of life insurance should I buy?
4. How should the life insurance death benefit be received?

QUESTION #1—DO I NEED IT?

Simple answer: *Yes*, if you have financial dependents. Children are the most obvious financial dependents. But remember, dependents might also include parents and/or siblings.

Other possible reasons: You have a lot of debt, you have expensive funeral plans, you have a dependent child or spouse with special needs or health problems, and so on.

QUESTION #2—HOW MUCH DO I NEED?

Enough to replace your lost earnings. *Life insurance is not for you, it is for your survivors.* Four methods for determining the needed amount of life insurance are shown below: multiple of income, desired income, human life value, and needs analysis.

1. Multiple of income method

The multiple of income method is a very simple approach in estimating the needed amount of life insurance.

$$\times \quad \frac{\text{Annual Income}}{\text{Insurance Multiple}}$$
$$= \quad \text{Needed amount of life insurance}$$

For example, a brochure from a life insurance company may suggest a life insurance multiple of 10. Using a multiple of 10, a married 40-year-old with an annual income of $40,000 and two dependent children would need approximately $400,000 of life insurance.

$$\begin{array}{r} \$40,000 \\ \times \quad 10 \\ \hline = \quad \$400,000 \end{array}$$

Obviously, using a larger multiple will suggest the need for greater amounts of life insurance. Larger multiples may be appropriate for people whom have multiple dependents and or people whom have young dependents.

2. Desired income method

In the event of your death, you want to provide your survivors with an annual income of $32,500 for an indefinite period of time (i.e., forever). Your survivors would invest the life insurance death benefit at a before-tax annual rate of 7%.

$$\frac{\text{Annual income desired for dependents}}{\text{Rate of return}} = \text{Needed life insurance}$$

$$\frac{\$32,500}{.07} = \textbf{\$464,286 life insurance needed}$$

The $464,286 is invested in an account that pays 7% annual interest. The annual interest (which is the annual income of your survivors) would equal $32,500. Recognizing that your survivors will need to pay tax on the interest earned you wish to account for the "tax bite" so that they will have *$32,500 of annual income after paying taxes*. This requires that an after-tax rate of return be calculated, as shown in what follows. A marginal tax rate of 15% will be assumed.

$$\text{Before-tax return} \times (1 - \text{marginal tax rate}) = \text{After-tax return}$$
$$7\% \times (1 - .15) = 5.95\%$$

Now, the desired income method is used again, but this time *using the after-tax rate of return* as the denominator.

$$\frac{\$32,500}{.0595} = \textbf{\$546,218 life insurance needed}$$

The $546,218 death benefit will produce $38,235 of annual interest *indefinitely* if the 7% before-tax return is achieved. After paying taxes of 15%, there will be $32,500 of annual after-tax income.

$$\$38,235 \times (1 - .15) = \$32,500 \text{ after-tax income}$$

3. Human life value method

This method involves converting future annual earnings to a present value. For example, you have 30 years until retirement, an annual income of $40,625, and a before-tax rate of return of 7%. You want life insurance to replace 80% of your annual income if you die. Assume a marginal tax rate of 15%.

Assuming 80% income replacement, the needed annual income received at the *beginning of each year* (or PMTad) is $32,500 as calculated by

$$\$40,625 \times .80 = \$32,500.$$

Next, the after-tax rate of return must be determined. Using the calculation shown earlier, the after-tax return is:

$$7 \times (1 - .15) = \textbf{5.95\%} \text{ after-tax rate of return}$$

$$\text{PMTad} = 32,500$$
$$n = 30 \text{ years}$$
$$i = 5.95\%$$
$$\textbf{PVad} = \textbf{<476,521>}$$

Using the *human life value* approach, $476,521 of life insurance is needed to provide a **constant (or nominal)** annual income of $32,500 to your survivors for 30 years assuming an annual after-tax return of 5.95%.

Obviously, the buying power of the $32,500 will decline each year owing to inflation. To account for inflation you must calculate the **real rate of interest** (or inflation adjusted interest rate). By doing so, you can determine the needed amount of life insurance that will produce $32,500 (or any other amount you select) of real annual income. *Real annual income is nominal income that increases by the rate of inflation.*

For example, if you expect annual inflation to be 3%, your dependents will need $33,475 ($32,500 × 1.03 = $33,475) 1 year from today to purchase the same amount of goods and services as $32,500 would purchase today. Similarly, they would need $34,479 ($33,475 × 1.03) in 2 years, $35,513 in 3 years, and so on.

This is known as a **serial payment**—a payment that increases at a given rate, in this case, the annual rate of inflation. Clearly, you would need a greater face value of life insurance to provide for an increasing payment. The calculation of a serial payment involves determining a "real rate of interest" (or inflation adjusted **i**).

If inflation is estimated at 3.0% per year, use the following formula to determine the *real rate of interest* (or inflation adjusted time value of money).

$$\frac{1 + \text{nominal after-tax interest rate}}{1 + \text{inflation rate}} - 1 = \text{real rate of interest}$$

$$\frac{1 + .0595}{1 + .03} - 1 = \textbf{.0286407 real interest rate (or 2.864\%)}$$

Using the real "i" you can now determine the needed amount of life insurance to produce a *real annual income of $32,500* using either the "desired income method" **OR** the "human life value" method.

How much life insurance must be purchased to produce annual *after-tax, real income* of $32,500?

Desired income method:

$$\frac{\$32,500}{.0286} = \textbf{\$1,136,364 life insurance needed}$$

Human life value method:

$$PMTad = \$32,500$$
$$n = 30$$
$$i = 2.86$$
$$\mathbf{PVad} = \mathbf{\$667,251 \text{ life insurance needed}}$$
(annuity due)

Using the human life value approach, the answer for PVad indicates that approximately $667,251 of life insurance is needed to provide an annual *real* income of $32,500 (received at the beginning of each year) for 30 years. This figure assumes a 7%-nominal before-tax rate of return, 15% marginal tax rate, and an annual inflation rate of 3%.

The annual income your survivors receive will increase each year at the rate of inflation (in this example, 3%) but will maintain the buying power of $32,500 from year to year.

4. Needs analysis

1. Estimate the total present value of economic resources *needed* by survivors.
   a. Debt liquidation (a present value)
   b. Final expenses (a present value)
   c. Annual future income needs as a present value* (*income needed beyond amount provided by Social Security)
   d. College education fund for children (if desired)
2. Determine all financial resources *available* to survivors.
   a. Savings and investments
   b. Current life insurance in force
   c. Other resources
3. Subtract the amount of resources *available* from the amount *needed* to determine the amount of additional life insurance required (if any). A negative number will indicate no additional life insurance is needed.

A very simple needs analysis is shown as follows:

NEEDS	
Debt liquidation (e.g., pay off mortgage)	$ 75,000
Final expenses (funeral, etc.)	$ 10,000
Present value of future annual income $\qquad PMTad = \$11,000$ (annual amount needed to supplement Social Security income) $\qquad I/YR = 4\%$ real return $\qquad N = 25$ years $\qquad PV = \$178,717$	$178,717
TOTAL NEEDS	$263,717
CURRENT RESOURCES	
Current savings	$ 12,000
Life insurance policy (group insurance offered by employer)	$ 50,000
TOTAL RESOURCES	$ 62,000
ADDITIONAL INSURANCE NEEDED (NEEDS MINUS RESOURCES)	**$201,717**

QUESTION #3—WHICH KIND OF LIFE INSURANCE SHOULD I BUY?

All life insurance companies use mortality tables to determine life insurance premiums. As can be seen in what follows, premiums for life insurance must increase with age. This is true for *all* life insurance policies. Do not believe anyone who tells you differently.

Among 20-year-old males there are 1.90 deaths per 1,000 during a year, or a death rate of .0019. Accordingly, if we were to ignore the costs and profits of the insurance company, the "pure" insurance premium will be $1.90 per $1,000 of life insurance. Therefore, a 20-year-old male would pay $190 for a $100,000 life insurance policy (or 1.90 × 100).

Understanding that the basic cost structure of life insurance is fundamentally based on mortality tables will make the following discussion of different types of life insurance policies more meaningful.

Age Group	Annual Deaths per 1,000 Individuals	Death Rate	Cost per $1,000 of Insurance
20-Year-Old Male	1.90	.0019	$ 1.90
20-Year-Old Female	1.05	.00105	$ 1.05
40-Year-Old Male	3.02	.00302	$ 3.02
40-Year-Old Female	2.42	.00242	$ 2.42
80-Year-Old Male	98.84	.09884	$98.84
80-Year-Old Female	65.99	.06599	$65.99

Discussions of different types of life insurance can often become emotionally charged—particularly between insurance agents with different perspectives. We simply want you—the reader—to understand the pros and cons of each type of life insurance product. Therefore, it is best to analyze insurance products rationally . . . rather than emotionally.

In simple terms, there are two types of life insurance: term and cash value (sometimes referred to as *permanent* insurance).

Term life insurance

With term, or "pure," insurance the face amount of the policy is paid to the beneficiaries if the policyholder dies while the policy is in force. There is no cash value building up within the insurance policy. As the policyholder gets older, the premium increases. Term insurance usually cannot be purchased beyond age 65, however, some policies can be purchased up to age 75. All term insurance policies may be classified as renewable, guaranteed renewable, and/or convertible.

Renewable term: It is a policy that may be renewed at the end of the "term."

Guaranteed renewable term: Policyholder is guaranteed the right to "renew the insurance policy" at the expiration of the term.

Convertible term: Policyholder may convert to a whole life policy.

There are several types of term insurance policies:

Straight term: Life insurance policies are written for a specified number of years, like 1, 5, 10, or 20. The face value or coverage remains constant throughout the effective term. If the insured dies during the term, his or her beneficiaries receive the full face value (or death benefit) of the policy.

Characteristics of **straight term** insurance:

> Death benefit—Fixed amount at policy inception.
>
> Premium—Annual premium increases with the age of the insured as the policy is renewed.
>
> Investment choices—Not applicable.
>
> Rate of return on the cash value—Not applicable.
>
> Access to cash value—Not applicable.
>
> **Decreasing term**: A term policy with a level premium over the term of coverage but the protection decreases. These are useful when the coverage needed declines over time, such as protection to pay off a declining loan balance (i.e., home mortgage).

Characteristics of **decreasing term** insurance:

> Death benefit—Face value decreases over term.
>
> Premium—Fixed annual premium.
>
> Investment choices—Not applicable.
>
> Rate of return on the cash value—Not applicable.
>
> Access to cash value—Not applicable.

Whole life insurance

Whole life insurance is sometimes called **permanent insurance** since it will always pay the face value if the insured dies while the policy is in force. In reality, it is a combination of a decreasing term insurance and a savings account. This occurs because the face value is constant and the savings portion increases over time. Since, at death, the beneficiaries receive the face value, the amount that is insurance, not savings, must have decreased. The Internal Revenue Service does, however, allow the cash value to grow without being taxed.

Characteristics of **whole life** insurance:

> Death benefit—Fixed amount at policy inception. Newer policies offer PUAs (paid-up additions) to the base amount of insurance.
>
> Premium—Fixed amount paid monthly, quarterly, or annually.
>
> Investment choices—None. **Bonds and mortgages** are the mainstay of most whole life portfolios.
>
> Rate of return on the cash value—Not disclosed, but a guaranteed accumulation of cash value.

Access to cash value via:

1. Policy loans (money can be "borrowed" from the cash value portion of the policy)
2. Withdraw cash (surrender the policy)
3. Paid-up insurance (or convert cash value into a term insurance policy or a single premium whole life policy).

> **Limited payment whole life** offers coverage for the entire life of the insured but schedules the premium payments to end after a limited period.

> **Modified whole life** has reduced premiums for a limited time period. This product is often marketed heavily to younger people (i.e., college students or newly married couples).

> **Single premium whole life** is an insurance product designed for those who need a tax shelter and little insurance. In essence, the insurance policy is entirely paid for in one lump-sum payment.

Universal life

Universal life insurance is a form of cash value insurance with flexible premiums and a flexible cash value. Tax-exempt growth of cash value is a common selling point. If the cash value is withdrawn prior to death, the gain (amount in excess of premiums paid) is taxed. Growth of the cash value is not taxed if distributed as a death benefit to the beneficiaries of the insurance policy (this is true for any form of cash value insurance).

Characteristics of **universal life** insurance:

Death benefit—Variable. One option allows for an increasing death benefit and slower cash value growth, while another option holds the death benefit steady while the cash value grows more rapidly.

Premium—Fixed *or* variable amount paid monthly, quarterly, or annually. Interestingly, the premium is "unbundled," allowing the insured to know what portion of the premium buys insurance and what portion goes to savings.

Investment choices—None. Basically, universal life policies offer rates of return comparable to **money market mutual funds**.

Rate of return—A minimum rate (say, 2%–3%) is generally guaranteed; above the minimum, the rate is variable. Rates change from day to day with changes in market rates of interest. Cash value grows tax-deferred.

Access to cash value—The cash value can be withdrawn tax-free until the amount withdrawn equals the total premiums paid. In other words, you can withdraw the money you have paid in (your premiums) without owing tax on it. After this point, all withdrawals are subject to taxation. Policy loans are also available. The entire cash value can be withdrawn by surrendering the policy, which may have tax implications.

Variable life

This type of policy attempts to combine the protection and savings function of life insurance with the growth potential of equities (stocks and/or bonds).

Characteristics of **variable life** insurance:

Death benefit—You choose when buying the policy and it will increase if your investments do well and possibly decrease if they do poorly.

Premium—Fixed amount paid monthly, quarterly, or annually.

Investment choices—**Stock and bond and money market mutual funds**. As such, variable life policies should be purchased using the same criteria one would use if purchasing a stock or bond mutual fund.

Access to cash value—Policy loans at some rate of interest.

Cash value—Is it for you?

Access to the growing, tax-favored cash value of a permanent life insurance policy (whole, universal, or variable life) is often promoted by many life insurance sales representatives. Individuals who purchase a permanent life insurance policy with the intent to borrow from it are essentially borrowing from the beneficiaries of the policy. If the insured dies while a policy loan is outstanding, the death benefit is reduced by the amount of the loan. Borrowing from beneficiaries, that is, life insurance policy loans, contradicts the primary purpose of life insurance, but does allow the insured access while they are living.

QUESTION #4—HOW SHOULD LIFE INSURANCE PROCEEDS BE RECEIVED?

When an insured person dies, the named beneficiary is entitled to a cash death benefit. How to receive the face value death benefit becomes an important decision.

Lump sum

The entire death benefit is paid to the beneficiary in one lump sum. The lump-sum settlement option is chosen by beneficiaries over 90% of the time. The life insurance death benefit received by beneficiaries is *not* taxable to them as income. However, the life insurance death benefit is added to the insured (but now dead) person's estate if the deceased person owned the insurance policy (meaning that the deceased person paid the premiums and was listed as the owner of the policy) and may be taxable to the deceased person's estate. Interest income subsequently produced by the death benefit is taxable.

Interest payment

The death benefit (or face value of the policy) is left with the insurance company to be invested. The interest from the investment is paid to the beneficiary over a stated period of years at the end of which the face value is paid to the beneficiary. A portion of the payments received by beneficiaries will be taxable.

Installment (annuity)

Instead of receiving a lump sum (i.e., the death benefit) from the insurance company, you receive the money over a period of time, generally monthly. In other words, you "annuitize" the death benefit. In many cases, it becomes a person's living allowance and a portion of it will be taxable as interest income.

For example, if the face amount of a life insurance policy was $75,000 and, as beneficiary, you choose to receive 120 monthly installments of $1,000 each, the tax-free portion of the payment would be:

$$\$75,000 \div 120 = \$625 \text{ per month or } \$7,500 \text{ for an entire year.}$$

The rest of each payment, $375 a month (or $4,500 for an entire year), is interest income to you and is taxable.

Two common methods for creating an annuity:

a. You choose an amount (PMT) to be received each month, and the insurance company tells you how long the annuity will last (n) given their assumed interest rate (i).

b. You choose a period of time (n) that you would like the annuity to last, and the insurance company tells you how much money you will receive each month (PMT) given an assumed interest rate (i).

Life annuity

With a life annuity, you (the beneficiary) are guaranteed to receive a monthly annuity payment for as long as you live. If you are willing to receive somewhat less each month, the annuity will last for a specified length of time, say 10 years, regardless of when you—the beneficiary—die. If, say, you die in 7 years, your beneficiaries (secondary beneficiaries) will receive the annuity payment for 3 years. For example: Husband dies first. Wife decides to receive a life annuity with a 20-year guaranteed period. Wife dies in 8 years. Her beneficiaries (two children) split the annuity for the next 12 years.

COMMON LIFE INSURANCE "RIDERS"

The term "riders" refers to additional forms of insurance coverage that "ride" alongside the primary policy.

Disability clause

Waives the premium if the insured becomes disabled. If the insured has adequate disability insurance, this is not necessary.

Accidental death

Double or triple indemnity (or payment) if death results from an accident. Do your beneficiaries need triple the death benefit if you die in an auto accident rather than from a heart attack? They do not.

Suicide

If the insured commits suicide less than 2 years after purchasing the policy, the death benefit is limited to the cash value (if it is a permanent insurance policy). Suicide after 2 years is, in most cases, treated as a "normal" death and the beneficiary receives the full face value of the insurance policy.

Period of contestability

Limits the period of time in which the company can contest the basis on which policy was issued. In other words, if you provide inaccurate information on the application, the company has a limited period of time in which it can contest the information and cancel the policy.

Joint death of husband and wife

Pays nothing when one dies and the entire face value when both die. These policies are useful for highly compensated couples.

Guaranteed renewable

Insured may renew the term insurance policy indefinitely without proving insurability.

Guaranteed insurability

Insured may purchase additional amounts of insurance at stated intervals without proving insurability, usually up to the age of 40.

Assignment 6.1 Life Insurance

Name _____

SHOW YOUR WORK

1. You are 40 years old and earn $65,000 annually. Based on a multiple of income of 12, how much life insurance should you purchase? How much life insurance would you purchase using a multiple of 20?

2. Using the "desired income" method, if you want to provide your survivors with a *nominal* annual income of $55,000 at the beginning of each year, how much life insurance is needed assuming your survivors can earn 7% interest annually? Assume a combined tax rate of 22%.

3. Using the "desired income" method, how much insurance would be needed if you want to provide your survivors with a *real* annual income of $55,000 at the beginning of each year? (Assume a before-tax rate of return of 7%, a marginal tax rate of 22%, and annual inflation of 3% per year.)

4. a. Using the "human life value" method how much life insurance should you purchase if you have 45 years until retirement, an annual income of $61,500 received at the start of each year, and a time value of money of 7%? (Assume 80% income replacement, ignore taxes and inflation.)

   b. How much life insurance would be needed if you take into account 3% annual inflation over the next 45 years? Assume 100% income replacement and a marginal tax rate of 15%.

5. List advantages and disadvantages for both whole life insurance and term life insurance.

	Advantage	Disadvantage
Term		
Whole Life		

There are two kinds of financial loss that are associated with health problems:
a. the cost of medical care

b. the loss of income

HEALTH AND DISABILITY INSURANCE

The risk of financial loss associated with medical care is dealt with by purchasing health or medical insurance. The risk of financial loss associated with loss of income (due to injury or illness) is dealt with my purchasing disability income insurance.

During the Open Enrollment Period insureds can choose their health insurance plan for the following year. The Open Enrollment Period for the governmental marketplace's health insurance plans start usually around the first of November and end around mid December. For example, in November 2018, you will choose your medical coverage for all of 2019. Changes cannot be made to your medical plan during the year, except for certain situation such as birth of a dependent, death of a dependent, adoption, divorce and marriage.

IMPORTANT HEALTH INSURANCE DEFINITIONS

Deductible: the dollar amount the insured pays before the insurance company pays any money (except for free preventative services). There may be different deductibles for medical services and prescribed medicines. Often insurance plans are based on calendar years.

- The cost of insurance premiums can be lowered by choosing a larger deductible; however, the insured should consider other costs beyond deductibles and premiums in order to obtain the best medical plan for themselves and or their family

Copayment: An amount that the insured pays for health care services, like a doctor's visit. This is usually a predetermined flat dollar amount that you to be paid per visit. For example, it may cost $10 to see your doctor for any reason.

Coinsurance: the portion of the expenses beyond the deductible that the insured person pays; it is a split between the insured and the insurance company. Coinsurance is usually calculated as a percentage of the amount of the service. For an example, an insured pays 20% after the deductible has been met and the insurance company will pay 80%.

Premium: The amount the insured pays to have a health insurance plan each month.

Out of Pocket Maximum: limits the total amount that the insured pays each calendar year for healthcare (includes co-pays, deductibles, and co-insurance). After this amount is reached, the insurance company pays 100% for the covered services

- $7,350 for self only coverage / $14,700 for family coverage (2018)
- $7,900 for self only coverage / $15,800 for family coverage (2019)
- Does not include cost of premiums

Lifetime Maximum Benefit: the maximum dollar amount a health insurance plan will pay in benefits for an insured during the insured's lifetime. The Affordable Care Act did away with lifetime maximums.

Pre-Existing Conditions: a medical condition that occurred prior to the insured obtaining a health insurance policy from a particular insurance company. Before the Affordable Care Act, insurance companies could refuse to pay for these medical condition, however, in 2014, pre-existing conditions can no longer be excluded from medical payments, factored into premium costs, or cause an application to be denied.

THE AFFORADABLE CARE ACT OF 2010

The Affordable Care Act (ACA) 2010 was created out of the need to reform the US health care system. The ACA focuses on provisions to (1) increase the number of people who are covered under a health care plan, (2) control health care costs to patients, and (3) improve the health care system in general. The chart below shows effective dates for various provisions of the ACA Act.

EFFECTIVE DATE 2010	
Pre-existing Conditions (Children)	Insurance companies cannot deny coverage to children who have pre-existing medical conditions. (Adults, 2014)
Lifetime Maximum Benefits Banned	Insurance companies are prohibited from placing lifetime limits on how much they pay out to an individual policyholder
EFFECTIVE DATE 2013	
Itemized Deductions	Increases the threshold for itemized medical deductions to 10% of adjusted gross income
EFFECTIVE 2014	
Individual Mandate	Individuals required to obtain health insurance or pay a fine
Health Insurance Marketplace	Created state-based health care marketplaces to compare and purchase insurance policies
Pre-existing Conditions (Adults)	Insurance companies cannot deny coverage to adults and children who have pre-existing medical conditions. Pre-existing conditions can no longer be excluded from medical payments, factored into premium costs, or cause an application to be denied
EFFECTIVE 2015–2016	
Individual Mandate - penalty increases	For individuals and families who do not have health insurance, fines will increase each year.
EFFECTIVE 2019	
Individual Mandate – penalty eliminated	Individuals and families will no longer have to pay a penalty for not having health insurance

Apply for health care coverage and FAQ's
https://www.healthcare.gov/

PENALTIES FOR NOT HAVING HEALTH INSURANCE

When you pay your taxes in 2019
The Affordable Care Act enacted a penalty which started in 2014 for those who do not have health insurance. The penalty was the higher of two different calculations. The first was a flat dollar amount based on how many people were in the household and the other was based on your household's income. Each year the penalty was increased and in 2016 it was

1. $695 per adult / $347.50 per child (up to a maximum of $2,085) for the flat feee or
2. 2.5% of family income above the tax filing threshold.

In December of 2017 the individual mandate penalty was appealed, however, it does not go into effect until 2019. Therefore, you may still have to pay a tax penalty when you file your 2018 tax returns in April of 2019 if you do not have health insurance.

CALCULATING INSURANCE PAYMENTS – how much will insurance pay?

Example 1: You are single and have a medical procedure that cost $2,500. Your health insurance has a $500 deductible, an 80/20 coinsurance Single. Remember that the maximum out of pocket for 2018 is (single) $7,350.

Medical bill	$2,500
Deductible	$ 500 (you pay)
Remaining Bill	$2,000
Coinsurance	x .20
Coinsurance payment	$ 400 (you pay)

Your total portion of the bill is $500 (deductible) + $400 (coinsurance) = $900

Make sure that your calculated amount does not go over the maximum out of pocket amount of $7,350 (for single) for the calendar year. Since it did not, you will pay $900.

Insurance company's portion of the bill = $2,500 - $900 = $1,600

Maximum out of pocket remaining for the rest of the year is $7,350 - $1,600 = $5,750

In this example, the maximum out of pocket of $7,350 was not reached, and thus you still have $5,750 of out of pocket remaining before the insurance company starts paying 100% of the bill.

Example 2: You had another accident during the same calendar year that required major surgery and the bill is $45,000. How much will you pay and how much will insurance pay towards this bill?

Medical bill	$45,000
Deductible has already been paid for the calendar year	$ 0 (you pay)
Remaining Bill	$45,000
Coinsurance	x .20
Coinsurance payment	$ 9,000 (you pay)

Your total portion of the bill is $0 (deductible) + $9,000 (coinsurance) = $9,000

Make sure that your calculated amount does not go over the maximum out of pocket amount of $7,350 (for single) for the calendar year. In the first incident you had $5,750 remaining in out of pocket expenses before the insurance company pays 100% of the bill. In this example your calculated amount was $9,000, however, you only had $5,750 remaining from your first incident. Thus you will only pay $5,750 instead of $9,000.

Insurance company's portion of the bill = $45,000 - $5,750 = $39,250

Maximum out of pocket remaining for the rest of the year= $7,350 -$7,350 = $0

In this example, the maximum out of pocket amount of $7,350 was reached, and thus the insurance company will pay 100% of any other medical bills that happen during the same calendar year.

Example 3: You have another incident during the same calendar year and the medical bill total was $3,000. Your health insurance has a $500 deductible, an 80/20 coinsurance Single. Remember that the maximum out of pocket for 2018 is (single) $7,350.

As you have reached your maximum out of pocket amount in example 2, insurance will pay 100% of this bill and you will pay 0%. Thus

Your total portion of the bill is $0 (deductible) + $0 (coinsurance) = $0

Insurance company's portion of the bill = $3,000

SOURCES OF MEDICAL INSURANCE

Although there are still some Americans who are still uninsured, through the Affordable Care Act, this number has decreased in the past 3 years. So where do most Americans who have health insurance coverage obtain it from? Most have health insurance through their employer. If you have health insurance through your job, your employer pays a portion of the premium for you. Others obtain health insurance through the Marketplace which was created by the Affordable Care Act. There are other options available depending on your situation like Medicare (for retirees) and Medicaid (for low income).

WHAT COVERAGE IS PROVIDED?

The Affordable Care Act required that health insurance plans provide at least 10 Essential Benefits for every plan. Whereas some plans offer more, all plans must offer at least there 10 items.

1. Care before and after your baby is born
2. Outpatient care
3. Emergency room
4. Inpatient care
5. Care for mental health and substance use disorders – includes behavioral health treatment, counseling, and psychotherapy
6. Prescription drugs
7. Rehabilitative and rehabilitation devices and services
8. Lab tests
9. Preventative care (counseling, screenings, vaccines and care for management chronic diseases such as diabetes)
10. Pediatric care for children up to age 19 (includes oral and vision)

TYPES OF HEALTH INSURANCE PLANS

Health Maintenance Organizations (HMO)

HMOs are health care providers that operate on a prepaid basis and emphasize preventative care. They usually have cheaper premiums, no deductibles and small co-payments, however, to keep costs lower than other types of health insurance plans, there are usually more restrictions. One such restriction is always consulting your primary care physician to determine treatment needs before seeing a specialist.

Also, there is financial incentives to see a doctor that is in network, if you see a doctor that is out of network, you will need to pay the entire cost of medical services yourself.

Preferred Provider Organizations (PPO)

PPOs provide more flexibility as you can go out of network to see a doctor and have some of it paid for through your health insurance plan, however, there are cheaper rates if you stay in network. With PPOs you will not need a referral from a primary care physician to see a specialist. These differences from an HMO will cost you as premiums for PPOs are usually more expensive and there is usually deductibles involved before the health insurance plan will start providing benefits.

High Deductible Health Plan (HDHP)

HDHPs have become more popular in recent years as consumers try to find ways to cut costs while still obtaining health insurance. HDHPs have low premiums, however, the costs are high if you use your health care plan. Employers usually provide funding to your Health Savings Account Plan (HSA) to help cover some of the medical costs.

Advantages and Disadvantages of HMOs, PPOs, and HDHPs

	Advantages	Disadvantages
HMO	- Lower out of pocket costs - Focus on wellness and preventative care	- Tight control - Care from non-HMO providers generally not covered
PPO	- Free choice of health care provider financial incentive to see in network - Out of pocket costs generally limited (deductibles and co-payments)	- Less coverage for treatment provided by non-PPO physicians - More paperwork and expenses than HMO – larger co-payments
HDHP	- Low premiums	- Large bills if you decide to use your health care plan

FLEXIBLE SPENDING ACCOUNT (FSA)

An FSA is a tax free account you put money into that you use to pay for certain out-of-pocket health care costs such as co-payments, deductibles, and other qualified expenses for medical, dental and vision. Also you can utilize funds in this account to help pay for child/dependent care expenses. If there is any money left in the account at the end of the year, you will lose those funds – so budget your contributions well or you will forfeit any funds still in the account.

HEALTH SAVINGS ACCOUNTS (HSA)

An HSA is an account that is created by an employer on behalf of an employee to save money towards medical expenses in high deductible health plans. Money in the account can be used to help pay co-payments, deductibles, and other qualified medical expenses. Eligible payments made to a HSA can be deducted from your federal taxes Typically, HSA plans have a larger deductible and co-payments. Unlike a Flexible Spending Account, your HSA balance rolls over from year to year, so you never have to worry about losing your savings.

EXAMPLES OF ITEMS THAT ARE USUALLY NOT COVERED BY HEALTH, DENTAL, OR VISION INSURANCE

- Cosmetic (elective surgeries)
- Travel vaccines
- Acupuncture
- Nursing home care
- Some weight loss surgeries

Assignment 6.2   The Appendectomy

Name _____

SHOW YOUR CALCULATIONS

In March you have an emergency surgery. You need to figure out your share of the total medical expenses. Your annual health insurance premium costs you $450. Your insurance policy has a $500 annual deductible after which it pays 80% of the charges. Your maximum annual co-payment is $1,000. The total bill for surgery was $7,500 (hospital bill of $6,500 plus doctor bill of $1,000).

   1. What is your *maximum* possible out-of-pocket cost per year?

   2. What is your portion of the surgery costs and how much will the insurance company pay?

This is not your year. It is now June of the same year. Just after recovering from the surgery you are rushed to the hospital with a massive blood clot in your leg. The total bill this time comes to $4,000. All costs associated with treatment of the blood clot are covered under your health insurance policy.

   3. How much of this $4,000 bill will you need to pay?

   4. Had the blood clot problem occurred in February of the next calendar year, how much of the bill would you have had to pay?

Assignment 6.3 Annual Out-of-Pocket Health Expenses

Name _____

SHOW YOUR CALCULATIONS

Mark Meweird has a comprehensive medical insurance policy with a $750 annual deductible, an 80/20 coinsurance clause. Mark's annual insurance premium is $785.

What is Mark's maximum annual out-of-pocket cost per year?_____

Does Mark's maximum annual out of pocket cost include the cost of premiums? _____

Medical Procedure	Deductible	Co-insurance	Out of pocket (based on insurance)	Cumulative out of pocket (based on insurance)
January 10—Accidental knife wound while peeling an onion which required stitches. Cost: $350				
March 15—Broken arm with x rays. Cost: $1550				
June 23—Cold leading to strep throat. Cost: $45				
September 9—Elective plastic surgery to give Mark something other than a Jimmy Durante nose. Cost: $4,350				
November 14—Heart attack after being mistaken for Tom Cruise required hospitalization and surgery. Cost: $35,000				
December 24—Severe gastritis after eating fried oysters at Dr. Weagley's home on Christmas eve which required a pumping of the stomach. Cost: $650				
TOTAL				

DISABILITY INCOME INSURANCE

Disability income insurance is designed to replace a portion of a person's income if they are unable to work because of a disabling injury or illness.

From a financial point of view, the impact of total disability can be more devastating than death. In fact, the probability of being disabled is higher than of dying prematurely. Through the ages of 35–65 the chance of being disabled for 6 months or less is about 33%, for 1 year or more it is 25%, and being totally and permanently disabled is 5%. All these percentages are far greater than the chance of death at these ages. Besides, death is a one-time experience, whereas disabling injuries can occur more than once.

Annually renewable disability income (ARDI) policies are generally more affordable than traditional fixed-price disability policies. The annual premium increases just like term life insurance.

High-income people can generally replace only 30%–60% of their income through disability income insurance. Middle income people can replace 60%–80%.

Due to the moral hazard of a self-inflicted disabling injury or falsely claiming such an injury, it is not possible to purchase disability income insurance that would totally replace your income.

SOURCES OF DISABILITY INSURANCE

Employer/union group plan

Federal government

Social Security

Department of Veterans Affairs

Mine Safety and Health Administration (Black Lung)

Aid to Families with Dependent Children

State government

Workers' Compensation

Cash Sickness Programs (some states)

Vocational Rehabilitation Programs (some states)

Auto insurance: This coverage applies only if one is disabled in an automobile accident.

Credit insurance: Coverage for your debt payments to be paid during your period of disability.

Personal investment income: Those with sufficient assets are able to maintain their level of living with investment-based income.

Determining your needs: Sum the disability benefits from the above sources (employer, federal, etc.), and if you need and qualify for more protection, purchase additional disability income insurance from a private insurance company.

IMPORTANT POLICY PROVISIONS

When shopping for disability income insurance, the following policy provisions are important to understand.

Elimination (or waiting) period: The elimination period you select determines how long you wait after becoming disabled to receive monthly benefits and acts as a deductible. In many cases, disability benefits begin when the disability has lasted 6 months.

Benefit period: The benefit period determines how long you can receive benefits. The range is from under 1 year to the remainder of your lifetime.

Residual clause: If you are not totally disabled, your disability benefit is proportionally reduced.

Social Security rider: Extra coverage in the event you do not qualify for Social Security benefits.

Cost of living adjustment: An important option, though at increased cost, that keeps your benefit increasing in pace with inflation.

Noncancellable: Your policy cannot be cancelled, nor can the company change the monthly benefit or raise the premium. The premium in a "guaranteed renewable" policy can increase.

Definition of disability: Are you unable to perform your previous job or *any* job? This is a very important provision because the insurance company may encourage you to take any job you can find if the definition of disability is an "any job" definition.

Limit of liability: The total amount payable from insurance to the disabled insured over the duration of the policy.

HOMEOWNER'S AND RENTER'S INSURANCE

Commonly referred to as property insurance. The typical policy has two sections, one to cover your property and one to cover payments to others.

SECTION I

A.   **Dwelling**

This portion of your homeowner's policy provides protection for losses that might occur to your home or other structures attached to your home.

Six common property insurance policies are as follows.
(HO refers to HomeOwner)

HO-1   *Basic Policy*: Provides protection from losses occurring as a result of specific risks, such as fire or lightening, windstorm or hail, explosion, riot, damage caused by aircraft or vehicles, smoke, vandalism, theft, breakage of glass, or volcanic eruption. No coverage for personal property. No longer sold in most areas.

HO-2   *Broad Form Policy*: In addition to the HO-1 perils list, HO-2 covers falling objects, such as weight of ice, snow, or sleet; collapse of building; leakage or overflow of water or steam from plumbing, heating, or air-conditioning system; cracking, burning, or bulging of a steam or hot water heating system or of appliances for heating water; freezing of plumbing, heating, and air conditioning systems and domestic appliances; and sudden and accidental injury from artificially generated currents to electrical appliances, devices, fixtures, and wiring. No coverage for personal property. No longer sold in most areas.

HO-3   *Comprehensive Policy*: Covers the dwelling and personal property. Rather than listing what it insures against, this replacement cost policy insures against *all* perils *except* named exclusions, such as, flood, earthquake, war, nuclear accident, and others which may be specified in an individual policy.

HO-4   *Renter's Policy:* Offers coverage for personal property as well as liability coverage. HO-4 does not cover the building (the landlord has insurance for the dwelling), but insures your property inside the building.

HO-6 *Condominium Policy*: Same coverage as HO-4. (Special liability insurance provisions to incorporate the undivided common interest in condominium association property apply in this policy.)

HO-8 *Older Home Policy*: Market value insurance for homes whose value is less than their replacement cost (typically older, classic homes). Coverage similar to HO-1.

B.   **Other Structures** (applies to all HO policies except HO-4)

Structures separated (not attached) to your dwelling (i.e., garage, workshop, greenhouse).

C.   **Personal Property** (applies to HO-1—HO-8)

Insures the personal property you own. Your limit under this part is often from 50% to 75% of the coverage for the dwelling under A. Coverage C has internal limits for particular types of property, such as collections, firearms, jewelry, and so on.

D.   **Loss of Use** (applies to HO-1—HO-8)

This coverage pays living expenses for similar housing while your home is being rebuilt, or until a suitable replacement home is found.

SECTION II

E.   **Personal Liability** (applies to HO-1—HO-8)

Insures you against liability arising from bodily injury or property loss of others when this loss is created by your negligence. This applies to all actions you may be responsible for except when driving or in conducting your professional practice.

F.   **Medical Payments to Others** (applies to HO-1—HO-8)

Insurance that will pay up to a stated maximum the medical expenses for each nonresident person injured on your property. Negligence does not need to be proven.

DETERMINING THE PROPER AMOUNT OF PROPERTY INSURANCE

The coinsurance feature of most property insurance contracts requires that you have, say, 80% of the replacement value of the home insured to receive full payment of replacement cost. However, many homeowners policies now offer **guaranteed replacement cost**, which is a superior policy though at greater cost.

$$\frac{\text{Amount of current insurance}}{80\% \text{ of replacement cost}} \times \text{Loss} = \text{Amount Received}$$

For example: You have a home that would cost $100,000 to replace. You have $50,000 in property insurance. Last Sunday morning you had a fire. The damage is estimated as $20,000.

$$\frac{50,000}{80,000} \times \$20,000 = \textbf{\$12,500} = \textbf{Amount Received}$$

If you had the needed $80,000 minimum:

$$\frac{80,000}{80,000} \times \$20,000 = \textbf{\$20,000} = \textbf{Amount Received}$$

AUTOMOBILE INSURANCE

Very few forms of insurance are mandatory . . . this is one of them. In many states, certain coverages in the standard automobile insurance policy are mandatory by law while other coverages are mandatory by lenders.

Liability coverage (legally required in many states)

The numbers **100/300/50** would mean:

$100,000 for bodily injury liability limit paid per person in an accident.

$300,000 for bodily injury liability limit paid to all persons in an accident.

$50,000 for property damage liability limit for damage to other people's property from a single accident.

For example, you have liability coverage in the amounts of 25/50/10, and your liability coverage annual premium is $90. What is the cost per $1,000 of liability coverage?

Cost per $1,000 of liability coverage = (annual liability premium) / (maximum liability payout / 1,000)

$$\text{Cost per } \$1,000 \text{ of liability coverage} = 90 / (60,000 / 1,000) = 90 / 60 = \$1.50$$

Therefore, the cost per $1,000 of liability coverage is $1.50.

Bodily injury liability provides coverage for the risk of financial loss from injuries suffered by anyone in or out of your car as a result of an accident.

Property damage liability protects you from financial loss when your car damages another's property.

Medical payments

Medical payments coverage covers the cost of health care for people injured while in your auto, or when entering or exiting your auto.

***Un*insured motorist protection** (legally required in many states)

Provides coverage to protect the insured from the financial cost of injuries resulting from an accident with an *un*insured motorist, a hit-and run driver, or a driver insured by an insolvent insurance company. In other words, if you are injured in an automobile accident and the person who hit you is at fault *and* they have no liability insurance, your own auto policy will pay for your medical expenses under this coverage.

***Under*insured motorist protection** (legally required in many states)

Provides coverage to protect the insured from the financial cost of injuries resulting from an accident with a motorist who has liability coverage below that of the cost of the damages they cause.

Collision and comprehensive

Collision coverage pays for damage to your automobile when it is involved in an accident, regardless of who is at fault. Collision is generally defined as "the upset, or collision with another object, of your covered automobile."

Comprehensive coverage is protection from risks other than collision, such as hail damage, theft, falling objects, and windshield damage. It will also reimburse you for contact with animals such as birds or deer.

WHAT IS NO-FAULT AUTO INSURANCE?

No-fault insurance, as applied to automobile coverage, is a type of indemnity plan in which those injured in an accident receive direct payment from the company with which they are insured. Originated (1947) in Saskatchewan, Canada, no-fault insurance eliminates the need for accident victims to establish another's liability, or fault, through a civil lawsuit. Lawyers' groups oppose no-fault, saying that it limits the citizen's right to sue. Supporters say that it leads to faster settlement of accident claims and lower premium rates than the traditional tort liability system because it reduces legal fees and court costs. The first comprehensive no-fault plan in the United States was adopted (1971) in Massachusetts. As of 2009, 12 states (FL, HI, KS, KY, MA, MI, MN, NJ, NY, ND, PA, UT) have no-fault auto insurance laws that in some way restrict the right of parties to file legal suits. Provisions defining when a person can sue in no-fault states vary, but motorists can generally sue for severe injuries. Recently, however, rising insurance costs have led some states to reexamine the effectiveness of no-fault insurance laws.

Sources: http://www.infoplease.com/ce6/bus/A0835799.html
http://www.autoinsuranceindepth.com/no-fault-insurance.html

COSTS VERSUS BENEFITS IN AUTO INSURANCE

Collision and comprehensive

As just discussed, the personal auto policy offers several different coverages. Are all the coverages necessary? For a new car, the answer is most likely yes. For an older car (6- to 10-years old), it may be prudent to either raise the deductible on collision and comprehensive or drop the coverage altogether. Raising the deductible reduces the size of your premium, but increases your out-of-pocket cost in the event of an accident. For example, assume you have a 4-year-old car with a book value (*i.e., market value or actual cash value*) of $3,500:

Collision Coverage **Book Value of Car = $3,500**	
$100 deductible	$1,000 deductible
$450 annual premium	$128 annual premium
$2,000 accident claim < book value	$2,000 accident claim < book value
Minus $100 deductible	Minus $1,000 deductible
$1,900 insurance settlement	$1,000 insurance settlement
$550 out-of-pocket cost	$1,128 out-of-pocket cost

As $2,000 is less than the book value (or actual cash value) of the automobile, the insurance company will pay the $2,000 claim minus your $100 deductible.

It is important to remember that if the cost to repair the car exceeds the book value you will be reimbursed only the value of your car.

What is the cost per $1,000 of collision coverage in this example?

Cost per $1,000 of collision coverage

$$= \frac{Annual\ premium\ for\ collision\ coverage}{(Book\ value\ of\ the\ car\ /\ 1{,}000) - (Annual\ deductible\ /\ 1{,}000)}$$

$$= \frac{450}{(3{,}500\ /\ 1{,}000) - (100\ /\ 1{,}000)}$$

= \$132.35 per \$1,000 of collision coverage for \$100 deductible on \$3,500 car value

$$= \frac{128}{(3{,}500\ /\ 1{,}000) - (1{,}000\ /\ 1{,}000)}$$

= \$51.20 per \$1,000 of collision coverage for \$1,000 deductible on \$3,500 car value (Emergency funds are key to financial success.)

Collision Coverage Book Value of car = \$750	
\$100 deductible	\$1,000 deductible
\$296 annual premium	\$104 annual premium
\$2,000 accident claim > book value	\$2,000 accident claim > book value
\$750 maximum reimbursement	\$750 maximum reimbursement
Minus \$100 deductible	Minus \$1,000 deductible
\$650 insurance settlement	\$0 insurance settlement
\$1,646 out-of-pocket cost	\$2,104 out-of-pocket cost

In this example, the cost to repair the car far exceeds the book value of the vehicle. This is a common scenario for older cars. In such a case, the value of collision or comprehensive coverage is questionable. Notice that the \$296 annual premium for the \$100 deductible policy equals almost 40% of the \$750 book value of the vehicle. After 2 years of paying a \$296 annual premium, you will have paid nearly \$600 in premiums—while the most you could be reimbursed would be \$650 (or \$750–\$100). Maximum reimbursement = book value minus deductible.

For very old cars (over 10-year old), collision and comprehensive coverage may be dropped. The reason for this is that older cars depreciate (lose value) and at some point the annual premium (*cost*) for collision or comprehensive coverage may exceed the maximum reimbursement (*benefit*) from the insurance company—obviously a losing proposition. In fact, these insurance coverages may be dropped whenever the insured has the financial means to self-insure and chooses to do so.

Guideline: As a vehicle's book value declines you might raise the deductible on collision and comprehensive, or choose to not purchase collision and comprehensive coverage.

Liability—The real insurance value

As indicated previously, liability coverage is legally required in many states and, as such, is not purchased on the basis of a cost-versus-benefit analysis. Whether you feel it is cost-effective or not, you legally need to have it. However, the *amount* of liability insurance purchased is up to the consumer. *We strongly suggest that the maximum amount of liability coverage be purchased—regardless of the age or market value of the vehicle.* The reasoning for our suggestion is very simple:

If a tree falls on a 1983 Ford Pinto Wagon and totally destroys it, the loss is minimal. The market (or book) value of such a vehicle is very low, hence having comprehensive coverage is next to worthless, as would be collision insurance.

If this same person is driving their Pinto Wagon and hits and kills a pedestrian, the potential loss to the driver (because of a potential lawsuit) is extremely large, in fact far beyond the value of the vehicle. Liability insurance offers protection in this type of circumstance. It is possible that a lawsuit could result in a large judgment against the driver. Hence, the driver needs a large amount of liability coverage. Liability insurance offers indemnification for the potentially disastrous event—precisely what insurance is for.

PREMIUM FACTORS

All insurance companies offer lower premiums when deductibles are increased. Companies vary with respect to the premium discounts they may offer.

Common discounts may include:

Completing a driver training program

Maintaining a certain GPA level

Participating in a carpool

Driving fewer than a certain number of miles per year

Insuring two or more vehicles with the same company

Establishing a safe driving record.

Rates may rise by the following:

- Age, sex, marital status (young, single males present insurance companies with the greatest risks)
- Where you live (e.g., Detroit would have higher rates)
- What the vehicle is primarily used for (higher rates for heavier usage), and high performance vehicles
- Frequent premium payment periods (unless premium payments are made by electronic funds transfer, or EFT)
- Risk factors caused by a person's driving record.

Assignment 6.4   Property and Auto Insurance

Name _____

SHOW YOUR CALCULATIONS

1. If you purchased automobile liability coverage of 75/200/30, describe what each number means.

2. Assume you own a 1996 Chevrolet Impala that has a book value of $800. The total annual premium for your auto insurance policy is $789. The annual cost for collision coverage is $284 with a $500 deductible. Liability coverage of 100/300/50 costs you $325 per year. What is the annual cost per $1,000 of coverage for collision insurance? What is the annual cost per $1,000 of coverage for liability insurance?

3. Assume you have an accident in which your 1996 Impala is totally destroyed, but you are not hurt. ACME Insurance Co. (your insurance company) writes you a check for the car. What is the dollar amount of the check?

4. Assume you have a home that would cost $120,000 to replace. You currently have the home insured for $85,000. Last night a tornado damaged your home, causing an estimated $25,000 in damage. How much will your insurance company pay for repairing the damage to your home?

5. What is the important difference between HO-2 and HO-3?

Section Six Extra Practice Problems

1. In a small city there are 400 houses worth $45,000 each. Based on historical data, 3 houses are expected to burn each year. Without insurance, every homeowner must "self-insure" their home for $45,000 (the cost to rebuild the home). To purchase insurance each (and every) homeowner must pay how much money into the mutual insurance fund?

2. You desire your dependents to have an after-tax income of $60,000 should you die. Assume a marginal tax rate of 15% and an annual rate of return of 7% (before taxes). Use the "desired income" method to determine the proper amount of life insurance to purchase.

3. You have 25 years until retirement, an annual income of $65,000, and a time value of money of 7.5%. You want life insurance to replace 100% of your annual income if you die. Using the "human life value" approach determine how much life insurance needs to be purchased. (Assume annuity due, meaning that survivors withdraw annuity payment at the beginning of each year.)

4. Now you decide that your survivors need a *real*, *after-tax* annual income of $65,000 (annuity due). Using a marginal tax rate of 28% and an inflation rate of 3.5%, how much life insurance will you need to purchase? Your time value of money is 7.5%.

5. You have emergency heart surgery. The total medical bill is $22,700. Your health insurance policy has a $600 annual deductible and 70%/30% coinsurance. The insurance company pays 70%, and your portion is 30%. Your policy has a maximum annual coinsurance payment of $1,200 and the annual premium for the policy is $650. How much of the bill will (a) you have to pay and how much will (b) insurance pay?

6. Assume you have a home that would cost $150,000 to replace. You currently have the home insured for $100,000. Last night a severe hailstorm damaged your home, causing an estimated $15,000 in damage. How much will your insurance company pay for repairing the damage to your home?

7. Each person has a personal auto policy with 25/50/10; $7,500 medical payments and a $500 deductible for collision. How much will insurance cover? How much are they out of pocket?
   a. Alex skids on ice and runs into a parked car causing $13,785 to unoccupied car and $6,350 to his own.

   b. John runs a stop sign and causes a serious accident badly injuring two people. The injured parties medical bills are $20,000 each.

   c. Mable backs in to a telephone pole and causes $450 worth of damage to the car.

Section Six Practice Problems Answers

1. Three homes burn $\times$ \$45,000 = \$135,000
   \$135,000 / 400 homeowners = **\$337.50 premium**

2. 7% $\times$ (1 − .15) = 5.95% after-tax return

$$\frac{\$60,000}{.0595} = \textbf{\$1,008,403 needed life insurance}$$

3. Using a financial calculator in annuity due (i.e., begin) mode:

   PMTad = 65,000 at the beginning of each year
   N   = 25 years
   I/YR   = 7.5%
   PV   = **<778,893> needed life insurance**

   The answer is negative on a financial calculator simply because the PMT was entered as a positive. Using algebra:

$$\textbf{PV} = \text{PMTad} \left(\frac{1 - (1 + i)^{-n}}{i} \right) \times (1 + i)$$

$$\textbf{PV} = 65,000 \left(\frac{1 - (1 + .075)^{-25}}{.075} \right) \times (1 + .075) = \textbf{\$778,893}$$

4. Gross rate of return   = .075
   After-tax rate of return = Gross return $\times$ (1 − MTR)
                            = .075 $\times$ (1 − .28)
                            = .054

   After-tax, real (i.e., inflation adjusted) rate of return:

$$\frac{1 + \text{nominal after-tax interest rate}}{1 + \text{inflation rate}} - 1 = \text{real rate of interest}$$

$$\frac{1 + .054}{1 + .035} - 1 = .01836 \text{ real interest rate (or 1.836\%)}$$

   PMTad = 65,000 at the beginning of each year
   N   = 25 years
   I/YR   = 1.836
   PV   = **<1,317,554> needed life insurance**

5.

Medical bill	\$22,700
Deductible	\$ 600
Remaining bill	\$22,100
Coinsurance percentage	$\times$ .30
Coinsurance payment	\$ 6,630

   However, \$6,630 > \$1,200, so your maximum co-payment is \$1,200

Your total portion of the bill	**\$1,800 (or \$600 + \$1,200)**
Insurance company's portion of the bill	**\$20,900**

6. $$\frac{\text{Amount of current insurance}}{80\% \text{ of replacement cost}} \times \text{Loss} = \text{Amount Received}$$

$$\frac{\$100,000}{\$150,000 \times .80} \times \$15,000$$

$$\frac{\$100,000}{\$120,000} \times \$15,000 = \textbf{\$12,500 maximum reimbursement}$$

7. a. Parked car: Insurance will pay $10,000 and Alex will owe $3,785 Alex's car: Insurance will pay $5,850 and Alex will owe $500 deductible

   b. Bodily liability: Insurance will pay $40,000 and Alex will owe $0

   c. Mable will owe $450 as her deductible is $500 (so she has not met her deductible yet)

Notes:

Housing

Be it ever so humble, there's no place like home.

John Howard Payne (1791–1852)

Property is desirable. It is a positive good in the world.

Abraham Lincoln (1809–1865)

Once the housing market begins to recover,
I would phase out the mortgage tax deduction.

Joshua A. Tucker

A strong housing market is the engine of economic recovery.

Ben Bernanke (1953–)

The American dream of owning a home turned into a nightmare for many in 2008 and 2009. Some households have been so severely hurt by the economic downturn that it will take years for them to recover and, perhaps, their retirement is now only a vague dream they once had. Yet, other households had their financial house in order and were able to weather the storm while prices stabilized. In many cases, those people took advantage of the downturn and purchased real estate as an investment. In many markets, prices now exceed what they were at the height of the bubble; while, in others, they still languish. One thing that we have learned from the Great Recession is that households need to better understand economics, markets, and financial products. We are also reminded of the toll taken when excess greed dominates sound financial principles.

It is interesting to observe how today's young adults were affected by the market downturn. We find them less likely than previous generations to want to purchase a home, even with low interest rates and a continuation of the tax deductibility of home mortgage interest. Coincidentally, we also find them less likely to buy a car as they are moving to multifamily housing in the core of many of America's cities. One thing is for certain, markets change and there are still many who want to own a home as a means of establishing their identity and to have an ownership interest in their communities. We will begin with trying to understand the reasons to help direct us through the home purchase versus rental housing decision.

RENTING VERSUS BUYING A HOME

Rental Housing

Advantages:

- More flexibility to move quickly, if the need arises
- If moving to a new area, renting allows you time to become familiar with the area before purchasing a home
- Costs are initially low
- Most unexpected repair expenses are paid by the landlord

Disadvantages:

- At the end of a lease, you may have to move
- At the end of a lease, you may face rent increases
- A neighborhood of rentals can be unstable
- Lack of freedom to remodel, as in major structural projects
- Less privacy
- Indirectly pay property taxes and mortgage interest with no tax benefit

Types of Leases

- Verbal lease—Month to month legal agreement. Either party can change the agreement with 30 days notice prior to the next anniversary of the agreement.
- Time lease—Most tenants prefer a time lease. A time lease prohibits price increases in rent during the time of the lease.
- Gross lease—Most rentals of houses and apartments use a gross lease. With a gross lease, the tenant pays monthly rent and the landlord pays property taxes, some utilities, repairs, and fire insurance.
  - Net lease—Tenant has to pay some of the above-mentioned landlord expenses.
  - Triple net—Tenant pays all expenses.
- Discount lease—Tenant receives a discount for performing some tasks, such as first $50 in repairs or by providing property management for a multifamily structure.

Buying a Home

Advantages:

- Mortgage payments are a form of forced savings (i.e., the house is viewed as an investment)
- Sociopsychological advantages of ownership
- Freedom to improve or modify the home
- Financial and geographic commitment
- Privacy

Disadvantages:

- High initial cost (closing costs + down payment)
- Commitment of time/money to maintain/repair the home/yard
- Cost to replace/repair appliances and other capital equipment
- Less flexibility to quickly relocate

STEPS OF BUYING A HOME

1. Carefully prepare and examine your monthly budget to determine how much you can spend on housing (principal + interest + taxes + insurance + maintenance).

2. Go to a lender (bank, credit union, savings and loan) and **prequalify** for a loan. In this process, the lender will help you determine how large of a loan you can reasonably borrow. This is a very healthy "reality check" and banks welcome working with you on this, as they want good customers. Once you have your budget figured out (step #1) and you are pre-qualified for a loan (step #2), you are ready to go house hunting in neighborhoods that you can afford!

3. Select the home you would like (and can afford) to purchase. Contact the seller of the home, either through a realtor or directly, if it is not being offered by a realtor.

4. Make a written offer of purchase price to the seller, with a statement of your intent to make an earnest money deposit. It is often the case that a larger earnest money deposit will signal a greater desire to purchase the home. If the seller accepts the offer and all terms of the contract are met, and you "change your mind," you lose your earnest deposit. Obviously, you should not casually make an offer to purchase a home if you have no serious intention of actually buying the home.

   Important contract items:
   - If the buyer needs to move in before the settlement date, or the seller needs to remain after the settlement date, the typical rental agreement is a triple net lease.
   - Make the sale contingent on your ability to obtain a mortgage loan with terms (interest rate, length, amount of loan) that are acceptable to you.
   - State what items actually sell with the house (such as drapes, appliances, etc.). If it is not affixed with nails, screws, or glue, it may not be included.
   - Specify who pays for repairs if a structural inspection reveals defective construction (leaky basement, sagging roof, water damage) or mechanical equipment (e.g., furnace, water heater, appliances, etc.)

5. The seller may or may not accept your initial offer. If your offer is not accepted, the seller may counteroffer with a price that is greater than your offer but, perhaps, less than the original asking price. It is possible that you may want to offer more than the asking price, if markets are moving quickly or you perceive they are asking too little for the home. Of course, there may be a good reason they are asking less so do not forget one of the lessons of home buying, "If you buy in haste, you can repent at leisure." Negotiating the price is a process that may take two or three iterations. For example, you find a home you like and it is listed at a price of $179,000. You submit a written offer to the seller of $168,000. The seller counters with a price of $174,000. You "counter" with $171,500. Eventually you both agree on a price of $173,000.

6. Once the contract has been agreed on, both parties (buyer and seller) sign it. Along with the signed contract you now make an earnest money deposit. An earnest money deposit is held in escrow to be given to the seller if you back out of the contract. It is an indication of your seriousness to purchase the home. If you actually purchase the home, the earnest money is applied toward the purchase price. If you decide that you do not want to buy the home, you lose your earnest money unless the reasons for your change of heart are specified in the contract.

7. At this point, you (as the buyer) need to go mortgage loan shopping, if you have not shopped for a loan before making an offer on a home. In this way, the period of time between signing a contract and "closing" is shortened. Closing refers to the actual transfer of property. This occurs when the seller and buyer, along with an attorney and/or loan officer, meet and sign all the necessary documents to seal the deal. Once you "close on a home," it becomes your legal property.

TYPES OF HOUSING

Single-family housing: One house on one lot. This is what most people envision, when they think about buying a home. Yet, there are many other options.

Duplex: Two dwellings under the same roof, but the two residences are considered to be one legal parcel of land. Two family units are in the structure but there is one owner for the lot. Many young people get their "start" in housing by owning a duplex and living in one side, while renting the other. This covers much of the mortgage costs and may allow them to save faster for a single-family home, while getting their start in real estate investing.

Split-lot duplex: A lot with two dwellings under the same roof, but the lot is legally divided (split) into two separate legal parcels.

Condominiums: You own your housing unit and you also own an undivided interest in the surrounding property to your housing unit, the common property. You are required to pay a fee for the maintenance of the surrounding property to the condominium owners' association.

Before you buy a condominium:
- Understand the rules regarding resale and renting of the condominium.Check the budget of the condominium owners' association. Make sure it is adequately managed to pay for known future repairs, such as paving the parking lot, as well as unknown issues.
- A sinking fund should exist for known maintenance repairs in the future. If not, you will be billed.
- Know the insurance policy of the association and share a copy with your insurance agent to ascertain it adequacy.

Cooperatives: Cooperatives often look like condominiums. The difference between the two is that the mortgage is with the cooperative, rather than with each unit. You also must "buy in" to the cooperative mortgage. Your share of assessments, operating costs, and property taxes are all paid to the cooperative. However, your portions of the cooperative's taxes and interest are tax deductible to you.

Mobile homes: Price is the attraction, but mobile homes have a history of depreciating. As such, they are often taxed by counties as personal property rather than real property. Moreover, lenders will typically charge higher rates of interest on mobile home loans.

COST OF HOUSING

The monthly cost of housing, in the form of a mortgage payment, is typically 25%–40% of the household budget. The Federal Housing Administration (FHA) allows homeowners to pay up to 29% of their income toward their home mortgage and 41% toward the sum of their mortgage payment and other household debt.

The following table shows the costs of home ownership by region in America. In the next table, there is a summary list of the cost of housing in different U.S. cities during 2009 and 2013.

As can be seen from the tables on the following pages, the difference in the cost of housing is very large based on where you live. Consider the difference in the median-priced home between Lima, Ohio and San Francisco, California. The monthly mortgage payment for a home costing $779,000 in San Francisco (assuming a 20% down payment, 30-year loan, 5% interest rate) would be $3,345 per month. The monthly mortgage payment for a home in Lima costing $96,000 (assuming a 20% down payment, 30-year loan, 5% interest) would be $412. A monthly difference of nearly $2,933! (If Lima, Ohio was a good enough location for Ben Roethlisberger to be reared, it might be good enough for you!)

Median Prices of Existing Single-Family Homes

Year	U.S.	Northeast	Midwest	South	West
2000	139,100	139,500	123,600	128,200	183,400
2005	219,000	281,600	168,300	181,100	340,300
2015	223,900	262,500	175,500	196,400	319,100
2016	235,500	265,400	184,400	209,200	342,900
2017	248,800	275,700	196,200	222,700	369,400
Percentage Change from 2015 to 2017	11.1%	5.0%	11.8%	13.4%	15.8%

Source: National Association of Home Builders
New and Existing Single-Family Home Prices by Region: http://www.nahb.org and www.realtor.org

Cost of Housing in Various U.S. Cities as of December 2009 / 2013

Metro Area	2009 Percentage of Homes Affordable for Median Income	2009 Median Family Income ($)	2009 Median Home Sales Price ($)	2013 Percentage of Homes Affordable for Median Income	2013 Median Home Sales Price ($)
10 Most Affordable U.S. Cities in 2009				2013 Data	2013 Data
Kokomo, IN	98.0	61,800	73,000	96.9	95,000
Monroe, MI	97.1	70,300	102,000	90.6	120,000
Flint, MI	96.3	58,500	85,000	84.1	92,000
Lima, OH	96.3	56,400	78,000	89.7	96,000
Bay City, MI	96.1	56,500	77,000	92.4	79,000
Lansing-East Lansing, MI	95.8	67,000	90,000	89.3	100,000
Indianapolis-Carmel, IN	95.7	68,100	106,000	93.3	93,000
Elkhart-Goshen, IN	95.3	59,200	94,000	84.9	122,000
Battle Creek, MI	94.9	55,700	75,000	86.4	87,000
Canton-Massillon, OH	94.7	57,700	84,000	85.5	107,000

(*Continues*)

Cost of Housing in Various U.S. Cities as of December 2009 / 2013 (*Continued*)

Metro Area	2009 Percentage of Homes Affordable for Median Income	2009 Median Family Income ($)	2009 Median Home Sales Price ($)	2013 Percentage of Homes Affordable for Median Income	2013 Median Home Sales Price ($)
10 Least Affordable U.S. Cities in 2009				2013 Data	2013 Data
Napa, CA	44.4	81,800	360,000	31.4	448,000
Nassau-Suffolk, NY	42.7	101,800	380,000	51.8	395,000
Ocean City, NJ	37.8	67,200	330,000	51.3	303,000
Santa Cruz-Watsonville, CA	37.7	83,800	431,000	20.3	540,000
Los Angeles-Long Beach-Glendale, CA	36.8	62,100	320,000	21.1	425,000
Santa Ana-Anaheim-Irvine, CA	34.5	86,100	435,000	22.1	540,000
Honolulu, HI	33.8	79,300	450,000	45.2	442,000
San Luis Obispo-Paso Robles, CA	32.1	70,800	372,000	26.6	412,000
San Francisco-San Mateo-Redwood City, CA	22.3	96,800	625,000	16.0	779,000
New York-White Plains-Wayne, NY-NJ	19.7	64,800	425,000	23.0	464,000

Source: National Association of Home Builders: http://www.nahb.org/hoi

From the earlier tables, you might have observed the large increase in median home prices from 2009—in the midst of the recession—compared to 2013, a time when we all believed the recession was behind us. In 2009, median prices in the most affordable city—Kokomo, IN—rose 30.14% in 4 years. This is a 6.8% annual rate of return on housing in Kokomo. However, not all cities experienced a rise. Note that median home prices actually decreased in Indianapolis (−12.26%), Ocean City (−8.18%), and Honolulu (−1.78%).

The table presented above points out that all investments are risky, including real estate. Due to the housing peak of 2008, many learned this lesson the hard way. Yet, this lesson provides us with a chance to mention the way **leverage** can work for you when markets are favorable. Leverage can also lay waste to your best laid plans if the market moves against you. To demonstrate this, read the following example.

For simplicity, we will assume that a $300,000 home was purchased both in Kokomo and in Indianapolis, with a 20% down, 5%, 30 year mortgage. For simplicity sake, we will also assume that all other factors are equal except for house price appreciation. Next, we will determine what the rate of return on the down payment will be for both cases.

An Example of Leverage in Two Indiana Markets 2009–2013

	Indianapolis	**Kokomo**
Purchase Price	$300,000	$300,000
Down payment (Purchase Equity)	$60,000	$60,000
4-Year Rate of Appreciation	−12.26%	30.14%
Sales Price	$263,220	$390,420
Mortgage after 48 Payments	$224,712	$224,712
Equity at Sale	$38,508	$165,708
Rate of Return on Purchase Equity	**−35.8%**	**176.2%**

Notice how the 30.14% positive return in housing was magnified to a 176.2% return by the use of leverage, borrowed money. During the same time period, a negative 12.26% return in median prices in Indianapolis was further decreased to a negative 35.8% return. Leverage can make the good times better, but it can also make the bad times worse. Had we assumed a lower down payment (less than 20%) these results would have been even more dramatic. On the other hand, if we had assumed no leverage, then the return would have been a negative 12.26% in Indianapolis and a positive 30.14% in Kokomo—due to the lack of leverage.

MORTGAGE FINANCING

Most of us do not have enough money initially to purchase a home by paying cash, so we must borrow money (i.e., use leverage). A **mortgage** is a loan from a lending institution (typically a bank or credit union) in which the home and/or property serves as the collateral for the loan. In the event the borrower does not make the payments on the loan, the collateral (home) is taken by the lender in an attempt to recover the money they have lent the borrower.

As of 2007, the total amount of residential mortgage debt in the United States was over $11.24 trillion. By 2014 it had shrunk to $9.94 trillion and, by 2017, if had grown to $10.62 trillion. With a 2017 U.S. population of about 326.5 million people in 2017 this equates to over $32,629 of mortgage debt *per capita* (i.e., for every man, woman, and child).

Mortgage Loan Amortization

Amortization is simply the process of determining the equal, periodic payment that will repay a loan (principal and interest) over the stated length of the loan. The algebraic formula below is used to amortize a mortgage loan (i.e., calculate the ordinary annuity payment). Or, you can use your financial calculator.

$$PMTa = \frac{PVa}{\left(\dfrac{1 - (1 + i)^{-n}}{i} \right)}$$

Assumptions: Mortgage loan = $172,960
Loan length = 30 years
Interest rate = 5.00% annually

Using the algebraic formula:

$$\frac{\$172,960}{\left(\dfrac{1 - (1 + .05 / 12)^{-(30\times12)}}{.05 / 12}\right)} = \textbf{\$928.49 monthly payment}$$

Using a financial calculator:

PV	=	172,960
I/YR	=	5 / 12, or use 5% and change P/YR to 12
N	=	30 × 12 = 360
PMT	=	**928.49 monthly payment**

The **interest portion of the monthly payment** is calculated by multiplying the loan balance by the monthly rate of interest. In this scenario, the first month is calculated as follows (where the monthly interest rate = .05 / 12 = .00416667):

Loan Balance		Monthly Rate of Interest		Interest Portion of Payment
$172,960	×	.00416667	=	**$720.67**

The **principal portion of the monthly payment** is calculated by subtracting the interest portion from the monthly payment. The first month was calculated as follows:

Monthly Payment		Interest Portion		Principal Portion
$928.49	−	$720.67	=	**$207.82**

During the early years of a mortgage loan, the majority of the monthly payment goes to interest, and not to principal.

Question: How much will be paid to the lender over the life of this loan?

Multiply the monthly payment by the number of months of the loan.

Monthly payment		$928.49
Multiplied by number of months	×	360
Gross repayment to lender		**$334,256.40**

Question: How much interest will be paid to the lender over the life of the loan?

Subtract the original loan amount from the gross repayment—the difference is interest.

Gross repayment to lender	$334,256.40
Minus original loan amount	− $172,960.00
Total interest paid	**$161,296.40**

As can be seen, if you repay this loan on schedule the amount of interest would be slightly less than the original loan amount. In essence, you pay for the mortgage on your house twice (one time for principal, and one more time for interest!).

During the life of your mortgage, you may want to calculate how much you still owe on your mortgage. You can ask the bank or they might print it on your monthly statement. On the other hand, you are empowered with a financial calculator! During the life of a loan (in this case a mortgage), you can always determine the remaining loan balance by use of the ordinary annuity formula to solve for PV.

Using the same information as above (PV = 172,960, n = 30 × 12, i = 5 / 12), the loan balance at the end of 2 years would be as follows:

The borrower would have 336 payments remaining (n = 360 minus 24) at a monthly rate of .004166667 (.05 / 12).

Thus, the remaining balance after making payments for 2 years would equal:

$$PV = PMT\left(\frac{1 - (1 + i)^{-n}}{i}\right)$$

$$PV = 928.49\left(\frac{1 - (1 + .004166667)^{-336}}{.004166667}\right) = \mathbf{\$167,726.46}$$

Using a financial calculator:

PMT = <928.49>
I/YR = 5/12, or use 5% and change your P/YR to 12
N = 28 × 12 = 336 (the number of months remaining after 2 years)
PV = 167,726.46 remaining balance on loan after 2 years

PAYMENT REDUCTION TECHNIQUES

You must repay the loan principal; therefore, the techniques described in what follows can be used to reduce the *interest portion* of the payments. Three common ways to reduce total interest paid to the bank over the life of the mortgage loan are:

Make a Larger Down Payment (Thereby Reducing the Loan Amount)

Obtain a Lower Interest Rate

The monthly principal and interest payment on a $172,960 loan over 30 years at 5% annual interest would be $928.49 (vs. $1,036.98 at 6%). This reduces total interest paid to $161,296.40 (vs. $200,354 total interest on a 6% loan). A lower rate is generally obtained by paying "points."

Shorten the Length of the Mortgage

Select a 15-year mortgage instead of a 30-year mortgage:

Using the same loan of $172,960 at 5% interest, a 15-year loan would cut total interest paid from $161,296.40 to $73,236.20. The monthly payment would, however, increase to $1,367.76. It is the case that a 15-year mortgage will almost always have a lower rate of interest than a 30-year mortgage. This will magnify the savings.

Self-determined acceleration of regular mortgage payments:

If you choose to pay more than the normal monthly mortgage payment, every extra dollar paid goes directly to principal (loan) reduction which shortens the length of the loan and the total interest paid. If you paid $975 ($928.49 plus $46.51 extra) on the loan of $172,960, you would pay the loan off in 324 months, or 3 years sooner. You would save over $18,356 in interest, to use toward your other financial goals.

Select a biweekly mortgage where payments are made every 2 weeks, or a total of 26 payments per year:

> A biweekly payment of $464.24 on a 30 year, 5% loan of $172,960 would be paid off in 25.2 years. Total interest paid would equal $131,610.58 compared to $161,296.40—a savings of $29,685.82. This is calculated as follows.
>
> PV   =   172,960
> I/YR =   5 / 26, or I/Y = 5, and P/YR = 26
> PMT =   <464.24> every 2 weeks (which is $928.49 / 2)
> **N   =   656.06 biweekly periods / 26 = 25.23 years**

INTEREST-ONLY OPTION ON A MORTGAGE LOAN

This type of mortgage loan "option" was extremely popular in the lead up to the Great Recession. It was very popular because it allowed for a smaller monthly payment. The downside should be obvious: you are not reducing the size of the loan unless you pay more than the stipulated payment.

For example, a 30-year fixed rate mortgage of $100,000 at 6% has a monthly payment of $599.55. This is the **fully amortizing payment**—the payment that, if maintained over the full term of the loan, will pay off the $100,000 loan.

In month 1, that payment divides into $500 of interest and $99.55 of principal. In month 2, the payment remains at $599.55 but the breakdown is $499.50 to interest and $100.05 to principal. Each month, the interest portion declines and the principal portion rises. After 5 years, the balance is $93,054. That is how mortgages amortize.

Now, attach an interest-only option to this mortgage, say, for the first 5 years. That means that the borrower needs to pay only $500 a month during the first 5 years. There is no payment to principal. If the borrower exercises this option, the loan balance after 5 years will still be $100,000. There is no amortization. Beginning in year 6, the borrower must begin paying $644.30. That is the fully amortizing payment for a 6%, $100,000 loan for the 25 years left to amortize the loan.

Whether or not an interest-only option is a good idea is up to you. But, here is one thought: If your main goal is to be out of debt—rather than prolonging it—you may want to avoid the interest-only option on a mortgage loan. Also, consider how unhappy you will be when your mortgage payment increases by $144.30 per month.

On the other hand, if you live in a time of house price appreciation and you do not plan to remain a resident in the home past the end of the interest-only period, this type of loan may work well. I know there are many ifs in the above statement, but the money you do not spend on housing can be invested in other ways, like your retirement plan. (Yes, you will need to pay for your retirement.)

Assignment 7.1   Home Mortgage Loan Calculations

Name _____

SHOW YOUR WORK

Scenario: Mortgage loan   = $150,000
            Loan length   =   30 years
            Interest rate   =   6% annually

1. What will be the monthly mortgage payment?

2. Assuming you do not pay the loan off early, how much total interest will you pay the lender?

3. If you decide to amortize the loan over 15 years, what will be your monthly payment?

4. Compared to the 30-year mortgage, how much total interest will you save by going to a 15-year mortgage?

5. Assume you select a 15-year mortgage with an interest rate of 7.50%.
   a. What will be your monthly payment?

   b. How much total interest will you pay to the lender?

The Mortgage Menu

As we write this edition, mortgage interest rates are still very low compared to the double digits we saw earlier in life. When interest rates are low, you will find that almost all mortgages will be fixed rate mortgages, as consumers want to lock in the low rate of interest. The trouble is that when interest rates increase—and they will—the lender (bank) will have to borrow money at the higher interest rate, while their assets (the loans they have made to borrowers) only pay them the lower rates of interest. This is not good for bank profits, which is not good for our banking system. Thus, we want to provide you a brief discussion of alternative mortgages that have been used, and can still be used, to meet the needs of borrowers and lenders.

Fixed Rate Mortgage

A fixed rate mortgage is where the **debiting rate** for the mortgage, the rate used to determine the interest owed the lender, is constant throughout the life of the contract. This allows the borrower to be certain of payments but the lender will be uncertain of the value of the payments as interest rates change.

If the fixed rate mortgage is a *first mortgage*, the home is collateral for the loan, and if the mortgage is for less than 80% of the appraised value, the home is the only collateral. For mortgages greater than 80% of the appraised value, **private mortgage insurance** (PMI) is required. PMI insures a maximum of 20% of the loan (if we assume a loan equal to the home purchase price). PMI protects the lender in the event that the homebuyer defaults. The PMI insurance premium is paid by the borrower. The law allows a homeowner to drop the PMI after 2 years of homeownership if:

1. Their home equity has risen to 20% or more because of home improvements or reductions in the mortgage loan principal
2. Their home equity is 25% or more because of market appreciation

The homeowner is able to drop PMI after 5 years if their equity is 20% or more due to appreciation.

Adjustable Rate Mortgage (ARM) or Variable Rate Mortgage

An ARM allows the interest rate to rise or fall with changes in the money market. This effectively shifts the risks of the future from the lender to the borrower. As stated above, borrowers prefer the certainty of a fixed payment when interest rates are low. On the other hand, when interest rates are high the interest rate extended to the borrower can be substantially lower if the interest rate is allowed to change with the market for debt. At renewal, the interest rate can change according to a contractually stated index. The four most commonly used indices to determine a loans interest rate are:

1. Short-Term Treasury Securities Rate
2. Federal Reserve District Cost of Funds
3. National Average Mortgage Contract Rate published by the Federal Home Loan Bank
4. Prime Rate, as published in the *Wall Street Journal*

Typically, ARMs have **interest rate caps** that restrict how much the rate of interest (or payment) can increase each year, and over the life of the loan. An interest rate cap might restrict interest rate increases to 2% annually and 5% over the life of contract. Let us look at an example for a $100,000, 30-year mortgage with an initial interest rate of 6% where the maximum increase in interest rates occurs each year.

Year	Payments Remaining	Mortgage Balance ($)	Interest Rate (%)	Monthly Payment ($)	Payment Increase (%)
1	360	100,000	6.00	599.55	
2	348	98,772	8.00	730.86	22
3	336	97,871	10.00	869.06	19
4	324	97,199	11.00	939.87	8

Such a dramatic increase in payments (57%) is unlikely but it could occur. To help borrowers overcome this fear, lenders began to offer payment caps which often walk hand-in-hand with negative amortization.

Negative Amortization

You may encounter an ARM with **payment caps**. Payment caps limit the size of the payment but they allow interest rates to go where interest rates need to go to adjust to the current economic climate. Using the earlier example with a *payment cap of $850*, we would have the scenario shown below. Notice that with the same interest rate scenario, but with a payment cap, the year 5 mortgage balance is greater than the year 4 mortgage balance. This occurs because the maximum payment of $850 is insufficient to amortize the loan. When the loan does not amortize, **negative amortization** occurs. Typically, negative amortization is limited to 125% of the original mortgage balance and if it reaches 125% of the original balance then the homeowner must either refinance or sell the home.

Year	Payments Remaining	Mortgage Balance ($)	Interest Rate (%)	Monthly Payment ($)	Payment Increase (%)
1	360	100,000	6.00	599.55	
2	348	98,772	8.00	730.86	22
3	336	97,871	10.00	850.00	16
4	324	97,438	11.00	**850.00**	0
5	312	**97,983**			

Other Mortgage Variations:

Balloon mortgages appear to be like a standard mortgage; however, there exists a due date 3, 5, or 10 years into the contract. At this time, all remaining principal is due. Some are selfamortizing, while some are interest-only mortgages. When the principal is due, the purchaser must either refinance or repay.

Graduated payment mortgages (GPMs) are designed to allow younger people and/or those with a growing income to qualify for a home mortgage by initially reducing mortgage payments with contractual increases in those payments. If payments are less than those implied by the debiting rate, negative amortization can occur.

Shared equity mortgage (SEM) grants the lender title to a portion of the property. For example, a home costing $200,000 could be bought for $160,000 if a lender buys $40,000. Then, if the home appreciates, the lender receives his or her share of the appreciation realized at sale. Typically, the lender's share will be less than 30% to encourage the resident homeowner to maintain the home. The borrower pays all insurance, property taxes, and maintenance, and, if the lender believes that appreciation will be less (greater) than his or her cost of funds, they will require higher (lower) interest rates.

Growing equity mortgage (GEM) is similar to a GPM in the sense that payments increase each year. However, unlike a GPM, no negative amortization is allowed. This means that the growing payments reduce the mortgage principal at a faster rate. (Note: If you make sure that your mortgage does not have a penalty for prepayment, you can create your own GEM with the option of paying the contractual payment if events occur which prohibit you from making the larger, required payment in a contractual GEM.)

Reverse mortgage will be increasingly seen in our mortgage marketplace, as elderly baby boomers attempt to fund their retirement from the equity in their home—without having to move! A reverse mortgage allows elderly homeowners to have access to their housing equity without selling the home. Their equity is annuitized over either a fixed period or life, and their mortgage balance grows to be repaid when they move or sell the home. The reverse mortgage is increasing in availability and popularity as a source of retirement income.

REFINANCING

If a homeowner has a high fixed rate loan and interest rates have decreased, the homeowner can refinance to a fixed rate loan with a lower rate of interest. In other words, a homeowner simply applies for a new loan (with a lower rate of interest) at the same bank, or a new bank, and pays off the original loan. Many borrowers will refinance for more than what they owe on the original loan and use the difference to finance other consumption, such as the purchase of a car or their children's education.

On the other hand, a consumer with an adjustable rate loan may want to lock in a low fixed rate loan. The benefits of a lower interest rate loan are lower payments every month as well as faster principal amortization. However, there are closing costs (loan origination, appraisal, and legal fees) and, possibly, a prepayment penalty and the payment of points on the new loan. Moreover, if the term of the new loan is greater than the number of years remaining on the original contract, those future payments are also a cost. In calculating the benefit of refinancing, the time value of money must be remembered. If one refinances for the remaining term of the original mortgage, then the sum of all costs of refinancing is a present value. The benefits occur over time, as each month the monthly payment is less.

A useful calculation is to sum all costs of refinancing as a present value (PV), enter the difference between the old and new payments as the payment (PMT), use the lower rate of mortgage interest as "I/YR" (entered as a monthly figure, or annually with your P/YR set to 12), and solve for "N."[1] This procedure will calculate the approximate time it will take to "break even," while accounting for the time value of money. That is, the time it takes for the monthly savings to equal the opportunity costs of refinancing. If your expected residency is as long or longer than the number of months (N) it will take to recoup your costs on a present value basis, then refinancing is preferred.

Consider the following; you are considering refinancing an 8.75% loan *1 year after* obtaining the loan. We will assume a loan for $84,869 for 20 years and your new loan rate will be 7.5%. The cost to

---

[1] For simplicity, we will ignore the tax-deductibility of mortgage interest in this example. Including it would lengthen the discounted payback period slightly.

refinance is $1,500. How long will it take for your monthly savings (due to a lower monthly payment with the lower rate loan) to equal the cost of refinancing?

> Cost to refinance 1 year after original loan obtained = $ 1,500
> Monthly payment on **original loan**   = $750.00
> ($84,869 loan @ **8.75%** for 20 years)

Remaining balance on original loan:

> PMT = <750>
> I/YR = 8.75 / 12, or 8.75% with P/YR = 12
> N   = 19 × 12 = 228 (the number of years remaining × 12)
> PV   = $83,231 (remaining loan balance after 1 year)

> Monthly payment on **new loan**   = $685.89
> ($83,231 loan @ **7.5%** for 19 years)

> Monthly savings   = $ 64.11
> ($750 − $685.89 = $64.11)

Number of months to break even (i.e., recover the cost of refinancing):

> PMT = 64.11 (monthly savings)
> PV   = <1,500> (cost to refinance)
> I/YR = 7.5 / 12 (the lower interest rate loan, or 7.5% with P/YR=12)
> **N   = 25.4 months**

If you plan to live in the home for more than 2 years, it will be profitable to refinance. If you plan to move out of the home in 1 year, do not refinance.

Sometimes the goal of refinancing may not be to reduce the monthly payment, but rather to pay off the loan more rapidly. This would be accomplished by refinancing at a lower interest rate and reducing the length of the new loan. For example, using the same example as above, if the new loan (the "refinance loan") is amortized over 15 years instead of 19:

> Monthly payment on **new loan**   = $771.56
> ($83,231 loan @ 7.5% for *15 years*)

The new monthly payment of $771.56 is more than the original monthly payment of $750. The rationale for choosing this option is to retire the mortgage loan faster and, in doing so, reduce the total amount of interest paid.

POINTS

A **point** equals 1% of the mortgage loan. "Paying points" to the lender allows the borrower to obtain a lower rate of interest on the loan. For example, consider the following two loans.

> Loan A: 30-year fixed rate of 9% with 0 points
> Loan B: 30-year fixed rate of 8.25% with 1.5 points

Using a loan of $172,960, Loan B be could be obtained if the borrower were willing to pay points equal to $2,594.40 (calculation is $172,960 × .015). By doing so, the monthly payment would be reduced to $1,299.39 from $1,391.67 with Loan A—a monthly savings of $92.28.

> *Question:* How long would it take for the monthly savings with Loan B to pay for the cost of the points? (often referred to as the "break-even period")

> Monthly savings of Loan B: $92.28
> Cost of points in Loan B: $2,594.40

To solve for the "break-even period" (n) use the following approach:

PMT = $92.28 (monthly savings)
PV = <2,594.40> (the cost of points)
I/YR = 8.25% / 12 (time value of money)
N = 31.35 months to "break even"

If the borrower lived in the home for at least 32 months paying the points to obtain a lower interest rate would be a wise choice. After 32 months, the monthly savings of $92.28 for the 8.25% loan would have fully reimbursed the owner for the initial cost of the 1.5 points. Every month after that, the home buyer would experience a savings of $92.28, which would hopefully be saved for other financial goals. Plus, the total amount of interest paid over the life of the 30-year loan would be reduced.

Loan A total interest paid = $1,391.67 × 360 = $501,001.20 − $172,960 = **$328,041.20**

Loan B total interest paid = $1,299.39 × 360 = $467,780.40 − $172,960 = **$294,820.40**

Paying points, to obtain a lower interest rate, is optional. Points make more sense when you plan to be in the home for a longer period of time.

Costs of Obtaining a Home Mortgage Loan

Closing costs and **mortgage insurance (MI)** are just two examples of a variety of costs incurred when originating a mortgage. Below is an example of common costs involved in buying a home, with and without mortgage insurance (assume 0.5% for 41 months).

	Without Mortgage Insurance	With Mortgage Insurance
Purchase Price of Home	$82,500	$82,500
LTV (loan-to-value) Ratio	.80	.95
Loan Amount	$66,000	$78,375
Number of Payments (15-year loan)	180	180
Down Payment	$16,500	$4,125
Annual Interest Rate	6%	6%
Estimated Loan Costs:		
Credit report	$40	$40
Appraisal	$250	$250
Recording fees	$45	$45
Loan fees (1 "point")	$660	$784
Owner's title policy		
Lender's title policy	$50	$50
Mortgage insurance (yearly amt)(PMI)		**$392**
Mortgage ins. (2 months escrow)(PMI)		**$66**
Property Insurance policy (1 year)	$300	$300
Property Insurance (escrow)	$50	$50
Taxes (escrow)	$154	$154
Legal fees	$45	$45
Prepaid interest		

	Without Mortgage Insurance	With Mortgage Insurance
Termite inspection	$48	$48
Survey		
Prorated taxes		
Total Estimated **Closing Costs**	**$1,642**	**$2,224**
Total Cash Required at Closing	$18,142	$6,763
Components of Monthly Payment (PITI & MI)		
Principal and interest (P and I)	$556.95	$661.37
Monthly property taxes (T)	$77	$77
Monthly homeowners insurance (I)	$25	$25
Mortgage insurance (PMI)		**$33**
Total Monthly Payment	**$658.95**	**$796.37**

The example on the previous page outlines many of the costs incurred when purchasing a home. *If* a person purchased a home by paying cash, some of the costs would be avoided, such as a credit report, loan fees, mortgage insurance, and prepaid interest. Yet, very few individuals have the ability to pay cash for a home.

MORTGAGE INSURANCE

The comparison on the previous page compares a mortgage loan with and without **mortgage insurance**. Simply put, mortgage insurance is required when the buyer of the home borrows more than 80% of purchase price (or in other words makes a down payment in cash of less than 20% of the purchase price). A lender (bank or credit union) takes greater risk in lending more than 80% of the purchase price to the home buyer, as homeowners with less equity are more likely to default on the loan.

Mortgage insurance may be obtained from several organizations such as: PMI companies, Federal Housing Administration, or Veterans Administration (VA) Mortgage Insurance. PMI is obtained through a private company instead of a governmental agency. In the example on the previous page, PMI was estimated at 0.5%, although the cost usually varies from 0.25% to 2.0%. The Federal Housing Administration under the U.S. Department of Housing and Urban Development (HUD) insures houses where the home purchaser meets specific standards. VA Mortgage Insurances promotes homeownership amongst military veterans. Borrowers can drop PMI when the equity in their home or the principal balance falls below the 80% threshold; however, this may take several years.

For example, consider a home selling for $100,000. Joe Dokes wants to buy the home. He obtains a mortgage loan for $95,000 (or 95% of the purchase price). Two months later, Joe Dokes disappears and so do his monthly mortgage payments to Union Bank. Union Bank now takes possession of the home (this is commonly referred to as **foreclosure**) and attempts to sell it on the open market. If the home sells for only $90,000, the bank would have lost roughly $5,000. Had Union Bank required Joe Dokes to purchase mortgage insurance, the loss of $5,000 would have been reimbursed to Union Bank by the mortgage insurance company.

Mortgage insurance insures the lender against loss down to 80% of the purchase price of the home. So, using the same example, if Union Bank sold the home for $80,000, they would have their loss of $15,000 reimbursed (loss = loan amount − foreclosure selling price).

In the prior example, the home loan with a LTV ratio of .80 does not require mortgage insurance. When the buyer makes a larger down payment, the lender is taking less risk of losing money if the buyer defaults. Compared to the 95% LTV loan (requiring MI), the 80% LTV loan has a:

- larger down payment ($16,500 vs. $4,125)
- smaller monthly payment ($658.95 vs. $808.37) and
- fewer closing costs (other than down payment) ($1,642 vs. $2,638)

To compare your cost with and without mortgage insurance, check out http://www.mortgageloan.com/calculator.

HOW MUCH HOME CAN YOU AFFORD?

There is a generally accepted rule that states that you can afford a house that costs 2.5 times your annual income. Or, stated differently, your annual income should at least equal 40% of the house price. Such rules are designed to get you in the "ballpark." But, we can do better than that.

Another method for determining how much house you can afford is to use debt ratios. We can calculate several debt ratios using the data from the previous pages. The total housing payment or PITI (principal, interest, taxes, and insurance) with a large down payment (and therefore no mortgage insurance) was $658.95. Assuming you want your total housing payment (PITI) of $658.95 to equal 25% of your gross income, how much monthly gross income would you need to earn?

$$\frac{\text{Monthly housing payment}}{\text{Housing debt ratio}} = \text{Needed monthly income}$$

$$\frac{\$659}{.25} = \textbf{\$2,636 monthly gross income needed}$$

A monthly gross income of $2,636 equals an annual gross income of $31,632. Using 25% as your housing debt ratio is fairly conservative. If you use a ratio of .30, you would need only a monthly income of $2,197. But are you really wise to use a higher ratio? It depends on how much other debt you have. If you have a lot of debt payments (such as an auto loan, student loans, credit card payments, etc.), you are wise to use a lower housing debt ratio—otherwise you will end up *house rich and cash poor*.

For example, assume you have the following monthly debt payments:

Student loan		$112
Auto loan	+	$143
Credit card payment	+	$63
Total non-housing debt payments	=	$318
Total housing debt payment	+	$659
Total monthly debt payments	=	$977

How much income will be needed to make total debt payments of $977 per month? Lenders will commonly allow a borrower to allocate from 30% to 35% of their monthly gross income to total monthly debt payments.

Using the more conservative ratio of 30%:

$977 / .30 = **$3,257 needed monthly gross income or $39,084 annual gross income.**

Using the more liberal ratio of 35%:

$977 / .35 = **$2,791 needed monthly gross income or $33,492 annual gross income.**

There is a great temptation for homebuyers to use the more liberal ratio. The problem is this:

> **As you allocate a higher percentage of your income to debt, you have less money left over for everything else (recreation, entertainment, saving, investing, landscaping, furniture, food, charitable giving, gifts to your university, etc.)**

> Repeat after me: *Avoid being house rich and cash poor.*

Assume you graduate and get a job which pays you $52,000 annually, or $4,333 monthly gross income. How much home can you afford, assuming you've student loans, auto loans, and credit card debt.?

$4,333 × .30 = $1,300 available for total debt payments

$1,300	available for total monthly debt payments
− $ 112	monthly student loan payment
− $ 143	monthly auto loan payment
− $ 63	monthly credit card payment
$ 982	**available for monthly housing payment**

How much home can you buy for $982 per month? We recognize this may not be the home of your dreams. To find out, we will first subtract the taxes and insurance (T&I) component out of $982. We will assume that monthly T&I equals $82. That leaves $900 available for payment on principal and interest (P&I). Assume a 30-year mortgage loan at 5% annual interest. Now we can solve for PV, or in other words, the amount of mortgage loan that a monthly payment of $900 would qualify for.

PMT = <900>
N   = 30 × 12 = 360
I/YR = .05 / 12 = .005 (or I/YR = 5, if P/YR = 12 on a financial calculator)
PV   = 167,653.45 mortgage loan

Assuming you have a 10% down payment, what is the most you could pay for a home? (Recall the following: (1) a 10% down payment equates to a 90% loan-to-value ratio, and (2) the PV in a housing scenario equals the loan amount.)

$$\frac{PV}{\text{Loan-to-value ratio}} = \text{Maximum home price}$$

$$\frac{\$167,653}{.90} = **\$186,281**$$

Just for comparison, the median price of an existing single-family home in the United States, in November of 2013, was about $271,000. What does all this mean? Three things:

1. You must not expect to leave school and promptly buy the house of your dreams. The home you remember leaving as an 18-year-old is often quite different than the one your parents started out in. Young home buyers have a tendency to base their expectations on the home of their teenage years. Before you go out looking for your first home, take a few minutes and look at pictures of the home your parents bought when they were first-time home buyers! That will help you "recalibrate" your housing expectations. People living in bigger homes are not necessarily happier.

2. Leaving school with debt (student loans, auto debt, and big credit card balances) makes it more difficult to qualify for a home loan. Do yourself a favor: *minimize your debt load now*.

   Now, let us run the numbers again without other monthly debt payments (student loan, credit card, auto loan). Assuming that your monthly T&I equals $200, your maximum monthly P&I would be $1,182.

   $$PMT \ = \ <1,182>$$
   $$n \quad = \quad 30 \times 12 = 360$$
   $$i \quad = \quad .05 \, / \, 12 = \text{(or I/YR = 5\%, with P/YR = 12; financial calculator)}$$
   $$\textbf{PV} \quad = \quad \textbf{220,185 mortgage loan}$$

   Max home price = 220,185 / .90 = $244,650

   Do yourself a favor. Borrow little, while going to school. Doing so will make it more feasible to purchase a home when the time is right.

3. You may be tempted to use a higher debt ratio so as to qualify for a greater mortgage loan. Try to resist the temptation to go beyond a total monthly debt payment of 35%. Reputable lenders will help you restrain yourself. Lenders do not want you to over-extend yourself on total debt payments. They want you to be able to make your monthly payments for years and years.

Assignment 7.2   Home Affordability

Name _____

SHOW YOUR WORK

You have just graduated from State University with a degree in Diesel Technology. Your new job takes you to Toledo, Ohio. You are now earning $35,000 per year. Your take-home pay is 70% of that gross total. You are anxious to purchase a home. You have the following monthly expenses:

Food	$275
Utilities	$145
Phone	$75
Medical	$30
Insurance	$130 (including auto, health, and life)
Clothing	$70
Student loan payment	$145
VISA payment	$65
MasterCard payment	$48
Car payment	$211
Miscellaneous	$100
Total	$_____

1. First calculate your monthly take-home pay. Next, add up the budgeted monthly expenses shown above. How much remains for a monthly mortgage PITI payment?

2. Assume that taxes and insurance (T&I) amount to $70 per month. How much remains to pay monthly mortgage principal and interest (P&I)?

3. Using the answer to question #2 calculate the size of mortgage loan you could obtain. Assume a 30-year loan at 5% annual interest.

4. Using the answer from question #3, and assuming you have 10% of the purchase price, what is the most you could pay for a home?

5. Assuming you do not pay the mortgage off early, how much interest will you pay the lender over the life of the loan?

Section Seven Extra Practice Problems

1. Assume a $170,000 mortgage loan over 30 years with a 7% annual interest rate.
   a. What will be the monthly mortgage payment?

   b. On your first payment, what portion of the monthly payment goes toward interest?

   c. On your first payment, what portion of the monthly payment goes toward principal?

   d. How much will you end up paying back to the lender over the life of the loan? How much of this is interest?

2. Assume a mortgage loan of $80,500 and 7% annual interest.
   a. If you pay the loan off over 30 years, how much interest will you pay?

   b. How much interest will you pay after 20 years?

   c. How much interest will you pay after 15 years?

   d. Compared to the 30-year mortgage, how much interest will you save by going to a 15-year mortgage?

3. Use the following information for the remaining problems:

   You earn $57,800 per year and take home 70% of that gross amount. Your monthly expenses are as follows:

Food	$325
Utilities	$120
Phone	$75
Medical	$45
All insurance	$120
Clothing	$60
Student loan payment	$200
VISA payment	$140
Car payment	$249
Miscellaneous	$120

a. What are your total monthly expenses?

b. What is your monthly take-home pay?

c. After monthly expenses, how much do you have left over for a monthly mortgage PITI payment?

d. Assuming taxes and insurance (T&I) are $90 per month. How much remains for monthly mortgage principal and interest (P&I)?

e. Calculate the size of a mortgage loan you can afford. Use a 30year loan at 6.5% annual interest.

f. If you have 10% of the purchase price for a down payment, what is the most you can pay for a home?

4. You are considering a 30-year mortgage loan of $195,000. You have been offered a rate of 6.5% with no points or 6% at 2 points.
a. What would be the cost of the 2 points?

b. What would your monthly savings be if you paid the points?

c. How long would it take for the monthly savings to break even?

Section Seven Practice Problem Answers

1. PV   =   170,000
   N   =   30 × 12 = 360
   I/YR   =   7 / 12, or I/YR = 7, and P/YR = 12

   a. PMT = **<1,131.01>**

   b. 170,000 × (.07/12) = $991.67 goes toward interest

   c. 1,131.01 − 991.67 = $139.34 goes toward principal

   d. $1,131.01 × 360 months = $407,163.60 total gross payments $407,163.60 − 170,000
           = **$3,237,163.60 total interest paid**

2. a. PV   =   80,500
      n   =   30 × 12
      i   =   7 / 12
      PMT =   **<535.57>**
                     $535.57 × 360 = $192,805.20
                     $192,805.20 − $80,500 = **$112,305.20**

   b. PV   =   80,500
      n   =   20 × 12
      i   =   7 / 12
      PMT =   **<624.12>**
                     $624.12 × 240 = $149,788.80
                     $149,788.80 − $80,500 = **$69,288.80**

   c. PV   =   80,500
      n   =   15 × 12
      i   =   7 / 12
      PMT =   **<723.56>**
                     $723.56 × 180 = $130,240.80
                     $130,240.80 − $80,500 = **$49,740.80**

   d. $112,305.20 − $49,740.80 = **$62,564.40**

3. a. (add all amounts) = **$1,454.00**

   b. (57,800 × .7) / 12 = **$3,371.67**

   c. $3,371.67 − $1,454 = **$1,917.67**

   d. 1,917.67 − 90 = **$1,827.67**

   e. PMT =   **<1,827.67>**
      n   =   30 × 12
      i   =   6.5 / 12
      PV   =   **289,157.17**

   f. 104,577.35 / .90 = **$321,285.74**

4. a. $195,000 \times .02 = $ **3,900**

   b. PV   =   195,000   PV   =   195,000
       n   = 30×12 n   = 30×12
       i   =   6.5 / 12   i   =   6 / 12
       PMT =   <1,232.53>   PMT =   <1,169.12>

                 $1,232.53 - 1,169.12 = $ **\$63.41**

   c. PMT =   <63.41>
       PV   =   3,900
       i   =   6 / 12
       n   =   **71.21 months**

Notes:

Investing

Invest in yourself. Your career is the engine of your wealth.

Paul Clitheroe (1955–)

You get recessions. You have stock market declines. If you don't understand that's going to happen, then you are not ready. You won't do well in the markets.

Peter Lynch (1944–)

I will tell you how to become rich. Close the doors. Be fearful when others are greedy. Be greedy when others are fearful.

Warren Buffett (1930–)

The most powerful force in the universe is compound interest.

Albert Einstein (1879–1955)

INVESTING VERSUS SPECULATING

Investing is, by definition and by its very nature, a long-term proposition. Parents invest a great deal of time and energy into children. Corporations often invest millions of dollars into new technology that will not provide a return for many years. People who take a long-run perspective understand the nature of investing. Investing implies stewardship, while owning an asset.

Speculating, on the other hand, is a desire for a gain in the short term. Such gains are only available by taking on greater risk. Speculation can be exhilarating. "Once-in-a-lifetime opportunities" are usually speculative. It is not possible to receive an extraordinary gain, without taking extraordinary risk. Let's repeat that point. Extraordinary gains are not possible without taking extraordinary risks. This is what makes financial markets work.

Financial stewardship implies an *investing* perspective. Lifelong investing is just that a disciplined process of saving the income that you earn in order to accumulate wealth to support your financial goals.

Investment Attributes

Investments can be characterized by the following five attributes:

1. **Return**
2. **Risk**
3. **Liquidity**
4. **Tax aspects**
5. **Manageability**

Return

Wealth can increase only if money is invested so that the average after-tax return exceeds the rate of inflation. Returns come in two forms: **periodic income** (in the form of interest, rent, or dividends) or **capital appreciation** (selling the asset for more than it was purchased). Return figures are most commonly reported as a percentage, such as 12.50% per year. For example, if you invest $10,000 in stock of ACME Corporation and 10 years later the stock is worth $29,500, what has been your *holding-period* return if it pays no dividends?

The equation to calculate the holding-period return (total cumulative percentage return) is:

$$\frac{\text{Sum of dividends + Selling price}}{\text{Purchase price}} - 1 = \text{Total cumulative return}$$

$$\frac{0 + 29,500}{10,000} - 1 = 1.95 \text{ or } 195\% \text{ holding-period return}$$

The above "holding-period return" formula is also known as "percentage change." You may have this function built into your calculator. The HP10II key strokes would be 10,000 <INPUT> 29,500 <yellow key> <%CHG>.

Another method of determining return is to calculate **average annual compound rate of return (i.e., average return per year).** This is not the arithmetic mean. It is the **geometric mean return.**

PV   = <10,000>
FV   = 29,500
N   = 10
I/YR = 11.425%

11.425% equals the compound rate of return over the 10-year period. Of the two measures of return shown earlier, the *average annualized, compound return* (i.e., 11.425%) is a more commonly reported figure than total holding-period return (195%).

Risk

Risk is not bad. Nor is it inherently good. Financial markets exist because people are willing to accept risk and the chance that the outcome will deviate from what is expected. This deviation is what we commonly call risk. On average, investors only accept greater risk when they expect a greater return. Those who will only accept low risk invest in low-risk investments and, on average, receive a lower return. Investors who can tolerate more risk create "a market" for higher risk investment products.

The sources of risk that exist in investments need to be understood by investors in order to appropriately manage and diversify their portfolios. The sources of risk are:

Business risk: The chance that a business may fail, or have lower success than expected. At the extreme, a firm could go bankrupt. On the other hand, a firm's earnings could grow at a rate that is much greater than expected. Both are deviations from expectations and are, therefore, risk.

Financing risk: The amount of debt (borrowed money) relative to equity (ownership) that finances the company is considering investing in is a measure of financial risk. Companies with less debt, like people, are better able to withstand economic downturns than their counterparts who rely heavily upon borrowed money. Moreover, companies that borrow money to finance their operations are much more vulnerable to changes in interest rates.

Market risk: A psychological risk where investors, as if *en masse*, become more willing (bullish) or less willing (bearish) to invest. When investors are willing to invest, the market is bid up. When a majority of investors are unwilling to invest, markets fall. Market risk is the most common "risk" (i.e., cause of deviations) in investing and can come from many sources; including Twitter.

Interest rate risk: If interest rates rise (fall), then the values of outstanding fixed rate securities fall (rise). Securities such as bonds pay periodic interest and income-oriented stocks pay dividends. Thus, they are more susceptible to interest rate risk.

Purchasing power (inflation) risk: The risk that the monetary return of an investment will have less "purchasing power" than expected due to rates of inflation exceeding the after-tax returns of the investment.

Exchange rate risk: With investments in foreign securities there is risk that the exchange rate between the dollar and the foreign currency will change. For example, when the U.S. dollar weakens (i.e., depreciates against foreign currencies), foreign currencies can purchase more U.S. dollars, which increases the returns on foreign investments for U.S. investors. Obviously, the opposite is true when the U.S. dollar strengthens against foreign currencies.

Liquidity

Liquidity refers to how quickly an asset can be converted to cash at its full value. Money market accounts are very liquid. Stocks are moderately liquid, since they can be sold quite readily and, depending on where the stocks are kept, the cash can be more, or less, quickly accessed. On the contrary, real estate can be difficult to sell immediately at the desired price and is, therefore, illiquid.

Tax aspects

If you are eligible to invest without paying taxes on the principal, it is generally preferred to invest the money without first paying taxes. If taxation of investment income can be delayed, it is generally best to delay taxation. This is true if tax rates are expected to stay the same or decrease. On the other hand, if taxes are expected to increase in the future, one would do better to pay taxes first and to not pay taxes later. (This is really a math problem that can be quite complicated, as it involves so many unknowns.)

All investments are not taxed identically. Hence, it is important to understand the taxation differences between investments.

Manageability

Ask, "How much work is required to manage my investments. Do I enjoy it?" Managing a portfolio of stocks and/or bonds will likely require less work (at least physically) than investing in llamas or real estate. Yet, if you know how to manage a stock of llamas and you have a place to do it but you do not know a stock from a bond, investing in llamas might be the best option for you.

INVESTMENT ALTERNATIVES

Investments are broadly classified as either equity investments or debt investments. An **equity investment** implies ownership, such as when purchasing shares of the common stock issued by a corporation. A **debt investment** implies lending, as when you purchase a bond (corporate or government). By this act, you are lending money to the original seller of the bond. Therefore, the originator of the bond is the debtor, while the buyer of the bond is the lender. Therefore, when purchasing a Treasury Bill you are actually lending money to the U.S. government. The Treasury, in turn, promises to pay you interest in addition to repaying the principal.

> **Equity Investments**
> Common stock
> Preferred stock
> Common stock mutual funds

Debt Investments

Government bonds

Corporate bonds

Bond mutual funds

Treasury securities (bills, notes, bonds)

Alternative Investments

Real estate

Precious metals

Commodities

Collectibles (i.e., paintings, coins, stamps, etc.)

EQUITY INVESTMENTS

Common Stock

Shares of common stock represent ownership of a publicly held corporation. Companies sell stock to acquire money to build buildings, buy more trucks, hire more people, and so on. When a company sells shares of stock, it gives up a portion of the ownership of the corporation to the investors purchasing the shares of common stock. Investors gain if the price of the stock increases and/or if the board of directors votes to pay out profits in the form of dividends[1].

Small, new companies offer the potential for dramatic growth in stock prices. For example, if we adjust the price of Wal-Mart, a small company in 1972, for all the stock splits since it became public, the stock sold for $0.04 per share in 1972. In mid 2018, however, Wal-Mart stock had risen in value to over $98.75 per share. In other words, had you purchased 100 shares in 1972 (at a 1972 cost of $1,650) you would have owned Wal-Mart shares worth $4,061,482 in 2018. That amount of gain over a 46-year period equates to a 18.5% compound return per year. Unfortunately, it is more common for the stock of new companies to decline—ultimately disappearing from the financial pages as the company goes out of business. Money invested in such a company is lost.

Established companies (e.g., Ford, DuPont, General Electric, etc.) generally do not offer the spectacular share price gains of smaller companies. As a result, larger, more established companies commonly pay dividends to stockholders. A dividend is either paid in cash or in stock—both are taxable in the year they are received. Investing in the stock of large companies does have the potential for capital gains, but they may not be as dramatic and they may take an extended period of time (5–10 years) to materialize.

Small, new companies generally do not pay dividends. All earnings are retained and "invested" back into the company to facilitate growth. For quality, new companies, the capital gain potential can be spectacular, even over a short period of time (1–3 years). It is also quite possible for your investment to be worth nothing more than the paper it is written on.

The "profit" (or total return) from owning common stock comes in two forms:

Income   = Dividends
Capital gain (loss) = Buying stock at a low (high) price and later
                        selling stock at a higher (lower) price

---

[1] In lieu of selling stock to raise money, companies can borrow money. When they borrow, the companies do not share ownership but, instead, are obligated to pay interest to a bank or to bondholders, as well as repay the principal. When companies sell stock, they share ownership with investors, but do not have to pay anything to equity investors.

Preferred Stock

Preferred stock is a hybrid security. It possesses some characteristics of common stock and yet preferred stock is very similar to a bond. Like common stock, it represents ownership (or equity) in a company. However, like a bond that pays interest, preferred stock pays a relatively high, fixed dividend. Moreover, preferred stock has no maturity when you are repaid the "principal." As a result, preferred stock is more like a perpetual bond—a debt that pays interest without the repayment of principal.

"Preferred" means that if a company goes bankrupt and is forced to liquidate its assets, the preferred stockholder receives the par value (the dollar value assigned to each share when originally issued) of the preferred stock before the common stockholders receive anything. As such, preferred stock is closer to a bond than a stock unless it is "participating preferred" stock. Participating preferred stock allows the dividends of the preferred stock to increase if the firm does well.

A firm's preferred stock offers a higher dividend—often substantially higher—yield than the firm's common stock. The dividend, however, is fixed, meaning that it is constant over time. The opportunity for dramatic capital gains (a large increase in the price per share) in preferred stock is much lower than for common stock and typically occurs only if interest rates decrease.

HOW TO READ STOCK LISTINGS

Below is an example of a stock listing from Yahoo.com. Similar listings are published in the *Wall Street Journal* and other websites such as http://www.nasdaq.com, among others. The company is Molson Coors Brewing Company. This information is from midday on August 16, 2018.

Molson Coors Brewing Company (TAP)

-NYSE
68.06 + 0.90 (+1.34%) 2:52 PM EST - Nasdaq Real Time Price
Add to Portfolio

Prev Close:	**67.18**		Day's Range:	**67.21 – 68.21**
Open:	**67.41**		52 wk Range:	**58.75 – 91.52**
Bid:	**67.39 × 200**		Volume:	**682,814**
Ask:	**67.45 × 100**		Avg Vol (3 m):	**2,447,387**
1 y Target Est:	**76.79**		Market Cap:	**14.696B**
Beta:	**0.43**		P/E (ttm):	**9.35**
Next Earnings Date:	**31-Oct-18**		EPS (ttm):	**7.28**
			Div & Yield:	**1.64 (2.41%)**

Following the name of the company, in parentheses you will see TAP. TAP is the symbol for Molson Coors, and every publicly traded security has a unique symbol. Some are quite intuitive. For example, the following are familiar companies and symbols: General Electric (GE), Ford (F), General Motors (GM), International Business Machines (IBM), and Minnesota Mining and Manufacturing (MMM). Others have familiar names with symbols you may not have guessed: Allegheny Corporation (Y), Nordstrom (JWN), and AT&T (T). While others are suggestive of their culture: Southwest Airlines (LUV), as well as Molson Coors (TAP). Regardless of the company, knowing the symbol is the fastest way to find information on the company, although most websites will translate from the company name to the symbol.

Let us take this line-by-line and explain the meaning of each term:

> Molson Coors Brewing Company (TAP) = the name of the company, followed by its symbol, TAP.
>
> -NYSE = the stock is traded on the NYSE (New York Stock Exchange)

68.06 + 0.90 (1.34%) 2:52PM EST - Nasdaq Real Time Price = The stock last traded at $68.06, which is up $0.90 from the previous day's close, or 1.34% more.

- The previous trading day the stock closed (Prev. Close) at $67.18.
- Today, the stock has traded (Day's Range) from a low price of $67.21 to a high price of $68.21.
- The stock's first trade of the day (Open) was for $67.41.
- During the last year (52 wk range), the stock sold for a low price of $58.75 and a high price of $91.52.
- The current price the market maker is willing to pay for the stock (Bid:) is $67.39 and he or she is willing to buy 200 shares at that price.
- The number of shares of TAP that have been bought/sold today (Volume:) has been 682,814 shares. (Volume, when multiplied by the current price would be $46,472,321 in TAP changing hands today!)
- The current price the market maker is willing to sell the stock (Ask:) is $67.45 and he or she is willing to buy 100 shares at that price. (Note that the difference between the Bid and the Ask price is $0.06 per share. This is where the market maker makes his or her money.)
- The average daily volume over the past 3 months (Avg Vol (3 m)) is 2,447,387 shares.
- The average analyst estimate of the price of this stock in 1 year (1 y Target Est:) is $76.79.
- If one multiplies all the shares of TAP times the current price of the stock, one calculates the Market Cap: which is $14.696 Billion.
- A measure of the relative volatility of this stock to the market as a whole is known as Beta. TAP has a Beta of 0.43, indicating that it moves with less than half of the volatility of the market the overall stock market, as it is equal to 0.43.
- If one takes the price per share of the stock and divides it by the earnings per share of the stock, one calculates the P/E ratio. This is a measure of how much you have to pay per dollar of earnings of the company. These vary by industry and, within an industry, by company. A low number indicates either greater value or that the market believes less in the future of this firm. It is true that it is generally preferred to buy a stock when its P/E is close to the lower end of its historical range.
- TAP will next report earnings on October 31, 2018 (31-Oct-18).
- Molson Coors had earnings per share of $7.28 during the past 12 months. Of course, one wants to see earnings increase over time and more data on this can be found under "key statistics" tab on the left margin of the Yahoo website. (Take an investments course, if you would like to be taught more about this!)
- From the Div & Yield: we determine that the current annual dividend is $1.64 per share that represents a dividend yield, as a percentage, of 2.46% ([1.64 / 68.06] × 100 = 2.41%, rounded to 2.3%).

Stock Exchanges

NYSE Euronext—The NYSE is, perhaps, the most well-known stock exchange in the world and was purchased in December 20, 2012 by the Intercontinental Exchange (ICE) for $8 billion. The NYSE Euronext was the holding company formed by combining the NYSE Group, Inc. and Euronext N.V.. Prior to the purchase by ICE, NYSE Euronext fueled the world of investing by providing trading in cash, equities, futures, options, fixed income, and exchange-traded products.

The Dow Jones Industrial Index (30 very large companies) is often reported by the media as a representative index of the performance of the United States' stock markets. However, the Standard and Poor's 500 Index (S&P 500) is a more reliable index as it includes 500 of the largest companies traded in the United States. An index of 500 stocks is more representative of the entire market than is a smaller sample of 30 stocks.

NASDAQ (National Association of Security Dealers Automated Quotation System)—Typically, the stocks of smaller, newer companies are traded in the NASDAQ market. However, the stocks of larger companies are also traded on this market, such as Microsoft, Intel, and Novell. The stock of over 3,000 companies are traded in the NASDAQ market.

STOCK ORDERS

Market Order

A market order is an order to buy or sell shares at the market price that exists when the order reaches the exchange. If you want to buy the stock of Twitter (symbol is TWTR), immediately, you would call a broker and place a market order to purchase Twitter. Within seconds after calling, you would own Twitter stock. This type of order assumes that you know what the current price of the stock is, and that you are willing to pay or receive, if you are selling, the price that exists at the time of trade. It may be different from the price you are told from the brokerage company.

Remember that a market order is an order to buy or sell a stock at the best available *current* price. Market orders do not require an execution at a specific price or within a price range. With market orders, the order is generally assured to be executed; however, there is no limit on the execution price. Unfortunately, if the price changes, you will pay (or receive) whatever the market price is when your order is executed.

Limit Order

When you place a limit order, you specify a price at which you want to buy or sell a stated number of shares. Limit orders guard against executions at prices the person or firm placing the trade is not willing to accept. There are trade-offs, of course. The order may not be executed if the market suddenly moves away from the suggested limit price and there is a greater cost of placing a limit order, compared to a market order.

Limit buy order—If you wanted to buy Ford Motor stock (symbol = F), but felt the price might decline in the near future, you could place a limit buy order. If Ford is currently trading at $9.51 per share, you might place a limit order to buy 100 shares at $9.45. Your limit buy order would be acted upon by the broker when Ford stock declines to $9.45 per share or lower.

Limit sell order—If you currently own Wal-Mart stock (symbol = WMT) and are willing to sell it at this price, you could place a limit sell order. If Wal-Mart stock was currently trading at $98 per share, you could place a limit sell order with a broker to sell the stock at $99 per share, not less.

Stop-loss order—A stop-loss order is a limit sell order where you set a price at which you would like the sale of stock to occur. Unlike the limit sell order, a stop-loss order will set a sales price below the current trading price of the stock you may want to sell, should prices fall. This is to protect you should prices fall quickly. As an example, you purchased 100 shares of Netflix (symbol = NFLX) stock 6 months ago. You paid $244 per share. Now, NFLX is trading at $323. You have made a tidy little profit ($79 per share $\times$ 100 shares = $7,900, less broker commissions).

Not knowing what the stock market is going to do, you may choose to place a stop-loss order to sell your NFLX stock at $315. In other words, if the price of NFLX stock starts to decline, the broker will sell the stock if it hits $315 per share. In this way you stop your loss. However, if the price of NFLX is falling very rapidly, the price may be even lower—through no fault of your broker—he or she simply could not find a buyer at $315.

Another use of a stop-loss order would be to combine it with limit orders . . . all in the same phone call with your stock broker. For example, you might place a limit order to purchase IBM stock (symbol = IBM) at $140 per share (the market price is currently $145.39). You could then place a limit order to sell IBM stock (obviously the limit purchase order had to occur first) at $165 per share. Finally, you could place a stop-loss order to sell IBM at $135.

In the earlier example, you would automatically purchase IBM stock if the price hit $140 per share. Your stock would automatically be sold if the stock price increased to $165 per share, *or* if it declined to $135 per share. By selling at $135 you would lose money on this particular stock transaction, but you would *stop your loss* at $5 per share.

The risk in placing a limit order is that you might select a price that is either too high or too low, and your order will expire (unless it is placed as a "good-until-cancelled" order). If this happens, either you will not have purchased the stock you wanted to purchase or you will still own stock you wanted to sell. On the other hand, when markets react wildly, as they did on May 6, 2010 and fall close to 1,000 points on an error, computer trades forced prices even lower. If you had a limit sell order on your holding, you would have sold your holdings when the price hit the limit. The actual price received, however, may have been much lower. Then, when the error is found, markets returned to sanity and you no longer own your securities. A limit order, thus, can put you at risk. It is true, however, that most of the exchanges in the world—outside of the United States—require limit orders on trades to reduce wide swings in security prices.

STOCK SPLIT

A stock "split" is almost always a good event for an investor. In January of 2010, Berkshire Hathaway, Inc. (symbol = BRK-B) was selling for $3,476 per share. In an event that was triggered by the purchase of a railroad, BRK-B had a 50 for 1 split, lowering the price of BRK-B to $70.51 per share on the next day. The price of BRK-B was $3,476 per share (making the stock too expensive for some investors), so BRK-B decided to split the stock 50 for 1 (or 2 for 1, 3 for 1, or 4 for 1, etc.). After the split, people who already owned the stock had 50 times as many shares and the price was, approximately, 1/50th of the price prior to the split. If BRK-B stock pays a dividend, it will also decrease proportionately.

So, if you owned 100 shares worth $3,476 per share before the split, after the 50 for 1 stock split you would own 5,000 shares worth $70.51 per share, at the end of the first day of trading post-split. People who owned BRK-B stock before the split are no better off or worse off after the split.

A reverse stock split is just the opposite. It is a split that causes your number of shares to decrease, but the price per share to increase. Reverse stock splits are relatively uncommon and are typically a "last ditch" effort to artificially raise the price of a stock.

CALCULATING TOTAL HOLDING-PERIOD RETURN

The total gain (or loss) from owning stock results from:

1. Income received from dividends
2. Capital gain realized (selling price > purchase price)

   or

   Capital loss realized (selling price < purchase price)

Total Return = Dividends + Capital Gain or Capital Loss

For example:

You purchased 100 shares of CAT stock in January 2010 for $48.03 per share. Each year, we will assume you received a cash dividend of $2.00 per share. In July 2018, you sold 100 shares of CAT for $140.00 per share.

What is your **total cumulative** return (in dollars) over the 4-year period?

Eight years of dividends = ($2.00 × 8) × 100 shares = **$1600**

Capital gain = Sales value − purchase price
= $14,000 − $4,803 = **$9,197**

Total dollar return = $1600 + $4,248 = **$10,797**

What is your **holding-period** return (in percentage) over the 4-year period?

$$\text{Total Percentage Return} = \frac{\text{Dividends} + \text{Selling Price}}{\text{Purchase Price}} - 1$$

$$= \frac{\$1600 + \$10,797}{\$4,803} - 1$$

$$= \textbf{2.5811 or 158.11\% total return}$$

What is your *average annual, compound* percentage return over the 4-year period?

An accurate approach recognizes that dividends were received earlier than the capital gain. This approach accounts for the $200 in dividends, which we will assume happens once per year at the end of each year. The inputs to the formula to solve for i (rate of return) are shown as follows.

$$FV = 14,000$$
$$PMT = 200$$
$$N = 8$$
$$PV = <4,803>$$
$$\textbf{I/YR} = \textbf{17.085\% per year}$$

Brokerage Commissions

Brokerage commissions have to be paid when purchasing or selling stock. Commissions paid to a stock broker increase the cost of buying stock and reduce the proceeds received from the sale of stock. Assuming brokerage commissions (the cost to purchase and sell stock through a stock broker) amount to 4% of the total transaction value, the following would be the case for the CAT example. (If you use an online broker like Scottrade or Schwab, these costs are less than $5 per transaction!)

Brokerage cost to *purchase* 100 shares of CAT stock in 2014

($48.03 per share × 100 shares) × .04 = **$192.12**

Brokerage cost to *sell* 100 shares of CAT in 2010

($140.00 per share × 100 shares) × .04 = **$560.00**

The brokerage cost to purchase stock is *added* to the total purchase price and brokerage cost to sell stock is *deducted* from the total sale value.

Net total purchase price = $4,803 + $192.12 = $4,995.12

Net total sales value = $14,000 − $560.00 = $13,440.00

What is your *total cumulative* period return (in dollars) over the 4-year period <u>after accounting for brokerage costs</u>?

$$\text{Eight years of dividends} = (\$2.00 \times 4 \times 100 \text{ shares} = \textbf{\$1600}$$

$$\text{Capital gain} = \$13,440.00 - \$4,995.12 = \textbf{\$8,444.88}$$

$$\text{Total dollar return} = \$800 + \$8,444.88 = \textbf{\$9,244.88}$$

What is your *total cumulative* return (in percentage) over the 5-year period, after accounting for brokerage costs?

$$\text{Total Percentage Return} = \frac{\text{Dividends} + \text{Selling Price}}{\text{Purchase Price}} - 1$$

$$= \frac{\$800 + \$13,440.00}{\$4,995.12} - 1$$

$$= 1.85 \textbf{ or } \textbf{185\% total return}$$

What is your *average annual* percentage return over the 4-year period, after accounting for brokerage costs? (Bottom line – transaction costs matter.)

$$
\begin{aligned}
\text{FV} &= 13,440.00 \text{ (before-tax sales proceeds)} \\
\text{PMT} &= 200 \text{ (before-tax dividends [end of year assumed])} \\
\text{N} &= 8 \\
\text{PV} &= {<}4,995.12{>} \\
\text{I/YR} &= 15.91\% \textbf{ per year}
\end{aligned}
$$

CALCULATING *REAL, AFTER-TAX* RETURN

The return on an investment is reduced by taxes and inflation, as well as brokerage costs. Recall that the term "<u>real</u>" <u>refers to return after accounting for inflation</u>.

Taxes

Each year's dividends are taxed as they are received. If we assume the investor is in the 25% marginal tax bracket, qualified dividends and long-term capital gains will be subject to a 15% tax rate. Therefore, the after-tax dividend is $170, as shown in what follows.

$$\$200 \text{ dividend} \times (1 - .15) = \$170.00 \text{ after-tax dividend}$$

In addition, 15% of the capital gain would be paid in taxes.

$$\$8,440.88 \text{ capital gain} \times (1 - .15) = \$7,174.75 \text{ after-tax capital gain}$$

(The tax on the capital gain = $8,440.88 × .15 = $1,266.13)

We can make the assumption that the capital gains tax will be paid from the proceeds from the sale of the stock, which we will use as the FV, so the after-tax FV equals:

$$\$8,440.88 \text{ (before-tax FV)} - \$1,266.13 \text{ (capital gain tax)} = \$7,174.75$$

To calculate the after-tax rate of return (or "i"), we must change all of our inputs from the time-value-of-money problem to after-tax values:

$$FV = 7,174.75 \text{ (after-tax sale proceeds)}$$
$$PMT = 170 - \text{ (after-tax dividend payments)}$$
$$N = 8$$
$$PV = <4,995.12> \text{ (stock price plus commissions)}$$
$$\textbf{I/YR} = \textbf{8.09\% per year}$$

Therefore, the average annual compound *after-tax* rate of return, after subtracting brokerage commissions, was 8.09%.

Inflation

To account for the impact of inflation, one must reduce the nominal rate by the rate of inflation. A simple way to do this is to subtract it; however, this will not provide the correct answer in many financial problems where a *serial payment*, one that increases with inflation, is required.

You need to be using the equation introduced in Section 6, shown as follows, to determine the *real* (or inflation adjusted) *rate of return*.

$$\frac{1 + \textbf{Nominal after-tax interest rate}}{1 + \textbf{Inflation rate}} - 1 = \textbf{Real rate of interest}$$

If inflation averaged 3% per year over the 4-year period, the *average annual after-tax real rate of return* would be:

$$\frac{1.081}{1.03} - 1 = .0495 \text{ or } 4.95\%$$

Therefore, the average annual return for CAT during a 4-year holding period—after accounting for brokerage costs, taxes, and inflation—*was 4.95%.*

From an original average annualized return of 17.085%, after accounting for transaction costs, taxes, and inflation, the resulting real, after-tax return was 4.957%. As discouraging as this may seem, investing in a diversified portfolio of stocks over the long run is a proven way to build wealth. Moreover, the investor's purchasing power has increased.

WHAT IS A GOOD PRICE FOR A STOCK?

Consistent with the approach of using time-value-of-money principles in problem solving, the following is but one quantitative technique of stock valuation and should be considered as an example of such an approach rather than a tried-and-true technique. One thing is for certain: If a tried-and-true technique existed for stock picking, everyone would use it. If everyone used it, it would no longer work. We present this technique as it is a simple example of how time-value-of-money is used in the investment world, although the models used by the stock market are much more complex.

You are considering buying a stock with expected year-end dividends of:

Year	Dividend
1	.80
2	1.05
3	1.35

After 3 years, you expect (possibly based on the opinion of market analysts) the stock will sell in the range of $18–$21 dollars per share.

To account for the risk of this investment, you want to earn at least 11% before taxes annually over the 3-year period. What is the most you would be willing to pay to purchase this stock?

Using the "TVM" approach, you will solve for the present value (PV) of each future dividend and the estimated selling price. By adding the three PV figures you estimate the price you are willing to pay today to purchase this particular stock.

"Worst-case" selling price ($18) in 3 years	"Best-case" selling price ($21) in 3 years

Year 1   FV = $.80
           N = 1
           I/Y = 11
           PV = $.72
	Year 1 FV = $.80
	           N = 1
	           I/Y = 11
	           PV = $.72

Year 2   FV = $1.05
           N = 2
           I/Y = 11
           PV = $.85
	Year 2 FV = $1.05
	           N = 2
	           I/Y = 11
	           PV = $.85

Year 3   FV = $1.35 + $18 = $19.35
           N = 3
           I/Y = 11
           PV = $14.15
	Year 3 FV = $1.35 + $21 = $22.35
	           N = 3
	           I/Y = 11
	           PV = $16.34

By summing the PVs, you determine that you would be willing to pay as much as $15.72 per share today to purchase this stock.	By summing the PVs, you determine that you would be willing to pay as much as $17.91 per share today to purchase this stock.

Assignment 8.1   Investing in Stocks

Name _____

SHOW YOUR CALCULATIONS ON A SEPARATE SHEET.

1. At the end of a month, you are trying to determine the market value of your portfolio. You own the following stocks and need to complete the following table as of the most recent closing prices. You will find stock prices in the *Wall Street Journal*, http://www.finance.yahoo.com, Motley Fool (http://www.fool.com), or your favorite online brokerage.

Date used was _____

Stock	Symbol	# of Shares	Current Market Price	Total Value (# Shares × Price)	Portfolio Proportion
Duke Energy	DUK	200			
IBM	IBM	100			
General Mills	GIS	150			
Bank of America	BAC	200			
Ford	F	100			
TOTAL					

2. Given the reported dividends and the current market price, what is the dividend yield of each security and the weighted-average dividend yield of your portfolio?

Stock	Dividend	Dividend Yield	Portfolio Proportion (from Part #1)	Dividend Yield × Portfolio Proportion
Duke Energy				
IBM				
General Mills				
Bank of America				
Ford				
WEIGHTED-AVERAGE DIVIDEND YIELD OF PORTFOLIO				

3. You purchased 1000 shares of TAC for $5.15 per share 6 months ago. The brokerage fee was 4% of the total dollar amount of the purchase. Today, you sold the shares for $5.75 per share. Brokerage fees were 4% of the total sale value. If you are in the 25% marginal a tax bracket, how much tax do you owe on this **short-term** capital gain? (show all the calculations.)

4. You purchased stock in FIS for $32.05 per share on December 2012. Over the next year (>365 days), you received $0.88 per share in dividends. On December 31, 2013, you sold FIS for $52.04 per share. What has been your total holding-period return (in percentage) over the 1-year period?

5. You purchased 1,000 shares of stock in FMC for $55.50 per share on December 31, 2009. Over the next 4 years you received 54 cents per share annually in dividends. On December 31, 2013, you sell all your shares of FMC for $74.08 per share. Brokerage commissions are 4% of the total transaction value when buying *and* selling.

    What has been your total holding-period return (in percentage) over the 4 years?

    What has been your average annual return over the 4 years?

6. Now, determine your average annual return (after taxes and inflation) on FMC. Assume a marginal tax rate of 33% and a rate of inflation over the 4-year period of 2.75% per year. (A 33% marginal tax bracket consumer would be taxed 15% for both dividends and capital gains.)

7. You owned 1,200 shares of Jamba Juice (JMBA) on the first of January 2013. On June 3, 2013, Jamba had a stock split. How many shares do you now own, and what would be the expected price per share? (Look on the interactive chart for JMBA on http://www.finance.yahoo.com.)

8. The present market price of a stock is $20, and the earnings per share are $1.50. Therefore, the price earnings ratio is 13.33. An 8% annual growth rate in earnings is anticipated over the next 9 years. The P/E is assumed to be the same in 9 years. What is the expected market price of the stock in 9 years?

9. You are considering buying a stock with expected year-end dividends of:

Year	Dividend
1	1.00
2	1.05
3	1.12

At the end of the third year, you expect to sell the stock for $18 per share. You want to earn at least 11% annually over the three periods.

    a. What would you be willing to pay for the stock today?

    b. If the stock is selling for $15, would you buy it? Why?

DEBT INVESTMENTS—BONDS AND NOTES

Bonds are corporate and government debt. A person who purchases a bond is lending money to the issuer of the bond. Hence, if you buy a bond, you are lending money to the issuer. If the bond is a coupon bond, the issuer promises two things: (1) they will pay you interest each year, and (2) after the bond expires they will pay you the face value of the bond. If the bond is a zero coupon bond, they promise to pay the face value of the bond when it expires at maturity.

Treasury Bonds

Treasury Bonds are negotiable and marketable debt of the U.S. government. Government bonds have a fixed rate of interest that is paid semiannually over a period of 30 years and are sold in increments of $1,000. The holder, therefore, accepts interest rate risk. To learn more, go to: http://www.treasurydirect .gov/indiv/products/prod_tbonds_glance.htm

Government Agency Issues

Many government agencies and federal corporations are able to issue debt (borrow money by selling bonds) in order to fund their mandated activities. A sampling is shown below.

Federal Farm Credit loans	World Bank Bonds
Federal Land Bank loans	Student Loan Marketing
GNMA and FNMA Issues	Federal Home Loan Bank Issues

Municipal Bonds

Municipal bonds (often called "muni" bonds) are issued by state and local governments and most are issued in $5,000 increments. Typically, municipal bonds are coupon bonds and are *not taxed by the federal government.* Municipal bonds may also be free from state income taxes (it depends on the state). Generally, if a municipal bond is issued by a state agency or a community within a state, they are free of that state's income taxes.

The principal and income is relatively safe, and municipal bonds are rated by Moody's and Standard & Poor's with respect to safety. Before you purchase a municipal bond you should be aware of the following types of bonds:

General obligation bonds have the full taxing power of the treasury of the state or local government behind them. These are the safest, as taxes may be increased in order to repay the bondholders.

Revenue bonds are used to develop a project that must earn the revenue to pay the interest and principal. Turnpikes and bridges that charge motorists for travel are often funded by revenue bonds.

Private activity bonds are used for nongovernment activities and may be subject to the alternative minimum tax. For example, a recent remodeling of Chicago's O'Hare airport was financed with private activity bonds.

Taxes and Municipal Bonds

Before you purchase a municipal bond, compare the taxable equivalent yield of a municipal bond to a corporate, taxable bond. If both bonds are equally rated for risk, choose the bond with the highest after-tax yield.

$$\textbf{Corporate bond rate} \times (1 - t) = \textbf{Required municipal bond rate}$$

- or -

Municipal bond rate / (1 − t) = Required corporate bond rate

where t = marginal tax bracket

For example: At a marginal tax bracket of 35%, a corporate bond with a 10% yield is equivalent to a municipal bond with a yield of 6.5%.

$$.10 \times (1 - .35) = .065$$

(6.5% is the tax-free municipal bond rate that is equivalent to a 10% taxable bond)

- or -

$$.065 / (1 - .35) = .10$$

(10% is the required taxable bond rate to be equivalent to a 6.5% tax-free municipal bond)

So, for an investor in the 35% marginal tax bracket with a choice between a 10% taxable bond or a 7% tax-free municipal bond, the correct choice would be the 7% tax-free bond. Why? Because a 7% tax free bond is equivalent to a 10.77% taxable bond as shown below.

$$.07 / (1 - .35) = .1077$$

Corporate Bonds

Corporate bonds are similar to government bonds but are typically issued in *$1,000 face value denominations*. They carry a fixed rate of interest; therefore, you are assuming interest rate risk. Companies with weaker balance sheets or uncertain earnings will pay a greater rate of interest, due to greater business risk. Bonds issued by companies in financial difficulty offer a higher interest rate (due to the greater risk accepted by the buyer of the bond). Such bonds are referred to as "high-yield" bonds or **"junk" bonds**.

Bondholders have a prior and fixed claim on the corporate assets, should the business fail and its assets liquidated. If the business does well, however, the bondholders do not share in the new found wealth—only stockholders (owners) benefit. Bonds are rated by Moody's and Standard and Poor's, with higher "grades" being granted to companies that are financially stronger, and, therefore, less likely to default on the bond interest payments.

Bond ratings (or grades) are similar to school grades, with higher rated bonds receiving A grades and lower rated bonds receiving C and D grades. The following grading systems are used by Standard & Poor's and Moody's.

Standard & Poor's	Moody's
AAA	Aaa
AA	Aa
A	A
BBB	Baa
---------- Investment Grade Bond Line ----------	
BB	Ba
B	B
CCC	Caa
CC	Ca
C	C
D	D

As can be seen, bonds rated by Standard and Poor's above BB (Ba, if Moody's) are considered to be investment grade. Bonds below the investment grade line are referred to as "high-yield" or "junk bonds," reflecting the higher interest they must pay to compensate for their greater risk. Bonds issued by companies in financial distress are generally regarded as junk bonds.

HOW TO READ BOND LISTINGS

An example of bonds listed in the *Barron's*, in mid-August 2018. We will focus on Starbucks (SBUX).

Company (Ticker)	Coupon	Maturity	Last Price	Last Yield	Estimated Spread	UST	Volume (000's)
Citigroup (C)	4.650	July 23, 2048	101.469	4.559	154	30	284,573
Citigroup (C)	4.075	Apr 23, 2029	98.585	4.254	138	10	260,677
Starbucks (SBUX)	4.500	Nov 15, 2048	100.071	4.496	146	30	418,097

SBUX	SBUX is the ticker symbol for Starbucks.
104.38	The lowest price the bond sold for during the past 52 weeks, 104.38% of the face value.
4.5	The coupon rate of the Starbucks bond. The bond promises to pay 4.5% of the face value per year. This will be paid as 2.25% in May and November of each year, until the bond matures in 2048.
Nov 15, 2048	This particular Starbuck's bond matures on November 15, 2048. At this time the final coupon payment of 2.25% of the face value of the bond will p be paid, along with the face value of the bond, equal to $1,000.
100.071	The last price the bond sold for this week. The 100.071 indicates that the bond sold for a premium (price is above its face value), of 100.071% of its face falue, or $1,000.71. Had it had a price of less than 100, it is said to be selling at a discount.
4.496	Since the bond is selling at a premium, the Last Yield of 4.496% is less than the coupon rate of interest (4.5%). This occurs, due to the fact that the premium of $0.71 will disappear, as the bond reaches maturity.
146	The estimated spread is equal to 146. This means that the bond's yield is 146 basis points (1.46%) greater than a comparable Treasury bond, with similar maturity.
30	The years to marurity for the comparable Treasury bond.
418,097	The estimated dollar volume (in 000's) of this SBUX bond sold this week, or $418,097,000.

Callable bonds may be "called in" (retired or paid off) at the discretion of the company by payment to the bondholder of principal (or face value) and a "call premium." The call premium is often 6-month's interest.

Convertible bonds are coupon bonds that can be exchanged for common stock at a predetermined number of shares per bond. If a corporation does well, a convertible bond takes on the features of common stock. If the corporation does not do well, the bond will have its value determined by the value of the bond. Thus, the bond value sets a floor to the price and the convertibility provides for upside potential. Of course, you have to pay higher prices for convertible bonds, compared to similar non–convertible bonds, due the greater upside potential of a convertible bond.

Zero-coupon bonds are sold at deep discount and have no interest payments until they mature. At maturity the bondholder receives the face value of the bond (generally $1,000). However, the interest that accrues is taxed as if it were, in fact, received (i.e., taxed on an accrual basis). As such zero-coupon bonds are great for "locking in" a rate of return to have money for a future fixed obligation.

BOND RATES OF RETURN

The following definitions are the most commonly used rates in the context of a bond. We will use the following bond in our examples:

Company (Ticker)	Coupon	Maturity	Last Price	Last Yield	Estimated Spread	UST	Volume (000's)
Starbucks (SBUX)	4.500	Nov 15, 2048	100.071	4.496	146	30	418,097

- **Coupon rate**, r = stated rate = i ÷ 1,000, where i is the fixed dollar annual interest payments. The coupon rate is fixed when the bond is issued. It does not change. The numerator is the annual interest payment and the denominator the face value of the bond. If we have a $45 annual coupon bond (0.045 × 1,000) with a $1,000 face value, the coupon rate:

$$\frac{\$45 \text{ annual interest}}{\$1,000 \text{ face value}} = .045 \text{ or } 4.50\% \text{ coupon rate}$$

- **Current yield (or current rate)** = i / Pc , where the annual dollar interest payments (i) are divided by the current market price of the bond (Pc). Current market prices decrease (increase), as the current yield increases (decreases). The current yield is that yield required by the market, as economic expectations or the fortunes of the issuing firm change. Assume the bond is currently selling for 100.71 or $1,000.71.

$$\frac{\$45 \text{ annual interest}}{\$1,000.71 \text{ current bond price}} = 0.044968 \text{ or } 4.4968\% \text{ current yield}$$

- **Yield to maturity (YTM)** is the average annual return from both interest payments and any capital appreciation (or depreciation) if the bond is held to maturity (n years) and sold for its maturity price (Pm) of $1,000. The YTM is truly the internal rate of return from purchasing the bond at its current price and holding it until maturity. A simplified approximation formula for YTM (*use only if you do not have a financial calculator*) is:

$$YTM = \frac{i + \dfrac{Pm - Pc}{n}}{\dfrac{Pm + Pc}{2}}$$

Where: Pm = Maturity price (face value of $1,000)

Pc = Current market price of the bond

i = Annual coupon (or interest) payment

n = Number of years until maturity

Example: Let's look at another example from the above Table.

Company (Ticker)	Coupon	Maturity	Last Price	Last Yield	Estimated Spread	UST	Volume (000's)
Citigroup (C)	4.650	July 23, 2048	101.469	4.559	154	30	284,573

What is the coupon rate?

The coupon rate is shown above as 4.65%, or 0.0464.

The annual dollar amount of interest you will receive if you purchase the bond is calculated as follows.

Face value × coupon rate = dollar amount of annual bond interest

$1,000 × .0465 = **$46.50 annual bond interest (or $23.25 every six months).**

What is the current yield?

$$\frac{\$46.50 \text{ annual interest}}{\$1,014.69 \text{ current bond price}} = \textbf{.045827 or 4.5827\% current yield}$$

What is the approximate YTM?

$$YTM = \frac{46.50 + \dfrac{1,000 - 1,014.69}{15.5}}{\dfrac{1,000 + 1,014.69}{2}} = 0.04522 \text{ or } 4.522\%.$$

Using a financial calculator, the exact YTM equals:

2.935% (assuming semiannual interest payments and that the bond matures in the year 2020, as noted by 20 to the right of $5^{3/8}$)

PV = <1,014.69>
FV = 1,000
PMT = 45.00 / 2 = 22.50
N = 30.5 years × 2 = 61 semiannual periods
P/YR = 2
I/Y = **4.4119% annual rate**

How is the market price of this CitiCorp bond determined?

Using a financial calculator:

PMT = 45.00 / 2 = 22.50 semiannually
N = 30.5 years × 2 = 61 semiannual periods
FV = 1,000
I/YR = 4.411916 (current annual market rate)
P/YR = 2
PV = **<1,014.69> current market price**

Using algebra:

You will need to break this problem into two parts:

First, solve the PV of the PMT.

Second, solve the PV of the FV.

Now, add the PVs together to obtain the market price.

First part:

$$PMT = 45.00 / 2 = 22.50 \text{ semiannually}$$
$$N = 30.5 \text{ years} \times 2 = 61 \text{ semiannual periods}$$
$$I/YR = 4.411916 \text{ (current annual market rate)}$$

$$PVa = PMTa \left(\frac{1 - (1 + i)^{-n}}{i} \right)$$

$$PVa = 22.50 \left(\frac{1 - (1 + .04411916 / 2)^{-61}}{.04411916 / 2} \right)$$

$$\mathbf{PV} = \mathbf{<750.48>}$$

Second part:

$$FV = 1,000$$
$$N = 30.5 \text{ years} \times 2 = 61 \text{ semiannual periods}$$
$$I/YR = .04411916 / 2 = .02205958 \text{ (semiannual market rate)}$$
$$PV = FV (1 + i)^{-n}$$
$$PV = 1,000 (1 + .02205958)^{-61}$$
$$\mathbf{PV} = \mathbf{<264.2110>}$$

Adding the PVs together gives you the market price of the bond = $1,014.691.

Assignment 8.2   Investing in Bonds

Name _____

SHOW YOUR CALCULATIONS

1. A 12% coupon bond that matures in 6 years is selling for $1,150. It pays interest semiannually. What is the bond's:
   a. Current yield?

   b. YTM?

   c. Why is the YTM less than the coupon rate of interest?

2. A 10% coupon bond that pays interest semiannually and matures in 9 years is selling for $915. What is the bond's:
   a. Current yield?

   b. YTM?

   c. Why is the YTM more than the coupon rate of interest?

3. If yield to maturities of comparable risk-classed bonds are 9%, what is the <u>approximate market price</u> of a 11% coupon bond with semiannual payments that matures in 6 years? What if the bond were a zero coupon bond with no coupon payments?

4. What if the bond in Question 3 matures in 26 years? What if the bond were a zero coupon bond with no coupon payments?

5. Explain what is going on in Questions 3 and 4. Why are the answers different?

6. Benny Hill wants to invest $35,000 in bonds. He can buy a corporate bond with a yield of 8% or a municipal bond with a yield of 6%. Benny is in the 31% marginal tax bracket. Which should he select?

Value versus Growth

Since 1973, a "value" approach to investing has been superior to growth, when one looks at the coefficient of variation. (The coefficient of variation is the average divided by the standard deviation. In this case, it could be interpreted as the return you receive (average return) per unit of risk (standard deviation).). Stocks and mutual funds that are classified as "value" have lower price-to-earnings ratios compared to growth stocks or growth mutual funds. Value stocks are "cheaper" than growth stocks. Growth stocks, on the other hand, have earnings that are demonstrating exceptional growth.

Risk & Return Tradeoff—Notice how as risk (standard deviation) increases, so do average returns over time. This relationship has to be true when markets are efficient. Consider the following: If there were a low-risk, high-return investment, everyone would want it; this would cause the price to increase which, in turn, would lower the return on the investment.

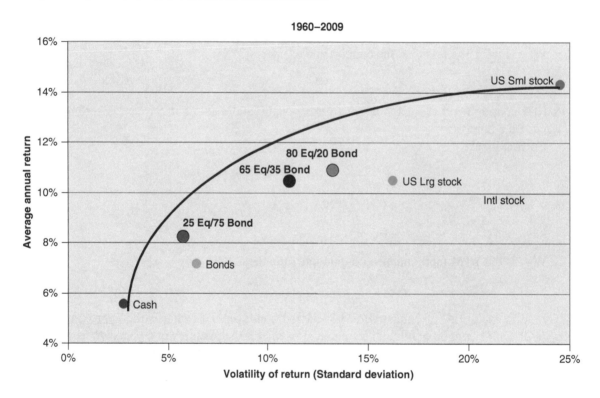

80/20 Asset Allocation
80 Eq / 20 Bond = A portfolio consisting of 45% U.S. Large Stock, 20% U.S. Small Stock, 15% International Stock, 12% Bonds, 8% Cash

65/35 Asset Allocation
65 Eq / 35 Bond = A portfolio consisting of 30% U.S. Large Stock, 20% U.S. Small Stock, 15% International Stock, 25% Bonds, 10% Cash

25/75 Asset Allocation
65 Eq / 35 Bond = A portfolio consisting of 15% U.S. Large Stock, 6% U.S. Small Stock, 4% International Stock, 55% Bonds, 20% Cash

Annual Returns (%)

Year	Inflation	US Stock Market	US Large Cap	US Large Cap Value	US Large Cap Growth	US Mid Cap	US Mid Cap Value	US Mid Cap Growth	US Small Cap	US Small Cap Value	US Small Cap Growth
1973	8.71%	−18.18%	−16.18%	−9.79%	−23.09%	−24.20%	−13.77%	−32.96%	−32.85%	−24.12%	−40.26%
1974	12.34%	−27.81%	−26.93%	−21.13%	−32.34%	−26.34%	−19.80%	−32.64%	−27.59%	−21.09%	−33.72%
1975	6.94%	37.82%	36.95%	40.67%	33.10%	48.69%	56.79%	41.95%	55.13%	53.94%	56.63%
1976	4.86%	26.47%	24.18%	33.32%	14.85%	36.67%	46.79%	26.54%	45.33%	54.78%	36.40%
1977	6.70%	−3.36%	−7.84%	−3.31%	−8.66%	1.30%	5.24%	−2.12%	15.67%	15.88%	15.36%
1978	9.02%	8.45%	5.87%	6.37%	7.11%	8.97%	9.05%	8.80%	17.74%	19.25%	16.60%
1979	13.29%	24.25%	18.05%	23.22%	17.44%	31.48%	29.84%	33.07%	41.02%	37.80%	45.21%
1980	12.52%	33.15%	31.92%	31.75%	35.59%	30.76%	17.60%	45.25%	35.78%	25.77%	46.32%
1981	8.92%	−4.15%	−5.21%	−1.48%	−6.20%	4.10%	10.20%	−1.74%	4.36%	15.69%	−5.82%
1982	3.83%	20.50%	20.97%	25.08%	20.33%	25.21%	29.36%	20.52%	29.27%	36.87%	22.36%
1983	3.79%	22.66%	21.29%	25.44%	16.92%	27.11%	32.69%	22.32%	31.64%	42.61%	20.54%
1984	3.95%	2.19%	6.21%	11.43%	1.56%	−1.74%	2.54%	−5.70%	−4.26%	5.69%	−13.51%
1985	3.80%	31.27%	31.23%	32.93%	33.57%	32.79%	32.31%	33.13%	33.70%	37.46%	31.17%
1986	1.10%	14.57%	18.06%	19.70%	16.96%	17.12%	18.13%	16.01%	9.77%	13.99%	5.71%
1987	4.43%	2.61%	4.71%	2.11%	6.44%	0.84%	−0.98%	2.64%	−6.42%	−3.51%	−9.10%
1988	4.42%	17.32%	16.22%	20.16%	13.21%	19.44%	24.96%	14.37%	23.78%	29.00%	18.42%
1989	4.65%	28.12%	31.36%	26.89%	35.83%	26.00%	24.92%	27.09%	19.41%	19.21%	19.62%

(Continued)

Annual Returns (%) (Continued)

Year	Inflation	US Stock Market	US Large Cap	US Large Cap Value	US Large Cap Growth	US Mid Cap	US Mid Cap Value	US Mid Cap Growth	US Small Cap	US Small Cap Value	US Small Cap Growth
1990	6.11%	−6.08%	−3.32%	−7.02%	1.54%	−10.73%	−16.75%	−4.02%	−18.13%	−19.05%	−14.26%
1991	3.06%	32.39%	30.22%	23.78%	44.61%	40.44%	41.56%	39.35%	45.26%	42.96%	49.22%
1992	2.90%	9.11%	7.42%	15.48%	6.61%	15.19%	19.50%	10.79%	18.20%	28.23%	10.18%
1993	2.75%	10.62%	9.89%	18.26%	1.53%	16.20%	17.18%	15.07%	18.70%	21.10%	11.25%
1994	2.67%	−0.17%	1.18%	−0.63%	2.89%	−1.72%	−3.03%	−0.60%	−0.51%	−0.07%	−3.63%
1995	2.54%	35.79%	37.45%	37.04%	38.06%	33.22%	33.38%	32.91%	28.74%	30.32%	30.07%
1996	3.32%	20.96%	22.88%	21.80%	23.74%	18.97%	20.15%	17.48%	18.12%	21.41%	10.24%
1997	1.70%	30.99%	33.19%	29.78%	36.34%	25.66%	35.08%	17.75%	24.59%	35.44%	14.37%
1998	1.61%	23.26%	28.62%	14.63%	42.21%	9.90%	3.67%	17.27%	−2.61%	−2.68%	3.52%
1999	2.68%	23.81%	21.07%	12.58%	28.76%	15.32%	3.12%	42.99%	23.13%	3.35%	19.80%
2000	3.39%	−10.57%	−9.06%	6.09%	−22.21%	18.10%	19.80%	−6.28%	−2.67%	21.88%	1.59%
2001	1.55%	−10.97%	−12.02%	−11.86%	−12.93%	−0.50%	−0.84%	−6.02%	3.10%	13.70%	−0.78%
2002	2.38%	−20.96%	−22.15%	−20.88%	−23.68%	−14.61%	−12.95%	−21.22%	−20.02%	−14.20%	−15.41%
2003	1.88%	31.35%	28.50%	32.25%	25.92%	34.14%	37.94%	35.59%	45.63%	37.19%	42.88%
2004	3.26%	12.52%	10.74%	15.26%	7.20%	20.35%	26.04%	13.00%	19.90%	23.55%	16.06%
2005	3.42%	5.98%	4.77%	7.10%	5.09%	13.93%	16.02%	8.11%	7.36%	6.07%	8.64%
2006	2.54%	15.51%	15.64%	22.13%	9.01%	13.60%	14.77%	11.79%	15.66%	19.24%	11.95%

(Continued)

Annual Returns (%) (Continued)

Year	Inflation	US Stock Market	US Large Cap	US Large Cap Value	US Large Cap Growth	US Mid Cap	US Mid Cap Value	US Mid Cap Growth	US Small Cap	US Small Cap Value	US Small Cap Growth
2007	4.08%	5.49%	5.39%	0.08%	12.56%	6.02%	−4.37%	17.30%	1.16%	−7.07%	9.63%
2008	0.09%	−37.04%	−37.02%	−35.97%	−38.32%	−41.82%	−36.64%	−47.07%	−36.07%	−32.05%	−40.00%
2009	2.72%	28.70%	26.49%	19.58%	36.29%	40.22%	37.61%	42.54%	36.12%	30.34%	41.85%
2010	1.50%	17.09%	14.91%	14.27%	16.96%	25.46%	21.63%	28.93%	27.72%	24.82%	30.69%
2011	2.96%	0.96%	1.97%	1.00%	1.71%	−2.11%	−0.44%	−3.84%	−2.80%	−4.16%	−1.58%
2012	1.74%	16.25%	15.82%	15.00%	16.89%	15.80%	15.91%	15.81%	18.04%	18.56%	17.52%
2013	1.50%	33.35%	32.18%	32.87%	32.16%	35.00%	37.42%	32.02%	37.62%	36.41%	37.98%
2014	0.76%	12.43%	13.51%	13.07%	13.47%	13.60%	13.84%	13.35%	7.37%	10.39%	3.88%
2015	0.73%	0.29%	1.25%	−1.04%	3.17%	−1.45%	−1.91%	−1.13%	−3.78%	−4.77%	−2.64%
2016	2.07%	12.53%	11.82%	16.75%	5.99%	11.07%	15.11%	6.62%	18.17%	24.65%	10.61%
2017	2.11%	21.05%	21.67%	16.99%	27.65%	19.12%	16.91%	21.72%	16.10%	11.67%	21.78%
Average Return	4.03%	11.79%	11.64%	12.71%	11.69%	13.92%	15.01%	12.59%	14.12%	16.37%	12.39%
Standard Deviation	3.13%	17.71%	17.51%	16.72%	20.05%	18.77%	19.10%	20.80%	21.28%	20.43%	22.27%
Coefficient of Variation	128.60%	66.57%	66.47%	75.97%	58.28%	74.16%	78.61%	60.56%	66.37%	80.10%	55.61%

INVESTMENT HOLDING PERIODS AND CHANCE OF LOSS

One of the secrets to successful investing in riskier investments is recognizing that there will be times when your investments will decrease in value. The chart below shows that, as the holding period increases, the percentage of those holding periods that resulted in a loss decreases as the length of the holding period increases. This statement holds true for every asset class. For example, every given year has a chance of a loss of 58% if we invest in small-cap U.S. stocks. Yet, if we agree (with ourselves) to leave the money for longer periods of time, five or 20 years in this chart, the chance of loss decreases dramatically. If one had had their money invested for the entire 1926–2012 time period, one would have earned 11.9% annually. If you missed any part of that time frame, it is not known what your return would have been. Thus, time is your friend when it comes to investing. (We will let you in on a little secret. You cannot have more time than if you start saving today.)

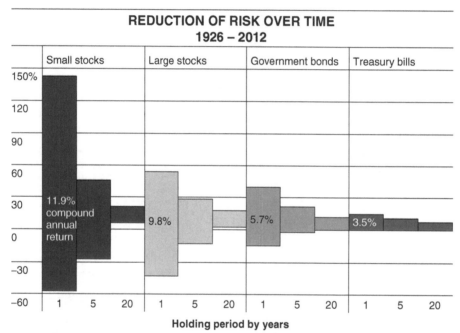

REDUCTION OF RISK OVER TIME
1926 – 2012

Holding period by years

Past performance is no guarantee of future results. • An investment cannot be made directly in an index. • Each bar shows the range of compound annual returns for each asset class over the period 1926-2012. This is for illustrative purposes only and not indicative of any investment. Licensed by Raymond James. • © 2013 morningstar, inc. All rights reserved. 3/1/2013

A similar story is told in the following chart. We find that as holding period increased, the maximum annualized return over each time period is less, the longer the holding period. In general, the same is true for average returns. Yet, for the minimum return, the longer the holding period, the greater the annualized rate of return. Investing for 1 year is much riskier than investing for 20. This is why we use low-risk, liquid investments for our short-term goals and higher risk investments for our long-term goals.

Buy and Hold for the Long Term			
Investors looking to smooth out returns and reduce the odds of suffering losses should hold stocks for 20 years. Annualized returns for S&P 500 index using rolling monthly returns between 1950 and 2010:			
Holding Pattern	**Max. Return (%)**	**Avg. Return (%)**	**Min. Return (%)**
1 year	53.4	8.4	−44.8
3 years	30.1	7.4	−17.3
5 years	26.2	7.5	−8.5
10 years	16.8	7.3	−5.1
20 years	14.4	7.2	2.4

Source: Oppenheimer Asset Management Investment Strategy.

MUTUAL FUNDS

A mutual fund is an investment company—a company that makes investments on behalf of individuals and institutions. The basic concept of mutual funds began in the 18th century in Britain. The first U.S. mutual fund was formed in Boston in 1924. Mutual funds pool the money from many investors and purchase dozens or even hundreds of stocks, bonds, or other securities. Meaning that mutual funds grant small investors the opportunity to invest in a diversified portfolio, which is one of the key methods for reducing the risks of a portfolio and reaching one's investment goals.

In January 1980, there were 458 stock and bond mutual funds; in January 1990, there were 3,079; and by the beginning of 2016, mutual funds in the United States reached their peak with 8,066. These 8,066 stock and bond mutual funds represented 25,115 fund classes. The majority of funds (about 73%) are funds that invest primarily in common stock (either in U.S. companies and/or in non-U.S. companies). The balance is composed of funds that invest either in corporate, government, or municipal bonds.

In the United States, as of the end of 2017, there was over 18.746 trillion dollars invested in all forms of mutual funds (open-end funds, closed-end funds, unit investment trusts, and exchange-traded funds). Worldwide, this figure increases to approximately $49.3 trillion. (Source: http://www.ici.org)

Mutual funds are a very convenient way to meet one's investment objectives. Funds vary by level of investment risk, type of securities held in the fund (i.e., stocks, bonds, real estate, precious metals, etc.), expenses and commissions, and management style. Mutual funds require an initial investment, often the minimum investment ranges from $250 to $2,500. Once the minimum is met, subsequent smaller investments can be made in almost all cases. Many funds waive the initial investment requirement for investors who start an **Automatic Investment Plan** (AIP). An AIP consists of authorizing the mutual fund company to automatically withdraw money from your checking or savings account and purchase shares of a mutual fund. An investment of $50 per month is a common AIP minimum requirement.

Once an account is set up, most mutual funds allow total flexibility in terms of the amount and timing of investments into the fund and withdrawals from fund —except for those with AIPs and for withdrawals from retirement accounts. A common characteristic among these funds is that regular investments are encouraged by all mutual funds.

Money is able to be withdrawn from a mutual fund at any time, unless the fund has been set up as a tax-deferred retirement account (such as a 401(k), 403(b), or IRA). Money going into and coming out of tax-deferred accounts is subject to different rules, where a penalty for early withdrawal may exist. (Section 9 discusses this more fully.) If you do not want to read that chapter, I suggest that before tinkering with your retirement account you visit with the employee benefits office at your place of employment. If you are self-employed, you should consult with a qualified tax advisor or a Certified Financial PlannerTM. In general, do not withdraw your money from your retirement accounts until you are retired. (After all, is not retirement what the account is for?)

When you are ready to redeem money from a mutual fund account, contact the mutual fund company, or your investment advisor, and instruct them to sell part or all of the shares. The mutual fund company buys the shares back from the investor (thus, the investor sells their shares back to the mutual fund company) at the net asset value at the close of the day of the redemption, and mails the proceeds to the investor.

When you purchase a mutual fund, there may be a commission on funds offered that average 5.3% and falling to 1% on actual paid commission, due to discounts on large contracts. Funds that charge no sales commissions are referred to as **no-load** funds. In recent years, many mutual funds have lowered or even eliminated front-end loads (class A shares)—a commission at the time of sale—and moved the load to the back end (class B shares). A **back-end load** (or deferred load) is a commission paid by the investor when he or she redeems money from the mutual fund account. Mutual funds that charge a low front-load commission (3% or less) are referred to as **low-load funds**. Funds that charge no commission of any kind are permitted to refer to themselves as **pure no-load** funds, often class C shares.

All funds assess an annual management fee, also referred to as the **annual expense ratio**. The average annual management fee for stock mutual funds is around 0.74%, or $0.74 per $100 invested. These fees can be lower for the same mutual fund, depending on the class (A, B, or C) of the mutual fund. It is quite common for class A shares, which charge a commission, to have relatively low annual expense ratios. The annual expense ratio is the percentage of your assets that you will pay in fees each year. Clearly, when everything else is equal, you would prefer to pay less than more for mutual fund management. Bond funds will typically have a lower annual management fee. For example, the Vanguard Group is a mutual fund company that is well known for two things: low expense ratios and lots of index funds to choose from. Index funds are mutual funds that are designed to mimic one of many different stock market indexes. The most popular index being mirrored by mutual funds is the Standard & Poor's 500 Index. Index funds typically have very low expense ratios and are often recommended as a very good investment for the novice investor who does not want to take an active role in the management of their assets.

Financial magazines regularly publish information regarding mutual fund performance. A major provider of mutual fund performance information is Morningstar (http://www.morningstar.com). An investor, however, is able to perform some analysis at http://finance.yahoo.com, where parameters may be set to reduce the number of mutual funds you are considering to purchase. You may set values for important variables, such as: expense ratios, loads, performance, ranking, category, fund family, among others to screen through the universe of mutual funds. After conducting your research, call the fund (usually a toll-free phone call) and ask to receive a prospectus and account application This can also be completed online, as most fund companies make their prospectus and annual reports available on their personal websites. Some mutual fund companies have excellent websites: T. Rowe Price (http://www.troweprice.com), Homestead (http://www.homesteadfunds.com), Dodge and Cox (http://www.dodgeandcox.com), Royce (http://www.roycefunds.com), and Vanguard (http://www.vanguard.com).

The "prospectus" of the mutual fund is an informational booklet provided by the mutual fund company that outlines the details of the fund. Such details include the fund's minimum initial investment requirement, investment objectives, annual expense ratio, historical return data, and so on. One must receive a mutual fund prospectus before you can invest. This does not mean that requesting a prospectus obligates a person to invest in a mutual fund; however, it is suggested that you read it, or at least a majority of it. It is strongly advised that the prospectus is studied before any money is invested in the fund.

There is no limit to the number of different mutual funds a person may invest in; yet, having a portfolio of more than 10 mutual funds is probably overkill. Investing in 5–7 mutual funds will typically meet the needs of most investors. However, a "portfolio" of even 1 mutual fund is an excellent starting point! An exception to wanting to maintain only 5–7 mutual funds is when you are limited in the mutual funds you can purchase for your retirement account, a 529 plan, or other investment platform.

Mutual fund companies provide investors with a broad array of mutual fund portfolios from cash reserve funds (money market mutual funds) to high-risk portfolios that invest in small, start-up companies (such as an aggressive growth mutual fund). However, there is no compelling reason to invest only in mutual funds within the same mutual fund company, other than to reduce the mail you receive.

It is common practice to move money from one portfolio (i.e., fund) to another mutual fund. However, the exchange is treated as a sale and a subsequent purchase, so consider the tax ramifications before you make this change. The convenience of being able to move money from one fund to another might be attractive, but one must remember that when you move your money you typically create a taxable event where you are mandated to pay taxes on any gain in your funds. If the funds involved are retirement accounts (i.e., traditional 401(k), 403(b), or IRA accounts) you do not have to worry about taxes until you withdraw the income.

Once you have invested in a mutual fund company, the company will provide you with performance reviews during the year. Financial magazines, daily newspapers, and many Web-based resources allow you to track your fund. Be careful about "chasing last year's winners," as opposed to having a disciplined program of diversified investments for the long term. Often, last year's winners turn out to be this year's losers. Knowing this makes the need to be well diversified apparent.

Many investors are surprised that they have to pay annual taxes on the dividends and capital gains distributed to them throughout the fund's year. These are always taxable, unless your account is a tax-sheltered retirement account. Dividends and capital gains in regular accounts (i.e., non–retirement accounts) are taxable whether or not you receive them. Repeat: even if you have them reinvested into the fund, dividends and capital gains are taxable.

One of the nice things a parent is able to do is to open a mutual fund account for their children or, for that matter, any child (niece, nephew, etc.). These types of accounts are referred to as **Uniform Gifts to Minors Accounts (UGMA)** and they are very easy to create. A UGMA account is an account that is established for a child with an adult acting as the custodian of the account. Though the child cannot be the legal owner of the account until they reach the age of maturity (between 18 and 21 depending on state law), the money in the account becomes the property of the child at the time the account is established. The custodian manages the account for the minor child, but the money belongs to the child and should, therefore, be used only for expenses that directly benefit the child—such as college expenses. Therefore, taxation of dividends and capital gains generated by the UGMA account is the child's responsibility, not the custodian's. As of 2018, one may give up to $15,000 per donor and per minor child. Minor children, in turn, can receive up to $1,050 in unearned income (i.e., dividends, interest, or capital gains) without owing tax on the money received. The next $1,050 will be taxed at the child's tax rate, while any unearned income over the sum, or $2,100, will be taxed at the parents' marginal tax rate. This continues until the child reaches the age of 19 years, at which point all unearned income is taxed at the child's tax rate. Obviously, some parents see this as a tax advantage because any returns to an investment account is in their name (not in a tax-deferred account), the interest, dividends, and capital gains are taxable at the parents' tax rate.

A potential "downside" of UGMA accounts is the college financial aid issue. Under current policy, investment monies in a child's own account are weighted more heavily than parental financial resources when considering whether the child (i.e., student) qualifies for financial aid. Many parents know that their children are unlikely to qualify for financial aid, in these situations not only is there a tax advantage to gifting to their children, but there is also a psychological positive given to children who now know their mother and father are making a financial commitment to his or her future. The same, however, could apply to money placed in a 529 plan—which is specifically designed for college savings.

The diversification provided by a portfolio of mutual funds makes it easy to contribute regular savings to reach your goal. Investing on a regular basis, such as $50, or more, per month is a wonderful approach to your future. If the stock market declines, your monthly investment will buy more mutual fund shares each month. On the other hand, if it goes up, you will buy fewer shares. This investment method is referred to as Dollar Cost Averaging (**DCA**). It is a technique that, over the long run, allows an investor to accumulate shares of a mutual fund, in which the average *purchase price* per share will be lower than the average *market price* per share, assuming the market goes up over time.

Most investors seek out mutual funds with the greatest rates of return. Often this takes them to last year's winners—which may or may not be this year's winners. The next page contains a table of mutual funds that we have followed in the various editions of this workbook. For each, we list the 5- and 10-year average return for each fund, the annual expense ratio, the manager's length of tenure, the size of the fund, and the funds recent 10-year alpha. While we want higher returns, we also seek lower expenses. Also, it is important that the returns we are "chasing" are, in fact, the result of the work of the current manager. Hence, the length of time the manager has been managing the fund is important. The size of the fund is an indication of popularity and some argue that larger funds have more trouble-making tactical moves with your money. Finally, we list the 10-year alpha for each fund. Alpha is a measure of manager effectiveness in outperforming, if positive, or underperforming, if negative, his or her benchmark. What follows is a sampling of mutual funds. It is an illustration. It is not meant as an endorsement.

No-Load Mutual Funds
A Sampling
Data as of December 31, 2013

Fund Name	5-Year Average Return	10-Year Average Return	Annual Expense Ratio (%)	Manager Tenure (Years)	Net Assets ($ million)	10-Year Alpha
Large-Cap U.S. Stock Funds						
Homestead Value	11.81	9.96	0.60	4	1,070	−1.36
T. Rowe Price Equity Income	9.23	8.78	0.65	3	21,800	−1.99
T. Rowe Price Capital Appreciation	10.58	9.92	0.71	12	30,560	2.44
American Century Large-Cap Value	9.19	8.25	0.83	2	863.64	−2.33
Mid-Cap U.S. Stock Funds						
T. Rowe Price Extended Market Index (Wilshire 4500 Index)	11.36	10.93	0.35	10	912.68	−1.05
American Century Mid-Cap Value	11.86	11.80	0.96	6	4,930	1.90
Invesco Mid-Cap Core Equity A	7.02	6.44	1.23	20	1,100	−2.93

Fund Name	5-Year Average Return	10-Year Average Return	Annual Expense Ratio (%)	Manager Tenure (Years)	Net Assets ($ million)	10-Year Alpha
Small-Cap U.S. Stock Funds						
Homestead Small Company Stock	8.28	11.96	0.88	4	921.7	0.32
T. Rowe Price US Small Cap	13.33	12.97	0.79	12	7,390	2.38
American Century Small-Cap value	10.96	11.20	1.26	6	1,600	–0.31
Invesco Small-Cap Growth A	13.16	11.91	1.20	14	3,200	0.59
International (Non–U.S.) Stock Funds						
T. Rowe Price Intl Value	4.00	2.96	0.83	1	13,320	–0.13
Homestead Intl Equity	6.68	3.86	0.99	2	78.82	0.86
Invesco International Growth A	5.01	4.31	1.31	21	7,550	1.42
Bond Funds						
T. Rowe Price Spectrum Income	3.56	5.23	0.00	7	6,720	2.10
Homestead Short-Term Bond	1.36	3.21	0.76	2	550.70	2.05

Invesco funds' initial investment start with $50 automated monthly investment.
Homestead initial investment is $500 ($200 if IRA)
American Century and T. Rowe Price funds initial investment is $2,500 ($1,000 if IRA).

Framework for Selecting a Mutual Fund

Evaluate Investment Objectives and Investing Approach

Find funds that match your investment needs and goals. Considerations often include: how long you want to invest the money, how often you want to withdraw money out of the account (i.e., annuitize the account), how often you want to add additional sums of money, how does the fund "fit" in relation to your other investments, and so on. The longer the term of your goal, the greater the risk you can take with your money, as you have more time to recover from a loss. Also, you will most likely gain from the higher return that exists when you assume greater risk. Be sure to compare the performance of funds within categories (growth funds, value funds, growth and income funds, balanced funds, international funds, etc.) rather than across categories. (Yes, you should attempt to have funds in multiple categories to assure proper diversification.)

Evaluate the Portfolio Manager's Performance

Try to choose funds with consistent performance over time through both bull and bear markets. Mutual funds are managed by people, singly or by committee. Choose managers or management teams who demonstrate skill in maximizing returns during bull markets, and minimizing losses during bear markets. Try to select funds that have managers with longer tenure.

Size of the Fund

Very small funds (under $100 million) may not be as well diversified as large funds. On the other hand, large funds (over $1 billion) may be more difficult for the fund manager to "manage" than smaller funds. In an attempt to keep the fund manageable, some mutual funds will close to new investors after reaching a certain size (say, $500 million in assets).

Annual Fund Operating Expenses

Mutual funds charge the shareholders for the expenses related to the management of the fund. Be cautious of equity (stock) funds with annual expense ratios in excess of 1.25% and .65% for bond funds. Funds that invest in international markets generally have higher expense ratios. These fees directly reduce the fund's annual return. Index funds generally have very low expense ratios, often under 0.20% per year, and index investing has been shown to be a good way for inexperienced investors to participate in the market.

 Services—Is the fund company easy to contact? Does the mutual fund company allow transfers from one fund to another fund? (Say, from a money market fund to a stock fund and vice versa.) Will they sell directly to a client or do you need to go through an advisor? Do they have helpful resources on their website?

Portfolio Diversification

A primary advantage of investing in mutual funds is diversification. Rather than attempting to assemble a diversified portfolio on your own (which would cost plenty in brokerage commissions and time spent researching the market) an investor can "buy into" diversified portfolios—known as mutual funds. Diversification has advantages . . . and disadvantages.

> The *advantage* is risk minimization. If one stock in a mutual fund portfolio of 100 stocks goes bankrupt, the impact on the entire portfolio is minimal. However, if your personal portfolio included three stocks and one went bankrupt, the impact is dramatic.
>
> The *disadvantage* of portfolio diversification is return minimization. If one stock in a mutual fund portfolio of 100 stocks goes up in price by 300%, the impact on the entire portfolio is minimal. However, if your personal portfolio included three stocks and one went up 300%, the impact is dramatic!

Properly done, diversification seeks to maximize return while minimizing the risk of loss. Diversification often involves allocating money in different types of investments, or "portfolio weighting." The amount of money to allocate to each type of investment is the key decision. For example, compare the returns of differently weighted portfolios (as shown in the table that follows) across 2 years.

Portfolio A	Portfolio B
25% in Stocks	60% in Stocks
50% in Bonds	20% in Bonds
25% in Cash (money market mutual fund)	20% in Cash

Year 1 (the "good" stock year):

Stocks	12% return
Bonds	3% return
Cash	4% return

Total Weighted-Average Return of Portfolio A in Year 1:

$$(.12 \times .25) + (.03 \times .50) + (.04 \times .25) = 5.50\%$$

Total Weighted-Average Return of Portfolio B in Year 1:

$$(.12 \times .60) + (.03 \times .20) + (.04 \times .20) = 8.60\%$$

Year 2 (the "bad" stock year):

Stocks	<8%> return
Bonds	7% return
Cash	3% return

Total Weighted-Average Return of Portfolio A in Year 2:

$$(-.08 \times .25) + (.07 \times .50) + (.03 \times .25) = 2.25\%$$

Total Weighted-Average Return of Portfolio B in Year 2:

$$(-.08 \times .60) + (.07 \times .20) + (.03 \times .20) = -2.80\%$$

What you should take away from the above is simple, yet profound. In year 1, stocks returned 12% and you wish, at the end of the year, that you would have had all your money in stocks. Let us assume you did and you kept it there for year 2, where you lost 8%. At the end of the 2 years, you have a total return of 3.04% (= $(1 + .12) \times (1 - .08) = 1.0304$). You are better off, but what if you had weighted the portfolio, as in portfolio B? Your return at the end of 2 years, with the diversified portfolio, would have been 5.56% (= $(1 + .086) \times (1 - .028) = 1.0556$). Clearly, you are better off with diversification.

HOW SHOULD YOU INVEST YOUR MONEY?

The most important part of investing is having the discipline to save money instead of spending money. This discipline needs to begin as soon, since the second most important aspect of investing is time. You need to invest for a long period of time to allow the power of compound returns to accumulate and, thus, help you reach your financial goals. If you have not started to save, today is the day to begin!

The third key to successful investing is diversification. An investor should diversify in a way that makes them comfortable. One should not be too conservative if they have long-term goals, or too aggressive if their investment horizon is shorter or if their personality is better suited for less risk. On the other hand, unless one ventures beyond what one knows and learns that the way to reduce risk in one's portfolio is to have investments in many different investment categories; one may fail to reach the financial goals that are important to them.

Below are three portfolios that have actually been used with clients: Aggressive, Moderate, and Conservative. You will note that the Aggressive is weighted toward equities while, at the other extreme, the Conservative is weighted toward bonds. It is important, regardless of the plan you choose, that you periodically rebalance your portfolio to "fit" the model you wish to have. In this way, you sell items that have increased in value (sell high) and buy securities that have decreased in relative value (buy low).

Investment Category	Aggressive	Moderate	Conservative
U.S. Large-Cap Growth	11.25%	6.75%	4.50%
U.S. Large-Cap Value	11.25%	6.75%	4.50%
U.S. Small-Cap Growth	11.25%	6.75%	4.50%
U.S. Small-Cap Value	11.25%	6.75%	4.50%
Real Estate Investment Trusts	5.00%	3.00%	2.00%
International Growth	9.00%	5.40%	3.60%
International Value	9.00%	5.40%	3.60%
International Small-Cap Growth	9.00%	5.40%	3.60%
International Small-Cap Value	9.00%	5.40%	3.60%
Emerging Markets	9.00%	5.40%	3.60%
ex-U.S. Real Estate	5.00%	3.00%	2.00%
Bonds 1–3 years	0.00%	12.00%	18.00%
Bonds 3–7 years Treasury	0.00%	20.00%	30.00%
TIPS Bond	0.00%	8.00%	12.00%
	100.00%	**100.00%**	**100.00%**

Assignment 8.3   Investing in Mutual Funds

Name _____

SHOW YOUR CALCULATIONS

1. Contact a mutual fund company (either go to their website or call them) and request (or print from the website) a prospectus and an application. A prospectus is a packet of information about their fund(s). After reading the prospectus, select a fund (or several funds) from the group that you would like to invest in. For each fund, write a paragraph describing (1) which fund(s) you selected, (2) why you selected it/them, and (3) what you intend to do with all the money you are going to earn!

2. If you were to invest $150 at the beginning of each month into a mutual fund that averaged a 9% annual return, what would be the mutual fund account value after 12 years? Ignore the impact of taxes and inflation.

3. What would your future account value be (after-tax and after-inflation) if you invested $125 each month into a growth mutual fund for 20 years? Assume an average annual rate of return of 12% (all in capital gains). Assume a combined federal and state income tax rate of 24% and an average annual inflation rate of 3.8% over the 20-year period. That is, what is the future value in terms of today's purchasing power.

4. Describe three distinct advantages of investing in mutual funds compared to investing in single issues of stock.

5. Dollar cost averaging is when an investor purchases the same dollar amount of securities every time period. In that way, he or she purchases more shares when the price is low and fewer shares when the price is high. If he or she invests $200 per month in a mutual fund at the following monthly prices, is he or she better or worse off compared to investing $200 per month in an account that pays a fixed 8% annual interest (compounded monthly)? The mutual fund ending account value will be determined by the total number of shares purchased during the year multiplied by the last known price of $5.50.

Month	Mutual Fund Share Price	# Shares Purchased
1	$5.00	40
2	$5.10	___
3	$4.30	___
4	$3.30	___
5	$3.75	___
6	$3.60	___
7	$5.00	___
8	$5.50	___
9	$4.30	___
10	$4.75	___
11	$5.00	___
12	$5.50	___

Section Eight Extra Practice Problems

1. If APC Corp. has a closing price of $70 per share and pays an annualized dividend per share of $1.44, what will be its dividend yield?

2. Using the same information as given in the preceding problem, calculate the earnings per share of APC stock assuming the P/E ratio is 12.

3. The current market price of ABC stock is $28 per share. If you placed an order to purchase 100 shares of ABC at $22 per share and an order to sell 100 shares of ABC at $20 per share you would have placed what two types of orders?

4. You purchased 100 shares of IBM stock in January 2011 for $154 per share. Each year you received a cash dividend of $3.80 per share. In December 2013, you sold your 100 shares of IBM for $188 per share. Brokerage fees amounted to 3.5% of the purchase price and 3.5% of the sales proceeds. What is your total holding-period return (in dollars) over the investment period?

5. Using the information from the preceding problem, what was the average annual return over the investment period for IBM? Assume the dividends were paid once per year, at the end of the year.

6. What would be the after-tax average annual rate of return for IBM using a 25% marginal tax rate?

7. Assuming an annual inflation rate of 4.5% over the same investment period, calculate the after-tax *real* annual rate of return for the investment in IBM stock.

8. You purchase a 9.75% coupon bond for $1,125 which will mature in 12 years. What is the bond's *current yield*?

9. What is the YTM of the bond in the previous problem? (Use semiannual interest payments if using a financial calculator. If using the approximation formula enter **i** and **n** as annual figures.)

10. You have a choice of purchasing a Missouri St Hwys bond (municipal bond) paying 4.92% annual interest or a Ford corporate bond paying 6.6%. If you were in the 28% marginal tax bracket, which bond would you purchase to earn the greatest amount of *after-tax* interest? Secondly, considering only federal tax, how much after-tax interest (in dollars) would you earn annually with the bond you select?

Section Eight Practice Problem Answers

1. If APC Corp. has a closing price of $70 per share and pays a annualized dividend per share of $1.44, what will be its dividend yield?

$$1.44 / 70 = .02057 \text{ or } 2.06\%$$

2. Using the same information as given in the preceding problem, calculate the earnings per share of APC stock assuming the P/E ratio is 12.

$$\frac{70}{\text{EPS}} = 12$$

Now, let the denominator and quotient trade places . . . and you get your answer.

$$\frac{70}{12} = \text{EPS} = \mathbf{\$5.83}$$

3. The current market price of ABC stock is $28 per share. If you placed an order to purchase 100 shares of ABC at $22 per share and an order to sell 100 shares of ABC at $20 per share you would have placed what two types of orders?

Limit order to buy at $22, **stop-loss order to sell** at $20.

4. You purchased 100 shares of IBM stock in January 2011 for $154 per share. Each year you received a cash dividend of $3.80 per share. In December 2013, you sold your 100 shares of IBM for $188 per share. Brokerage fees amounted to 3.5% of the purchase price and 3.5% of the sales proceeds. What is your total holding-period return (in dollars) over the investment period?

Dividends	=	($3.80 × 3) × 100 shares	=	$1,140.00
Capital Gain	=	Sale proceeds - Purchase price		
Sale proceeds		($188 × 100) × .965	=	$18,142.00
Minus			−	
Purchase price		($154 × 100) × 1.035	=	$15,939.00
Capital Gain				$ 2,203.00
plus			+	
Dividends				$ 1,140.00
Total return in dollars			=	**$ 3,343.00**

5. Using the information from the preceding problem, what was the average annual return over the investment period for IBM?
Using a financial calculator:

PV = <15,939.00>
FV = 18,142.00
PMT = 380
N   = 3
I/YR = **6.696%**

6. What would be the after-tax average annual rate of return for IBM using a 25% marginal income tax rate? Recall that a 25% marginal income tax rate corresponds to a 15% tax rate for dividends and capital gains.

Using a financial calculator:

Tax on capital gain	=	$2,203 × .15	=	$ 330.45
After-tax capital gain			=	$1,872.55
Tax on annual dividends	=	$ 380 × .15	=	$ 57.00
After-tax annual dividends			=	$ 323.00

PV = <15,939>
FV = 17,811.55 (18,142.00 − 330.45 = 17,811.55 after-tax FV)
PMT = 323 (380 − 57 = 323)
N   = 3
I/YR = 5.727%

7. Assuming an annual inflation rate of 4.5% over the same investment period, calculate the after-tax *real* annual rate of return for the investment in IBM stock.

$$\frac{1 + .05727}{1 + .045} - 1 = .01174 \text{ or } \textbf{1.17\%}$$

8. You purchase a 9.75% coupon bond for $1,125 which will mature in 12 years.

What is the bond's *current yield*?

$$\text{Current yield} = \frac{\text{Annual Interest}}{\text{Current Price}} = \text{Current yield}$$

$$\text{Current yield} = \frac{\$97.50}{\$1,125} = .0867 \text{ or } \textbf{8.67\%}$$

9. What is the YTM of the bond in the previous problem? (Use semiannual interest payments if using a financial calculator. If using the approximation formula enter **i** and **n** as annual figures.)

Using a financial calculator:

PV = <1,125>
FV = 1,000
N   = 24   (semiannual interest payments, P/Y =2)
PMT = 48.75   (97.50 / 2 = 48.75)

I/YR = 4.0509%, if P/Y = 1 you must multiply by 2 = **8.10%**,
(I/YR = 8.10%, if P/Y = 2 is entered in your calculator)

Using approximation formula:

$$\text{YTM} = \frac{97.50 + \dfrac{1,000 - 1,125}{12}}{\dfrac{1,000 + 1,125}{2}} = .082 \text{ or } \textbf{8.20\%}$$

10. You have a choice of purchasing a Missouri St Hwys bond (municipal bond) paying 4.92% annual interest or a Ford corporate bond paying 6.6%. If you were in the 28% marginal tax bracket, which bond would you purchase to earn the greatest amount of *after-tax* interest? Secondly, considering only federal tax, how much after-tax interest (in dollars) would you earn annually with the bond you select?

Municipal bond:

$$\text{Taxable equivalent yield} = \frac{\text{Tax-free rate}}{1 - (\text{marginal tax rate})}$$

$$= \frac{.0492}{1 - .28} = \textbf{6.8\%}$$

As 6.8% > 6.6% of corporate bond you should **choose the municipal bond.**

After-tax interest earnings:

Municipal bond:

$1,000 \times .0492 = $ **\$49.20 interest (after-tax)**

Corporate bond:

$1,000 \times .066 = 66 before-tax interest

$66 \times (1 - .28) = $ **\$47.52 after-tax interest**

Notes:

Retirement Planning

The question isn't at what age I want to retire, it's at what income.

George Foreman (1949–)

I have now the gloomy prospect of retiring from office loaded with serious debts, which will materially affect the tranquility of my retirement.

Thomas Jefferson (1743–1826)

I believe that the biggest mistake that most people make when it comes to their retirement is they do not plan for it. They take the same route as Alice in the story from "Alice in Wonderland," in which the cat tells Alice that surely she will get somewhere as long as she walks long enough. It may not be exactly where you wanted to get to, but you certainly get somewhere.

Mark Singer

Sadly, retirement planning, in many circumstances, has become nothing more than planned procrastination.

Richie Norton

Believe it or not, one day you will receive an invitation to join the American Association of Retired Persons (AARP; http://www.aarp.org). That is, if you are lucky enough to live until you reach your age of retirement. Yes, it should be "your age of retirement" on your terms with your past decisions made in such a way that they support the retirement of your dreams. The trouble for the lucky ones who are blessed with longevity in life is that they often live longer than their money. Living longer than your money is not a result of sound financial planning. (Living longer may, however, have something to do with a sound exercise regime.) Living longer than your money reflects either poor financial planning or some very bad luck. You cannot do much about your luck, but you can do something about your retirement plan along with your savings and investment decisions. We will address this issue by helping you understand a simple mathematical model of retirement savings goals. Hopefully, this will help you with your planning. We will then move forward to discuss the various sources of retirement income, and how your decisions create or destroy your retirement. Good decisions will enable you to enjoy your golden years.

STEPS IN PLANNING FOR YOUR RETIREMENT

The steps to planning for your retirement, like most problems, are pretty simple. At least they sound simple. You can do them today even though most of you are 40–50 years from retirement. Yet, doing them today can provide a powerful motivator to help you make better financial decisions going forward. The steps are:

1. Determine the level of living you desire for retirement and how much that will cost you per year of retirement.
2. Estimate your income from Social Security retirement, pension benefits at work, as well as investments.
3. If your expectations for your level of living are greater than your expected retirement income, either save more money or reduce your expectations.

Does not that sound simple? If it were that simple, would we be in a baby-boom retirement crisis?

ESTIMATING RETIREMENT NEEDS

a. Estimate the age you plan to retire. Compared to the past, many people are choosing to retire later in life for two reasons: (1) they are living longer and enjoy working or (2) they cannot retire because they do not have the money! For many, the age of retirement is when they qualify for full retirement benefits from Social Security, have served a minimum number of years to qualify for retirement, or at some target date, such as when their children have finished their university educations. We will assume you want to retire at the age of 67 and that you are currently 21 years old.

b. Estimate your life expectancy to determine the length of time you need financial resources. (We will use the number of years between your age of retirement and your anticipated death in an annuity due calculation.) To estimate your life expectancy, refer to a mortality table or consider the longevity of family members. A life expectancy table may be found at the following: https://www.ssa.gov/oact/STATS/table4c6.html.

   Another useful website to help you determine your life expectancy, given your family history and personal choices is http://www.livingto100.com. We will assume you will live to be 90 years old for our example as this is actually longer than the average life expectancy.

c. Imagine that you are retired today. Determine the amount of annual income (call it Y_{now}) that would be required to maintain your desired retirement lifestyle at today's prices (i.e., nominal dollars). In doing this, the following guidelines may be useful:
   - Make estimates based on your goals and desires during retirement.
   - While some living costs may *decline* in retirement (no mortgage payment, generally no need for life insurance, reduced work-related expenses, no more tuition expense for children!), other costs may *increase* (medical insurance premiums, medical costs, special needs such as travel, relocation, etc.).
   - Many financial professionals assume that living costs will decrease and, therefore, use *60%–80% of current income* (at midlife) as an estimate of retirement income needs.

   We will assume that you will need $75,000 in today's dollars to afford your retirement.

d. *Subtract* your anticipated annual Social Security and pension benefits to be received in retirement from your needed retirement income estimate ($75,000 from step C). These may be obtained from the Social Security Administration (phone 1-800-234-5772, ask for a *Personal Earnings and Benefit Estimate Statement*), the employee benefits office at work, or from the website (http://www.ssa.gov/planners/calculators.htm) of the Social Security Administration. Using that website and assuming you earned $75,000 each year for the past 8 years. (You child prodigy violin player, you!) Your Social Security benefit is projected to be $2,214 in today's dollars, or $26,568 per year—if Social Security is a part of your retirement plan. We will assume you participate in a defined contribution retirement plan (401(k), 403(b), individual retirement account [IRA], simplified employee pension [SEP], etc.), and you have to save all your retirement income yourself.

The difference (if a positive number) is the current value of additional income from personal investments you will need at retirement to provide for your retirement needs. If the difference is zero or negative, no additional financial resources are needed to fund your retirement.

$$Y_{now} - (SocSec + Pension) = \text{Annual Net Income Need (or } Y_{need})$$
$$\$75,000 - \$26,568 = \$48,432 = \text{Annual Net Income Need (or Yneed)}$$

e. If the net income need (denoted Y_{need}) is positive, the next step involves adjusting for inflation. To solve this, let Y_{need} be a present value (PV), N be the number of years until retirement, and assume a rate of inflation over the period until retirement. In 2018, inflation was a mild 2.4%, but in 2008 it was 3.85%. What do we use? We will use a 64-year average. Since 1950, inflation has averaged 3.67% with a standard deviation of 2.82%. We do not have to inflate Social Security, since current law allows it to increase with inflation.

$$Y_{need} \times (1 + \text{rate of inflation})^N = Y_{\text{inflated need}}$$
$$\$48,432 \times (1 + .0367)^{(67-21)} \text{ or } \$48,432 \times (1 + .0367)^{(46)} = \$254,200!!$$

If we want to calculate our need without Social Security, the need would be $393,644 per year. (Let us hope Social Security is there to help you!)

The future value ($254,200) represents the number of dollars you will need in the *first year of retirement* to ensure the purchasing power that you need, if you receive Social Security.

f. Given the fact that $Y_{\text{inflated need}}$ is required at the start of every year during retirement, one must calculate the lump-sum amount that should be available at the start of retirement to fund this annual need. To accomplish this, calculate the PV of an annuity due where $Y_{\text{inflated need}}$ equals the annuity due payment (PMT_{ad}), N is the number of years you expect to live in retirement ($90 - 67 = 23$ years), and r equals the <u>real</u> rate of return. The real rate of return is calculated as:

$$\frac{1 + \text{after-tax rate of return}}{1 + \text{inflation rate}} - 1$$

Assuming one can earn 7% after-tax rate of return.

$$\frac{1 + .07}{1 + .0367} - 1 = \text{I/YR} = 3.2121154\% \text{ (when calculated, save it immediately)}$$

PMTad = <$254,200>
    FV = $0 (we will assume you cannot take it with you!)
    N = 23
I/YR = 3.2121154%
   PV = ? = $4,220,603

The answer from step f is the amount of money you would need to have accumulated in your retirement savings account the day you retire. This amount will not only provide you with $75,000 in today's purchasing power but it allows your withdrawals to increase at the rate of inflation we assumed, 3.67%. This is your **retirement savings goal, $4,220,603!**

g. Subtract from your retirement savings goal the future value of general investment accounts you would be willing to liquidate and the future value of your retirement plans (e.g., 401(k), 403(b), Keogh, IRA, and SEP plans).

h. Repeat the process with contingency plans ("what if" scenarios)
   1. Disability before you retire
   2. Divorce
   3. Long term nursing care (insurance?)
   4. Your spouse dies, following a long-term, financially draining illness
   5. Whatever calamity you want to assume

An example of the process using different information is as follows:

Mr. and Mrs. E. Nuff have decided that they need $60,000 in today's dollars (Y_{now}) to fund their retirement. They are currently 42 years old and plan to retire at age 67. They estimate that their Social Security benefits will be $1,838 per month and that their combined pension income will be $1,500 per month. They assume:

a. Inflation will average 3% throughout their life.
b. They will earn a 6% **after-tax** return on their investments.
c. They will live to be 87 years old.

The first step is to estimate their deficit from Social Security and pension income.

$$Y_{now} - (SocSec + Pension) = \text{Net Income Need (or } Y_{need})$$
$$\$60,000 - ((\$1,838 + \$1,500) \times 12) = \$19,944\ Y_{need}$$

The $19,944 is in today's dollars so that figure must be adjusted for 25 years of anticipated inflation at 3% per year.

$$Y_{need} \times (1 + \text{rate of inflation})^n = Y_{inflated\ need}$$
$$\$19,944 \times (1 + .03)^{25} = \$41,758 = Y_{inflated\ need} \text{ (in inflation-adjusted dollars)}$$

This $41,758 is their projected *need* during their first year of retirement. The retirement need is for the start of each year and they need it to grow by the rate of inflation each year (i.e., a serial payment). The PV of a stream of annuity due payments of $41,758 (or PMTad) for 20 years of retirement (n) which earns a real rate of interest (r, or I/YR for calculations) of 2.9% [as calculated by $((1.06\ /\ 1.03) - 1 = .029)$] is their *retirement savings goal*.

PMTad	=	<$41,758>
I/YR	=	2.9% (inflation-adjusted return during retirement)
N	=	20 years
PV	=	**$645,220 retirement savings goal**

In other words, they need to have about $645,220 saved by the time they retire.

This amount of money would produce the needed retirement income until age 87. The retirement savings goal of $645,220 would be reduced by the future value of any retirement savings plans the Nuffs are willing to liquidate at retirement, if these have not previously been accounted for.

This $645,220 value can be used as the future value of their retirement savings goal to determine what additional investments are needed *prior to retirement* to achieve the needed FV goal of $645,220.

For example, if they currently had no money invested in accounts for retirement (such as a 401(k), IRA, etc.), how much would they need to invest each month to achieve their needed retirement savings goal? Assuming they are in the 25% federal marginal tax bracket and that their state tax rate is 6%, the *before-tax* rate of return will be 8.6957%. (Recall that money invested in traditional tax-deferred retirement accounts is not taxed until money is withdrawn during retirement.)

(6% after-tax return / $(1 - (.25 + .06)) = 8.6957\%$ before-tax return

FV	=	$645,220
N	=	25 years until retirement × 12 = 300 months
I/YR	=	8.6957
P/Y	=	12
PMTad	=	**<$600.96> monthly annuity due payment**
or		
PMT	=	**<$605.32> monthly ordinary payment**

Bottom line: they need to start saving about $600 per month for the next 25 years to meet their retirement savings goal of $645,220.

If they had started saving for retirement 10 years earlier (at age 32), they would need to save only about $240 per month.

Here is the real kicker: if they had started saving for retirement 20 years earlier (at age 22), they would need to invest only about $100 per month!

FV	=	$645,220
N	=	45 years until retirement × 12 (starting at age 22)
I/YR	=	8.6957
P/Y	=	12
PMT	=	**<$96.00> monthly annuity due payment**
	=	**<$96.70> monthly ordinary annuity payment**

This is a great place to stop and make the point about how important it is to start saving for your retirement now, like today. It is not about lattes, baubles, and beads. It is about reaching your goals. Retirement is but one.

- Retirement
- Children's college education
- Buy a home
- Periodically drive a newer car
- Vacation
- Vacation home
- Boat
- Dream, dream, dream and save, save, save. . . .

SOURCES OF RETIREMENT INCOME[1]

There is much talk about the failure of people to adequately plan for their retirement, this is due to the lack of saving sufficient income to support the retirement they aspired to obtain. As a result, we have seen changes in the sources of retirement income over time. The following table lists the sources of retirement income for those age 65 and over in both 1974 and 2010.

---

[1]http://www.ebri.org/pdf/publications/books/databook/DB.Chapter%2007.pdf

Source of Income	1974	2010	Percentage Change
Social Security	42.0%	39.5%	−5.95%
Pensions and Annuities	14.0%	19.7%	40.71%
Income from Assets	18.2%	11.8%	−35.16%
Earnings	21.3%	26.9%	26.29%
Other	4.5%	2.1%	−53.33%

What is striking in the above table is the decrease in the importance of income from assets and the increase in the importance of income from pensions and annuities (which includes defined contribution plans, which did not exist much in 1974) and earnings form paid work. Clearly, the low-hanging fruit for elderly income is to increase savings to provide income from assets. It is NOT to depend more on Social Security.

Another view of retirement income for the elderly by race is depicted in the following chart. The chart (U.S. Bureau of the Census, 2010) is a little different from the table, as asset income has been divided into interest and dividends. Moreover, a person could report more than one source of retirement income and this is not, necessarily, the one they think of as the most important. What do we see?

It is pretty obvious that White citizens (the darkest bar) have greater access to the income sources of Social Security, Pensions and Retirement Savings, Interest and Dividends, all of which indicate greater levels of wealth from past savings. On the other hand, both Hispanic (lightest bar) and Black households report greater reliance on current earnings and Supplemental Security Income than do White households.

A final picture of retirement income is provided in a 2013 poll by the Gallup annual Economy and Personal Finance survey.[2] By breaking up the sources of retirement income into more distinct categories, they compare all retirees, to those with less than $50,000 in income and those with $50,000 or more in income. Expectedly, Social Security is a major source of retirement income for 73% of those with less

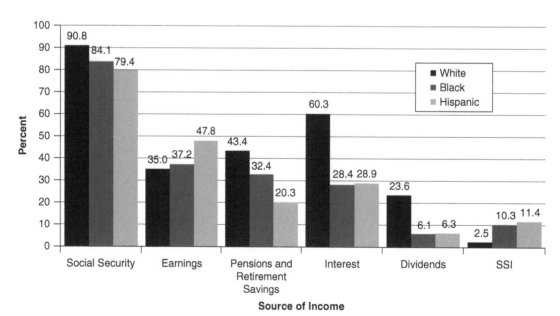

Figure 1 Sources of Family Income of Persons Age 65 and Older by Race/Ethinicity in 2009

Data Source: U.S. Bureau of the Census, March 2010 Current Population Survey Annual Social and Economic Supplement

---

[2]http://www.gallup.com/poll/162713/pensions-top-income-source-wealthier-retirees.aspx?version=print

"Major" Sources of Income, Current U.S. Retirees

Source of Income	All Retirees	Less Than $50,000	$50,000 or More
Social Security	61%	73%	49%
Work Pension	36%	27%	55%
401(k), IRA, Other "Self"-Retirement Savings	23%	18%	36%
Home Equity	20%	19%	22%
Stock Equity Investments	13%	9%	21%
Other "Cash" Savings	14%	14%	15%
Annuities or Insurance	9%	9%	12%
Part-Time Work	3%	5%	2%
Inheritance	3%	4%	3%
Rent and Royalties	4%	3%	6%

than $50,000 in income but is a major source for less than half of those with over $50,000 in income. Notice that stock equity investments are only a major source of income for 9% of the population whom have an annual income that is less than $50,000, but stock equity investments are more than twice as common, at 21% of the population, for those whom have an income of at least $50,000 annually. Similarly, annuities and insurance are a major source for 21% of the $50,000 and over income group, but only 9% of those with under $50,000. Most disappointing, especially for those that have to work in retirement is the result that 5% of those with less than $50,000 are engaged in part-time work but only 2% of those with income over $50,000 continue to work in retirement. A snapshot to take away is that to have a greater income in retirement, one is aided by pensions, self-retirement savings, home equity, stock equity, and insurance products. That is, you should take your savings and try to have several income sources, while taking advantage of as many tax-favored products as possible: IRAs, 401(k)s, housing, annuities, rents, and royalties.

The point to this discussion is simple. Start saving for your retirement.

To help motivate you to begin saving, the tables on the following two pages are powerful. The first, Future Value of Various Investing Strategies, shows five different investing scenarios. Scenario 4 depicts the traditional IRA account, that is, a person starts investing $5,500 per year (the 2018 maximum) at age 35.

As demonstrated earlier, you are much better off investing sooner, rather than later—regardless of whether it is a tax-deferred account or a regular, taxable investment account. Investing $275 per year (as shown in Scenario 3) up through age 35 followed by the traditional $5,500 per year makes a tremendous difference. Despite only investing an extra $5,225, the future value in Scenario 3 is over four times the future value of that in Scenario 4!

If you invest money into a tax-deferred account (such as an IRA, 401(k), 403(b), etc.), there is no taxation on the money in the account from year to year. It grows tax-deferred. When money is withdrawn from the account (which can begin at 59.5), it will be taxed. However, in retirement most people are in a lower tax bracket.

Remember that tax-deferred accounts must be funded by earned income (or alimony). For that reason, most of the scenarios in the following table would not likely be retirement accounts because not many children of age five have earned income or alimony checks coming in! Nevertheless, any of the scenarios below are possible—in real life—through a regular investment account in the child's name (via the Uniform Gifts to Minors Act). The money could be deposited in the child's account by a parent, grandparent, uncle, friend, and so on.

If that table does not convince you to start investing, the table that follows it, one page further in the book, entitled, "Save 10% and Be Happy," will.

Future Value of Various Investing Strategies
(Assuming a 10% annual return and not adjusted for taxes or inflation)

Age	Scenario 1 Annual Investment	Scenario 2 Annual Investment	Scenario 3 Annual Investment	Scenario 4 Annual Investment	Scenario 5 Annual Investment
5	$275	$2,750	$275	$0	$5,500
6	$275	$0	$275	$0	$5,500
7	$275	$0	$275	$0	$5,500
8	$275	$0	$275	$0	$5,500
9	$275	$0	$275	$0	$5,500
10	$275	$0	$275	$0	$0
11	$275	$0	$275	$0	$0
12	$275	$0	$275	$0	$0
13	$275	$0	$275	$0	$0
14	$275	$0	$275	$0	$0
15	$275	$0	$275	$0	$0
16	$275	$0	$275	$0	$0
17	$275	$0	$275	$0	$0
18	$275	$0	$275	$0	$0
19	$275	$0	$275	$0	$0
20	$275	$0	$275	$0	$0
21	$275	$0	$275	$0	$0
22	$275	$0	$275	$0	$0
23	$275	$0	$275	$0	$0
24	$275	$0	$275	$0	$0
25	$275	$0	$275	$0	$0
26	$275	$0	$275	$0	$0
27	$275	$0	$275	$0	$0
28	$275	$0	$275	$0	$0
29	$275	$0	$275	$0	$0
30	$275	$0	$275	$0	$0

Age	Scenario 1	Scenario 2	Scenario 3	Scenario 4	Scenario 5
	Annual Investment	Annual Investment	Annual Investment	Annual Investment	Annual Investment
31	$275	$0	$275	$0	$0
32	$275	$0	$275	$0	$0
33	$275	$0	$275	$0	$0
34	$275	$0	$275	$0	$0
35	$275	$0	$5,500	$5,500	$0
36	$275	$0	$5,500	$5,500	$0
37	$275	$0	$5,500	$5,500	$0
38	$275	$0	$5,500	$5,500	$0
39	$275	$0	$5,500	$5,500	$0
40	$275	$0	$5,500	$5,500	$0
41	$275	$0	$5,500	$5,500	$0
42	$275	$0	$5,500	$5,500	$0
43	$275	$0	$5,500	$5,500	$0
44	$275	$0	$5,500	$5,500	$0
45	$275	$0	$5,500	$5,500	$0
46	$275	$0	$5,500	$5,500	$0
47	$275	$0	$5,500	$5,500	$0
48	$275	$0	$5,500	$5,500	$0
49	$275	$0	$5,500	$5,500	$0
50	$275	$0	$5,500	$5,500	$0
51	$275	$0	$5,500	$5,500	$0
52	$275	$0	$5,500	$5,500	$0
53	$275	$0	$5,500	$5,500	$0
54	$275	$0	$5,500	$5,500	$0
55	$275	$0	$5,500	$5,500	$0
56	$275	$0	$5,500	$5,500	$0
57	$275	$0	$5,500	$5,500	$0
58	$275	$0	$5,500	$5,500	$0
59	$275	$0	$5,500	$5,500	$0
60	$275	$0	$5,500	$5,500	$0
Total Invested	$15,400	$2,750	$146,025	$137,500	$27,500
FV at age 60	$569,154	$571,904	$1,083,017	$254,909	$4,335,932

Save 10% and Be Happy

Age	Annual Income (3% annual increase)	10% of Gross Income Invested	# Years Money is Invested	Future Value at . . .				
				4% Annual Interest	6% Annual Interest	8% Annual Interest	10% Annual Interest	12% Annual Interest
20	12,000	1,200	45	7,009	16,518	38,305	87,469	196,785
21	12,000	1,200	44	6,740	15,583	35,467	79,517	175,701
22	45,000	4,500	43	24,302	55,127	123,150	271,080	588,285
23	46,350	4,635	42	24,069	53,567	117,448	253,830	541,012
24	47,741	4,774	41	23,837	52,051	112,011	237,677	497,538
25	49,173	4,917	40	23,608	50,578	106,825	222,552	457,557
26	50,648	5,065	39	23,381	49,146	101,880	208,390	420,789
27	52,167	5,217	38	23,156	47,755	97,163	195,128	386,976
28	53,732	5,373	37	22,933	46,404	92,665	182,711	355,879
29	55,344	5,534	36	22,713	45,090	88,375	171,084	327,282
30	57,005	5,700	35	22,495	43,814	84,283	160,197	300,982
31	58,715	5,871	34	22,278	42,574	80,381	150,003	276,796
32	60,476	6,048	33	22,064	41,369	76,660	140,457	254,554
33	62,291	6,229	32	21,852	40,198	73,111	131,519	234,099
34	64,159	6,416	31	21,642	39,061	69,726	123,149	215,287
35	66,084	6,608	30	21,434	37,955	66,498	115,313	197,987
36	68,067	6,807	29	21,228	36,881	63,419	107,975	182,078
37	70,109	7,011	28	21,023	35,837	60,483	101,103	167,446
38	72,212	7,221	27	20,821	34,823	57,683	94,670	153,991
39	74,378	7,438	26	20,621	33,837	55,013	88,645	141,617
40	76,609	7,661	25	20,423	32,880	52,466	83,004	130,237
41	78,908	7,891	24	20,226	31,949	50,037	77,722	119,771
42	81,275	8,128	23	20,032	31,045	47,720	72,776	110,147
43	83,713	8,371	22	19,839	30,166	45,511	68,145	101,296
44	86,225	8,622	21	19,649	29,313	43,404	63,808	93,156
45	88,811	8,881	20	19,460	28,483	41,395	59,748	85,670
46	91,476	9,148	19	19,273	27,677	39,478	55,946	78,786
47	94,220	9,422	18	19,087	26,894	37,650	52,386	72,455
48	97,047	9,705	17	18,904	26,132	35,907	49,052	66,633
49	99,958	9,996	16	18,722	25,393	34,245	45,930	61,278
50	102,957	10,296	15	18,542	24,674	32,660	43,008	56,354
51	106,045	10,605	14	18,364	23,976	31,148	40,271	51,826
52	109,227	10,923	13	18,187	23,297	29,706	37,708	47,661
53	112,504	11,250	12	18,012	22,638	28,330	35,308	43,831
54	115,879	11,588	11	17,839	21,997	27,019	33,062	40,309
55	119,355	11,936	10	17,667	21,375	25,768	30,958	37,070
56	122,936	12,294	9	17,498	20,770	24,575	28,988	34,091
57	126,624	12,662	8	17,329	20,182	23,437	27,143	31,352
58	130,423	13,042	7	17,163	19,611	22,352	25,416	28,832

Age	Annual Income (3% annual increase)	10% of Gross Income Invested	# Years Money is Invested	Future Value at ... 4% Annual Interest	6% Annual Interest	8% Annual Interest	10% Annual Interest	12% Annual Interest
59	134,335	13,434	6	16,998	19,056	21,317	23,798	26,515
60	138,365	13,837	5	16,834	18,516	20,330	22,284	24,385
61	142,516	14,252	4	16,672	17,992	19,389	20,866	22,425
62	146,792	14,679	3	16,512	17,483	18,492	19,538	20,623
63	151,195	15,120	2	16,353	16,988	17,635	18,295	18,966
64	155,731	15,573	1	16,196	16,508	16,819	17,130	17,442
65	160,403	16,040	0	16,040	16,040	16,040	16,040	16,040
Total Gross Income Earned from Age 20 to 65	**2,505,355**							
Start Investing at ...		**Preretirement Investments**		**Total Ending Account Value ($) at Age 65** (pretax and without inflation)				
Age 20		403,118		889,027	1,429,205	2,403,378	4,190,797	7,509,789
Age 25		386,809		803,070	1,236,360	1,976,997	3,261,225	5,510,469
Age 30		360,702		687,279	997,386	1,490,090	2,281,359	3,561,986
Age 35		330,438		576,949	790,369	1,105,928	1,576,034	2,280,268
Age 40		295,353		471,821	611,035	802,831	1,068,329	1,437,150
Age 45		254,680		371,652	455,682	563,693	702,873	882,544

Major retirement income sources

Each of the retirement income sources needs to be well understood in order to be able to use them to your advantage. They are really not as difficult as the media and the marketing professions make them out.

1. Social Security which is more properly called: Old Age, Survivors, Disability Income, and Hospital Insurance (OASDHI)
2. Employer-sponsored defined *benefit* retirement plans
3. Employer-sponsored defined *contribution* plan (tax-advantaged retirement accounts such as 401(k), IRAs, 403(b), SEPs)
4. Annuities
5. Life insurance
6. Equity in your home
7. Other investment accounts
8. Part-time employment

Social Security (OASDHI)

For 2018, 6.2% of all earnings (12.4%, if self-employed) must be paid on salary and wages up to $132,000 (for Old Age, Survivors, and Disability Insurance). Medicare tax (HI) of 1.45% (2.9%, if self-employed) is collected on <u>all</u> earned income—there is no upper limit. After your earned income exceeds $132,000 (in 2019), your liability to pay OASD taxes ceases. Payment of Medicare taxes, however, continues.

The OASD income limit is increased each year and the total tax rate is 7.65% (6.2% OASD and 1.45% HI), which is matched by your employer. If you are self-employed, you pay both. Thus, the total tax rate is 15.30% when you include both the employer's and the employee's contribution, or the total self-employed contribution.

Regular full retirement benefits are available at age 65 for those who were born prior to 1937. Recognizing that few people of that vintage will be reading this text, for those born between 1943 and 1954, they can receive full benefits at age 66, while the full-benefit age will be age 67 for those born after 1959. For those born between 1954 and 1959, their age of full benefits will increase, over time from 66 years to 67 years. Early retirement is possible. One may currently retire at 62 but, when one does take "early" retirement, there is a permanent reduction in one's retirement benefits. Benefits are reduced to 80% of full benefits if one retires at 62, and the percentage of full benefits received increases as one approaches full-benefit age. Moreover, delaying retirement past the age of full retirement benefits increases benefits by 8% per year, until age 70. (To estimate your benefits go to: http://www.ssa.gov/planners/benefitcalculators.htm or http://www.socialsecurity.gov/estimator)

As a result of your work, your family members may also receive retirement benefits:

- Spouse, if over 62 years of age. (The spouse receives the larger of either their benefit from their employment history or the amount they would receive as the spouse of the retired worker. Not both.)

- Spouse under age 62 if he or she is caring for a child under the age of 16 or over the age of 16 if the child is disabled.

- Unmarried child under 18 (19 if still in high school).

- Unmarried children 18+ and who were disabled before age 22.

Some Social Security pensioners may have to pay taxes on their benefits. This occurs if the recipient has substantial income in addition to Social Security (e.g., interest, dividends, wages, self-employment income that must be reported). If you file a federal tax return as an individual and your income is between $25,000 and $34,000 ($32,000 and $44,000, if married and file a joint return), you have to pay tax on 50% of your Social Security benefits. If your combined income is greater than $34,000 ($44,000, if joint filer), up to 85% of the recipient's Social Security benefits are subject to federal income tax.

Employer-sponsored defined benefit and defined contribution pension plans

You will have a job where you will need to understand the benefits that are offered to you. If not, you will be in business for yourself and you will need to make all these decisions. The following will be presented as important questions pertaining to employer-sponsored pension plans. The answers can, of course, be generalized to you, if you are the employer.

Q1. The first question is whether you, the employee, need to make contributions to the plan? Plans may be either contributory or noncontributory.

Noncontributory—These are fewer and fewer in number and more likely to be found in the public sector. In a noncontributory plan, the employer pays 100% of cost. The employer must demonstrate, moreover, that the plan is well funded—meaning that there is sufficient money in the fund to pay for the retirement of his or her workforce. With these plans, the employee is not taxed on the contributions until he or she receives those funds while in retirement.

Contributory—These are growing in popularity, as the employer is not required to demonstrate that they are funded. Instead, the cost of maintaining adequate retirement savings falls to the employee. The employee pays the cost, although some employers also match a portion of the employee's contribution. If the employer matches, the lesser of $56,000 or 100% of compensation is currently allowed for employer contribution to defined contribution plans. If you contribute through a traditional 401(k) or 403(b) plan, the contribution is an adjustment to income (meaning whatever you contribute lowers your taxable income).

In 2019, up to 20% of pretax income, up to a maximum of $19,000 (with scheduled increases), may be contributed to a 401(k) or 403(b) retirement account. While these are the most common, other types of plans are available for specific situations such as profit-sharing plans, 457 deferrals, IRAs, SIMPLE pensions, and SEPs. These may also be created to be Roth, as opposed to traditional tax-deferred plans, where the employee pays taxes on the earning first and then is not taxed on withdrawal. More on that later. . . .

Q2. What happens if you change jobs?

If the job is terminated or the employee quits, the employee has full rights to the money he or she has contributed to the account. However, since the employer also can make contributions, those contributions may or may not be able to transfer with the employee when he or she departs. The employee does not have full rights to these contributions until fully vested.

Vesting is a technical term designating the time at which the employee obtains legal rights to the funds in his or her retirement benefits. This is important at the point of retirement or when a person changes jobs. Remember, you are immediately vested in your contributions. However, the contributions of your employer become vested after you have worked for the employer for a specified number of years. The schedules that are used must follow one of these three vesting schedules:

1. Graded Vesting

Completed years Of service	Vested percentage
Fewer than 3	0
3	20
4	40
5	60
6	80
7 or more	100

2. Cliff Vesting (example only, full vesting can occur sooner than 5 years.)

Completed years Of service	Vested percentage
Fewer than 5	0
5 or more	100

3. Immediate vesting. The employer's contributions are immediately vested in the employee's name. Thus, when considering a job change it is important to consider the impact on retirement benefits. The increase in salary at a new job may not be worth the benefits you sacrificed at your current job. You might like that money during your retirement years. This is especially true with "cliff" vesting (example #2 shown above), if one has less than the required number of years with the company.

Q3. Is the plan insured?

The Employee Retirement Income Security Act (ERISA) was created by the Pension Benefit Guaranty Corporation (PBGC) to provide insurance to employees to insure that their pension income will be available when they need it. It guarantees a minimum pension to each employee, if the plan is a defined benefit plan, with premiums collected from the employer of $1 per year per employee.

Q4. How does the employer determine your retirement benefits?

To be strict in our conversation, the only benefits that are predetermined are **defined benefit** pensions. With a defined benefit pension, the level of benefits is fixed and based on income and/or years of employee service. This is usually a percentage or fixed flat amount.

Example 1: defined benefit of 2% *per year of service*

30 years service
Average salary = $56,000

$$.02 \times 30 \times \$56,000 = \$33,600 \text{ per year in benefits}$$

Be sure to ask the income figure that they use in the calculation. In some cases, it is the average of the last 5–10 years of service. In others, it is earnings over one's career.

Example 2: $100 monthly pension income *per year of service*

Same service record as above,

$$\$100 \times 30 = \$3,000 \text{ per month or } \$36,000 \text{ per year in benefits.}$$

When you take a job with a **defined contribution** pension plan, the amount of money the employer and employee contribute is either variable or clearly specified. With these plans, however, the benefit received in retirement is unknown, depending on the success of the investments in the fund. As mentioned earlier, there is a shift toward defined contribution plans and away from defined benefit pension plans. This shift increases the level of personal responsibility for one's retirement. That is, you need to start saving for your retirement today.

Q5. How will your benefits be received when you reach retirement?

There are three basic ways benefits are received by the worker.

1. Life Option—This is where installment payments are received for lifetime of worker. These are either defined by contract, as above, or where the worker pays himself or herself payments based on actuarial assumptions about interest rates and the life expectancy of the retiree given the amount of money in the account. This is difficult and many will purchase an annuity (more later). If not, the person has to "annuitize" the retirement fund, himself or herself. This may require some professional assistance but, generally, one can expect to withdraw no more than 3%–4% of the balance in the account the first year of retirement. Many people get in trouble when they withdraw more than that amount and, just when they do not expect it to happen, their investments fall in value and their retirement dream becomes a nightmare.
2. Joint Life Option—Installment payments are made for the life of the annuitant and, on the annuitant's death, the payments are continued to the annuitant's spouse. The payments, even initially, are lower than in the life annuity, for the time is over two lives, instead of one. If one is married, their spouse must sign a form agreeing to a life annuity option being chosen, for they know that this means they will receive no further benefits on the death of the first spouse.
3. Installment Certain Option—This is where annuity payments are made for a certain number of years such as 5, 10, 15, 20, or whatever the option chosen may be and the payments continue for that length of time, regardless of whether the annuitant(s) are alive or dead.
4. Life with a Guaranteed Term—An annuity which pays the annuitant for life or, if the annuitant dies, pays for a guaranteed term that is specified at purchase.
5. Lump-Sum Payment—You receive either the entire or partial balance as a lump sum on retirement. If you choose this, be sure to maintain the tax character of the account. For example, if your money is in a 401(k) plan, move the money to a self-directed IRA to avoid taxation on the entire withdrawal. In this case, you have to manage your money to make it last your lifetime by making systematic withdrawals from the account. (This is why people buy an annuity.)

Q6. How are your retirement benefits integrated with Social Security?

It is common for the inflation adjustment to occur within Social Security. These may or may not be offset by decreases in defined benefit pension benefits. Take as an example a 50% offset.

Example:	$ 600	Monthly Social Security benefit
	+ $ 900	Monthly pension
	$1,500	Total benefit

A $30 increase in monthly Social Security benefit leads to a $15 pension decrease using a 50% offset rule. $30 × .50 = $15 decrease in the monthly pension.

	$ 630	Social Security
	+ $ 885	Pension
	$1,515	Total benefit

Q7. Does your surviving spouse receive benefits?

As mentioned before, the answer depends on a choice. ERISA requires the employer (if the plan is tax qualified) to offer the option of spousal benefits being paid to the spouse of the employee should the employee die before his or her spouse. If this option is taken, the spousal benefit must be at least 50% of the benefit received while the retired worker was alive. The cost is borne through a reduction in the periodic pension amount of the retired worker to reflect the fact that two people (two lives) are now able to collect benefits, as opposed to solely the worker (one life). The amount of the reduction depends on the age of both spouses at the time of the employee's retirement. The worker may reject the option with the consent of their spouse, in order to increase monthly benefits. If the worker dies before normal retirement age, the retirement plan also provides survivor benefits to the vested worker.

Tax-favored retirement accounts

Traditional IRA

People who qualify can contribute up to $6,000 annually, into a tax-deductible retirement account. Money in the account grows tax-deferred and is taxed on withdrawal during retirement. For married couples with only one working spouse, an IRA account can be established for the nonworking spouse in which up to the annual maximum can be contributed. Thus, a total of $12,000 can be deposited into IRA accounts for such a couple in 2019.

Money in an IRA that is withdrawn prior to the age of 59.5 is assessed an early withdrawal tax penalty. Prior to age of 59.5, however, money in an IRA can be withdrawn without a tax penalty as long as it is reinvested into another IRA account within 60 days. *Individuals/couples with high incomes may not be able to deduct their IRA contributions if one or both of the couple are covered by a plan at their place of work.*

Roth IRA

The Roth IRA is just the opposite. Contributions are not tax deductible (i.e., they do not lower your taxable income) and the worker must include them in income to be taxed. The "opposite" is that no federal income tax is owed on money when it is withdrawn (under normal conditions the earliest you can withdraw is age 59.5). Contributions (money you invested) can be withdrawn *tax-free at any time for any purpose.* Earnings in a Roth IRA account (dividends and capital gains) can be withdrawn prior to the age 59.5 and still be tax-free under certain conditions. These conditions are:

1. First, the account needs to have been established for at least 5 years.

2. The money can be used only for certain purposes: first-time home purchase (with a lifetime maximum of $10,000), postsecondary education expenses, medical expenses exceeding 7.5% of your adjusted gross income, health insurance premiums (after you have received at least 12 consecutive weeks of unemployment compensation), disability, or the death of a spouse.

The annual maximum contribution limits are the same as the traditional IRA. In 2019, individuals are eligible to make a full contribution to a Roth IRA if their modified adjusted gross income is below $122,000 if you are a single filer or $193,000 if you are filing jointly under age 50.

For most people, the Roth IRA is the best choice—particularly for young investors, currently in a relatively low marginal tax bracket. The money you are contributing grows tax-exempt, and in an emergency you would have access to all of the money you have contributed.

401(k)

A 401(k) is a corporate payroll deduction plan whereby employees can annually contribute up to $19,000 (as of 2019) into either a tax-deferred retirement account or a Roth retirement account. The maximum contribution changes annually. Money in the account grows tax-deferred and is taxed on withdrawal during retirement (traditional) or is taxed when earned and not taxed on withdrawal (Roth). Many employers have a policy of "matching" the contributions of employees. If you have access to a 401(k) plan in which your employer matches your contribution (or makes any contribution in addition to your own), you are making a serious mistake to not make a contribution—at least enough to receive the full employer match!

403(b)

A 403(b) is identical to the 401(k) except that it is for employees of nonprofit organizations (say, a university or YMCA). Maximum yearly contributions are $19,000 (in 2019) or 20% of your pay (whichever is lesser), and changes annually.

SEP

SEP plans are tax-deferred retirement plans for self-employed people. The maximum annual contribution in 2019 is $56,000 or 25% of income, whichever is less. Money in the account grows tax-deferred and is taxed on withdrawal during retirement.

457

A 457 is for government and certain nongovernmental employers. Unlike a 401(k), there is no 10% penalty for withdrawal before the age of 59½. The maximum annual contribution in 2019 is $19,000.

Annuities

The possible payout structure is described earlier for annuities, but we need a deeper understanding before we jump into the annuity market. By definition, annuities are a contract with an insurance company designed for tax-deferred retirement savings with the company agreeing to make periodic payments to the investor for a specified period of time. Annuities are designed for retirement savings. They should be considered as a long-term savings vehicle.

Annuities are partially tax sheltered. First, annuities may be purchased with after-tax dollars, if outside of a tax-deferred retirement plan such as a 401(k) or 403(b) plan. If so, there is no investment limit as to how much money an investor may deposit into an annuity as there are in the above *before-tax* savings plans. This allows you to put as much money into an annuity as you would like, and enables the money to grow on a tax-deferred basis. The benefits of tax deferral continue to be great.

For example, assume you are able to earn 8% annually on your investments and are in the 33% marginal tax bracket (25% federal plus 8% state). If you deposit $50,000 today, at age 44, and allow the money to accumulate until age 67 and pay your taxes annually, the *non–tax-deferred* vehicle would have a lump-sum value of $141,965, which you could spend over your remaining life. If, instead, one deposits the $50,000 in a tax-deferred savings vehicle, they would have $259,587 in the account at retirement. This is a difference of $117,622 (or 83% more). If you were to withdraw the $259,587 in one lump sum and pay your 33% taxes, you would have $190,432. You were able to compound at a greater rate of return since taxes did not reduce the amount you had invested.

As you have been paying taxes on the non-tax-deferred savings plan as the money accumulates, you will not have to pay taxes on withdrawals. However, on the tax-deferred plan you will pay taxes on the amount of each withdrawal that is not a portion of the original principal that is invested. For example, if you withdrew the $259,587 as one lump sum, taxes would be due on $209,587 (i.e., 259,587 − 50,000). The taxes would equal $69,164, if your tax bracket remained 33%. This would leave you with a principal to spend of $190,432 (or, 34.1% more than $141,965).

On the other hand, annuities may be purchased with before-tax dollars (e.g., as a part of a 401(k) or 403(b)). If this is done, all the proceeds are taxable at withdrawal.

Fixed annuities are the most common type of annuity. With a fixed annuity, the amount of the payment to be received is fixed and never changes. These are typically backed by bonds or mortgages with a known yield over time, and expose the purchaser to the risk of inflation, since the payments are fixed.

In addition to the tax-deferral benefit, **variable annuities** provide the additional benefits of tying the rate of return to a mutual fund product that is chosen by the investor. Variable annuities may provide some protection from inflation since the underlying investments are equity and bond mutual funds. As such, variable annuity contracts should be analyzed on the basis of the underlying mutual fund that is being purchased.

Most investors will save before-tax dollars for their retirement through the use of a 401(k) or 403(b) plan, or perhaps through an IRA or SEP. Such investors should take full advantage of these plans before using an annuity as a retirement savings vehicle. With tax-deferred retirement savings plans, the owner may not withdraw the money or use the income from the annuity before the age of 59½ without incurring a 10% penalty tax in addition to regular taxes. (This penalty is only assessed on the earnings, not the initial principal deposit.) In contrast to tax-deferred savings plans, an annuity that is purchased with after-tax dollars does not require the owner to begin withdrawing at 70½. The investor can typically wait to begin disbursements until the age of 85.

As with any investment product, the following list should be considered before purchasing a variable annuity.

a. Only invest in annuities if you are investing for a long-time horizon.

b. Buy only from a top-rated insurer with outstanding mutual fund options.

c. Compare surrender periods. Most annuities have surrender charges that range from 6% to 8%. These fall to zero in about 7 years.

d. If investing for a longer time horizon, avoid fixed rate annuities. Only purchase annuities from firms that grant you the maximum flexibility in taking the money out. Avoid annuities that prohibit lump-sum withdrawals.

e. When investing in variable annuities, stick with contracts that offer at least five different investment accounts (referred to as subaccounts) to enable you to have proper diversification within your annuity.

f. Generally, avoid variable annuities with total fees higher than 2%. If there are two contracts that earn the same rate of return but one has a 1% fee compared to the other's 2% fee, the difference in value at the time of withdrawal is quite staggering.

Life insurance

One may purchase permanent life insurance contracts that have a savings component, as well as a life insurance component. Typical examples we learned in Section 6 are whole life policies, variable life policies, and universal life insurance policies, among others. It is often said that one can save for one's retirement with an insurance contract without payment of any taxes. You need to understand how this is true.

First, most life insurance policies are purchased with after-tax dollars that accumulate tax-free after payment for insurance and sales commissions. On one's death, the proceeds are paid to the beneficiaries and those proceeds are not subject to taxation. If, however, the insured would like to access the wealth that has accumulated in the cash value prior to their death, they may withdraw money without owing taxes <u>if they take the money out in irregular amounts at irregular periods</u>—so as the product does not appear to be an annuity. These withdrawals are seen by the Internal Revenue Service as policy loans—which they are—and the loans accrue interest that is payable to the life insurance company. On the death of the policy holder, the face value of the policy will be reduced by the amount owed to the life insurance company, including the amounts withdrawn and the interest owed on those withdrawals.

Equity in your home

First you must decide if you are willing to move or remain in your home.

<u>If you are willing to move:</u>

Under current tax law, you can sell your home and avoid paying any capital gains tax on the first $500,000 of profit if you are married. For single people, the tax-free amount of capital gain is $250,000. The home has to be your primary residence and you must have lived in it at least two of the past 5 years. This capital gains exclusion can be utilized repeatedly.

<u>If you are not willing to move:</u>

1. **Refinance** your home with either a first or second mortgage and take the principal to purchase an annuity (or other investment) to provide income. However, remember that the mortgage payments must be made. Acquiring debt in retirement is generally not recommended.

2. **Home equity lines of credit** will allow you to borrow from the equity in your home as you need the money. For many elderly, this may be a nice cushion against adversity or a temporary lack of liquidity.

3. **Home equity conversion loans** allow you to live in your home and the lending institution mails you a monthly check. These are called *reverse mortgages* because the mortgage balance continues to grow with each month's payment. Typically, the lender restricts the borrowing to 60%–80% of the appraised value of the home at loan origination. These mortgages may be for a fixed term or a life term. Greater payments are possible if the lender is able to share in the appreciation of the home.

4. **Sale/leaseback** may be used to receive income from your home . . . if you can trust the one to whom you sell your home. You can legally sell your home to, say, your child who then becomes your landlord. The sale can be accomplished through a mortgage that requires the buyer/landlord to make mortgage payments to the tenant/seller greater than the rent the tenant pays the landlord. Many of the costs of home maintenance, if paid by the landlord, become tax deductible to the landlord, as is the cost of the interest and the depreciation of the home.

For families with a high income child, who could benefit from the tax breaks and afford the mortgage payments, this option might be a realistic choice. For others, this is probably not the best scenario. Be sure that a lawyer, who is qualified in real estate law, is employed at the initiation of a contract.

Notes:

Estate Planning

*Planning is bringing the future into the present so that you
can do something about it now.*

Alan Lakein (1941–)

*Put not your trust in money,
but put your money in trust.*

O.W. Holmes (1809–1894)

*A son can bear with equanimity the loss of his father,
but the loss of his inheritance may drive him to despair.*

Machiavelli (1469–1527)

*When planning for a year, plant corn. When planning for a decade, plant trees.
When planning for a life, train and educate people.*

Chinese Proverb

This may come as a surprise to you, and I hate to be the one to break the news to you: "*You, like all of us, will die.*" This is even more certain than taxes. Death, moreover, does not depend on your religious beliefs. You will cease to be a part of life, as we now know it, and you need to have your personal affairs in order when that time comes. You need to educate those you love and who love you about what you want done when that time arrives. You cannot make effective, earthly decisions when you are no longer a part of life. Estate planning is not just for the wealthy. All of us have something we wish to leave to someone, we have preferences about how heroic we expect the medical profession to act on our behalf, or we have a desire for how we wish our family and loved ones to say goodbye to the body we leave behind. One thing is for certain, you do not want to leave these decisions to the government, and you do not want to ask your loved ones to do one more chore as a result of your death. They will be much more concerned about their loss than they will be with proper preparations and, frankly, why would you want to make work for those you love? Thus, we need to actively plan for the inevitable.

LETTER OF INSTRUCTION

A letter of last instructions is not legally binding but has a tremendous effect on your relatives' decisions regarding your funeral, your final rite of passage. The typical contents of a letter of instruction are:

1. The location of your will.
2. A list of those you would like to be notified of your death. This should include those who must be notified: lawyers, insurance agents, business associates, and friends who live outside the local area.

3. The location of all of your assets.

4. Copies of your birth certificate, marriage certificate, and divorce decrees or where they are kept.

5. The location of any deeds, important business papers, and military discharge papers.

6. Include your requests for your funeral. What music do you want played? Who would you like to ask to eulogize your life? Do you prefer to be cremated or embalmed? (You may always prepurchase many of these items and really make it easy on your family.)

LAST WILL AND TESTAMENT

A will is a legal instrument that is written by any competent person according to the prescribed statutes of the state in which they reside. Thus, once you have a will, it is very important to have it reviewed if you move to a different state than the state where it was written. This document allows the decedent (the person who dies) to state their desired disposition of their property, to be distributed upon their death. A will may only distribute property to heirs, if the property is:

1. Property owned individually with no named beneficiary.

2. One-half of **community property**. If one lives in a community property state, one-half of everything owned by a married couple belongs to each partner to the marriage and they can bequest it to whomever they wish.

3. Property held as a **tenant in common**, where one's percentage ownership of property is defined by deed.

In other words, if you *do not* own it after death, you *cannot* will it. This also means that there are ways you can distribute your property through ownership such that the use of a will is less necessary. For example, property you own as **joint tenants** or **tenancy in the entirety** will automatically pass to the surviving owner and cannot be transferred through a will. The same would apply for property where you have a named beneficiary or hold title to the property with a **transfer on death** (**TOD**) provision.

If you do nothing else, you should write a handwritten will (known as a **holographic will**) that is signed, dated, witnessed, and notarized. A holographic will that does not have a witness is valid in some states, but do not take the chance. A will that is not witnessed, typed (as opposed to written), unsigned, and undated is never valid. (You see, knowing how to write in cursive does matter!)

Other points of interest:

If your lineal heirs are given unequal shares, do the executor a favor by explaining *why* in your will, by letter, or tape recording.

Naming both a guardian for dependent children and a trustee for their inheritances are the two most compelling reasons to have a will.

Execute only one copy of your will (i.e., sign only one copy). Otherwise the probate proceedings will be delayed until all the signed copies are located. Make photocopies, if extra copies are needed.

You should state bequests in percentage terms rather than dollar amounts (your estate value can change over time, percentage terms allow the distribution to change with it).

Joint wills should be avoided because they are too difficult to change if situations change.

What happens if you die without a will (this is known as *dying intestate*):

1. Not all of your property will go to your spouse, as some property will be transferred to your children. On the other hand, all of it could go to your spouse and you may want to leave some to your university. (Just a thought.)

2. The court system, not you, will appoint a guardian for your child(ren).

3. Stepchildren will usually receive nothing.

4. The likelihood of your family fighting among themselves, and with the courts, is much greater.

5. A **testamentary** trust, one that is created after your death, cannot be established to manage the estate for young children (in the case of the death of both parents).

6. A closely held (family) business may need to be sold in order to distribute its assets.

WHAT A WILL *CAN* AND *CANNOT* ACCOMPLISH

Can Accomplish:

- Distribute property to persons other than lineal heirs.
- Place property into trusts.
- Preserve a portion of estate for payment of taxes and debts.
- Allocate property so that it qualifies for the marital and charitable deductions. This can be very important if your wealth is substantial.
- Name fiduciaries, guardians, conservators, and trustees to enable them to take care of your dependents.

Cannot Accomplish:

- Cannot disinherit a spouse. (If you want them left out of your inheritance, divorce them before death.)
- Cannot transfer property that will be transferred by an operation of law (e.g., joint tenancy with right of survivorship or tenancy by the entirety).
- Cannot make excessive charitable bequests when a spouse, children, or other legal heirs/dependents survive the decedent.
- Cannot ensure that all of the maker's wishes and commands will be met. For example, the choice of attorney is the executor's decision not the decedent's decision.
- Cannot accomplish provisions that are illegal.

PROBATE COSTS

Probate is derived from Latin and means, simply, "to prove." In the case of wills, the probate court is appointed to prove the authenticity of the will. The attorney, executor, accountant, appraiser, and the court may all get in the probate line to be "rewarded" for their efforts. The amount of probate costs will vary by the complexity of the estate but legal fees for a $100,000 estate in Missouri, for example, will be at least $3,300 and could be more. (Yes, it could cost you much more to die, than it did to be born. I will proffer that being born has a much greater promise of a return on your money than does death.)

In order to minimize probate expenses, one should reduce the property that is subject to probate. Also, assets held in defined manners will lower the necessity of having a will, if you are finding it difficult to get a will written but love the idea of sharing ownership with your family and friends.

The following assets do not have to go through the probate process:

a. Assets held in joint tenancy. Joint tenancy allows the surviving owner (tenant) to become the sole owner following the first owner's death.

b. IRA, pensions, and/or other assets where a beneficiary has been named. If you have not named a beneficiary, assets will go through probate. If you have named a beneficiary, make sure this is updated as circumstances change.

    c. Life insurance proceeds with a named beneficiary, unless your estate is named as the beneficiary. In this case, probate will determine who received the proceeds. (Thus, do not name your estate as beneficiary.)

    d. Assets held in a trust belong to the trust. If your trust is the named beneficiary, the trust will determine who benefits from the corpus of the trust. The trust will cease, when it is no longer necessary.

    e. Assets titled transfer on death to the desired heir will pass to the desired heir should the heir survive to receive the asset.

    f. Personal property.

The following assets <u>do</u> have to go through the probate process. They make up your **probated estate**:

    a. Property owned solely by you (sole ownership property).

    b. Property held as tenants-in-common.

    c. Life insurance proceeds payable to the estate.

    d. One-half of all community property.

DUTIES OF THE EXECUTOR OF A WILL

The executor (if male) or executrix (if female) of another person's will is the person who performs all the tasks of settling the deceased person's estate:

    1. Identify and verify all the assets of the deceased.

    2. Notify creditors.

    3. Pay final bills and taxes.

    4. Claim life insurance death benefit.

    5. Communicate with heirs and determine who receives miscellaneous personal items. (This can be a difficult and emotional task.)

REASONS TO CHANGE YOUR WILL (OR AMEND WITH A *CODICIL*)

    1. You experience a large change in your net worth.

    2. You have a new child (birth, adoption, or marriage).

    3. You experience a marriage, separation, or divorce.

    4. A child gets married, separated, or divorced.

    5. A child becomes old enough to be responsible for their self.

    6. A named heir in your will dies.

    7. A beneficiary becomes terminally ill or incapacitated.

ESTATE TAXES

Your gross estate for tax purposes includes <u>your probated estate</u> plus:

- Life insurance proceeds of policies owned, and paid for, by the decedent.
- One-half of property owned jointly (with rights of survivorship), unless the survivor can prove what they contributed solely to the purchase.
- Gifts made within the last 3 years (property is often excluded).

The estate is reduced by:

- Estate settlement costs,
- Income taxes owed,
- Mortgages owed,
- Marital deduction (100% of what is left to the spouse is deducted from the gross estate), and
- Charitable bequests (100% of what is left to charities is deducted from the gross estate).

The remainder is the **taxable estate** on which taxes are calculated. Estate taxes can be very expensive and, while it is true that you cannot take it with you, most people prefer to not give it to the government. The estate tax schedule has historically been similar to a progressive income tax table, where lower valued estates are taxed at lower rates while higher valued estates are taxed at progressively greater marginal rates (currently 40%). For 2019, all estates up to $11,400,000 are exempt from estate taxes. Above that amount, estates are taxed at a rate of $0.40 per dollar, or 40%.

ESTATE TAX PLANNING

If you have a large estate that will be subject to a tax that, the three basic options that one may use to reduce the taxes on the estate are:

1. Make full use of the **marital deduction** (if married).
2. Use the **credit shelter** or **bypass trust**.
3. Use a **bypass trust with estate equalization**.

Marital Deduction—Make full use of the unlimited marital deduction or the simple will (the "I-love-you" will) where all property is left to the surviving spouse.

No estate tax is due on the first spouse's death due to the existence of an unlimited marital deduction, where all money left to the surviving spouse is not considered a part of the decedent's estate.

There may be tax on the second spouse's estate if the gross estate of the final spouse to die exceeds the exemption equivalent amount. Recall that the exemption equivalent amount is the size of the estate where the entire unified tax credit is applied.

The Credit Shelter (or Bypass Trust)

The exemption equivalent amount ($11,400,000 in 2019) is placed in trust for the benefit of the surviving spouse during his or her lifetime only. In other words, the income produced by the assets in the trust is used to support the surviving spouse. The trust is created where the surviving spouse has no power to control the ultimate dispersion of the property and the trust provides that, upon the surviving spouse's death, the assets of the trust are passed to another person(s).

This type of trust is referred to as a "bypass" trust because the surviving spouse does not receive the corpus (principal used to fund the trust) of the trust but is supported by the income produced by the trust during his or her lifetime.

Any amount of estate over and above the exemption equivalent amount from the first decedent spouse's estate is given to the surviving spouse, and qualifies for the unlimited marital deduction. Then, upon the death of the surviving spouse, only this amount is included in the second spouse's estate.

The advantage of this option is that there is no tax liability on the first estate, and a lower tax liability exists on the surviving spouse's estate. In as much as each spouse has a unified tax credit, this method alone allows for, at most, twice the exemption equivalent amount escaping estate taxation ($22,800,000).

It is important to remember that assets placed in a bypass trust cannot be owned jointly with one's spouse. They would have to be owned as tenants-in-common, by a trust, or sole ownership.

Assuming an estate valued at $32,400,000, a $11,400,000 exemption equivalent amount, and no increase in value of estate corpus.

	With Bypass Trust	**Without Bypass Trust**
Husband dies first	$11,400,000 of assets deposited in a trust for children ESTATE TAX FREE. Surviving spouse has access to income produced by the trust during her lifetime. $21,000,000 of assets given to spouse ESTATE TAX FREE.	Entire estate ($32,400,000) given to spouse ESTATE TAX FREE.
Wife dies second	$11,400,000 of assets is passed to children ESTATE TAX FREE. Children pay *$4,240,000 in taxes* on the $10,600,000 of estate that exceeds the $11,400,000 exemption.	$11,400,000 of assets is passed to children ESTATE TAX FREE. Remaining $21,000,000 given to children (assuming the estate maintained a value of $22,000,000) is subject to *ESTATE TAX in the amount of $8,800,000 (or, 40%)*
Total amount given to children	$18,160,000 ($11,400,000 from trust funded at father's death + $6,760,200 from trust funded at mother's death)	$13,600,000
Total Estate Tax Paid	$4,240,000	$8,800,000

POWER OF ATTORNEY AND LIVING WILL

Power of Attorney

A power of attorney allows someone else to act in your behalf; such as to write checks for you, sell stocks, or even make health care decisions if you are unable.

Limited power of attorney—Someone else can write checks on your account.

Ordinary power of attorney—Grants broader authority to manage your finances.

However, both limited and ordinary powers of attorney expire if you become mentally disabled. To prevent this lapse, you should appoint someone with a **durable power of attorney**, which is enacted if you become mentally disabled, in a coma, and so on. A new durable power of attorney needs to be executed every 4–5 years.

Durable Power of Attorney for Health Care

A durable power of attorney for health care allows someone, whom you appoint, to make health care decisions for you in the event that you are unable to do so. The advantage of a durable power of attorney is that a *person*, as opposed to a *document*, is empowered to make life-and-death decisions for you.

Unlike a written living will or an advance medical directive, the person appointed as your agent (via a durable power of attorney for health care) can discuss specific, and often unforeseeable, health care situations with doctors before making a decision on your behalf.

Living Will

A living will is a legal document in which you request that you not be kept alive by means of life support technology should you be terminally and irreversibly ill. Most states allow family members or legal guardians to "stand in the patients shoes" and make life-or-death decisions. However, two exceptions are New York and Missouri, where no surrogate decision can be made unless the individual expressed a clear preference not to be kept alive by artificial means while still alive (and coherent).

The more specifically a living will (or advance medical directive) is worded the more useful it will be to the family and doctors.

TRUSTS

A Trust is a legal relationship in which one person transfers property to a new legal entity to be managed by a second person for the benefit of a third person (or group of people). The person creating the trust is the **grantor**. The person managing the trust property is the **trustee**. The person (or persons) for whose benefit the trust is created is the **beneficiary** (or beneficiaries). Interestingly, the same person can be a grantor, trustee, and beneficiary all at the same time.

Using a trust, an individual can transfer property from their personal name to a trust and name themselves trustee of the trust. As the trustee, they can hold the property for themselves or for someone else. Under the instructions of a revocable living trust, the trustee (or cotrustees) can see to it that when the grantor dies all trust property is transferred to the beneficiary or beneficiaries. When the grantor dies, the trust property automatically is held by any cotrustee or successor trustee for the benefit of the beneficiary. All of this is accomplished *without* any probate process, or any other type of court proceedings. You do not need to be wealthy to take advantage of a trust. If you own only your home or automobiles, you can use a trust to make sure that when you die everything automatically transfers to whomever you wish.

A revocable living trust is the answer to almost all of the problems that can be encountered by probate court. It can be entered into easily at little cost and it can be revoked by the stroke of a pen.

TYPES OF TRUSTS

Revocable living trust—The *grantor* creates this type of trust while living and maintains the right to *revoke*. A revocable living trust is *not* a completed gift and is included in the grantor's estate. However, if it is funded (i.e., assets retitled and placed within it), it avoids probate.

Irrevocable living trust—The grantor creates this while living without retaining the right to revoke the trust. An irrevocable living trust is a completed gift and is not included in the grantor's estate. Income may be taxed to the beneficiary, trust, or grantor.

Testamentary trust—Created by the decedent's will to be effective at death. The corpus of the trust is included in the grantor's estate and it does not avoid probate.

Discretionary—Decisions regarding whether/how much income is to be distributed from the trust to the beneficiaries is the decision of the trustee.

Sprinkling or spray—Trust that permits trustee to distribute income or corpus among various beneficiaries according to perceived needs.

Support—Establish a support trust for the purpose of providing income to a beneficiary, in order to discharge the grantor's obligation of support.

Spendthrift—A trust that is structured such that the trust beneficiaries may not transfer interest in income until the income is actually received.

Clifford trust—An *irrevocable trust* created for a limited time (life expectancy of the beneficiary or 10 years and 1 day). At which time the corpus reverts to the grantor. Income is, however, taxed to the grantor, and the trust is considered a completed gift for estate tax purposes.

Generation skipping—A generation-skipping trust is created in the attempt to bypass inclusion in a lower generation's estate, such as the children's estate. There is a separate generation-skipping tax on this property. However, it will avoid successive probate. For example, a trust is created where the trustee is asked to manage the trust for your *grandchildren*—who are the beneficiaries of the trust. However, while your *children* are living, all trust income is stated to be used for your children's needs.

Grantor retained annuity trust—Grantor retains an annuity interest for a term of years that is actuarially equivalent to the value of the property placed in the trust. The goal is for the property to appreciate at a rate greater than the assumed rate of return on the "annuity." Thus, the gift is valued at the time of creation, income can be pulled for the grantor, from the gift, and any remaining corpus passes to the beneficiaries without taxes due.

Standby—A trust structured to take effect when the grantor becomes temporarily or permanently disabled. Usually, a standby trust is revocable in nature.

Pourover—A revocable or irrevocable living trust established to provide a receptacle for assets passing outside of the will. Often used when there are multiple beneficiaries. These assets are not subject to probate. The pourover trust is a useful device for checking account funds and personal property.

Simple—A simple trust is a trust that is required to distribute all of its income each year.

Complex—A complex trust is a trust that is not required to distribute all of its income each year.

ADVANTAGES OF A TRUST

Revocable Living Trust

1. Avoids probate and probate administration fees and expenses.
2. Assigns someone else (the trustee) to manage your financial affairs in the event that you become incapacitated.
3. You are able to test (in advance of your death) the managerial ability of the trustee.
4. Distributes assets as you desire (the trust takes precedence over a will).
5. Avoids unnecessary delays in estate settlement.
6. Avoids publicity resulting from probate.
7. Attempts to avoid creditors (not always possible or wise).
8. Minimizes or eliminates the potential for will disputes.
9. Provides for uninterrupted income and access to principal for beneficiaries.

A Revocable Living Trust *Does Not:*

1. Save income or estate taxes.
2. To avoid estate taxes, assets must be placed in an *irrevocable* living trust. Only those assets that are permanently removed from your estate (via the irrevocable trust) escape estate tax.

Under the management of a trustee (whom the grantor names), a trust can:

1. Hold money until a dependent child grows up.
2. Manage money and property for the remaining spouse.
3. Provide financial care for a developmentally challenged child.
4. Prevent children of a prior marriage from being ignored in your will.

For example, a bypass trust can be established to provide your second wife with annual income until her death, at which point the children of your first marriage receive the corpus (or principal) of the trust.

Notes:

Index